Dreamers & Defenders

Douglas H. Strong

Dreamers & Defenders

American Conservationists

University of Nebraska Press

Lincoln and London

The paper in this book meets the minimum require-
ments of American National Standard
for Information Sciences—Permanence of Paper for
Printed Library Materials, ANSI Z39.48–1984.

Library of Congress Cataloging-in-Publication Data
Strong, Douglas Hillman.
Dreamers and defenders.
Rev. and enl. ed. of: The conservationists. 1971.
Bibliography: p.
Includes index.
1. Conservationists–United States–Biography.
I. Strong, Douglas Hillman.   Conservationists.
II. Title.
S926.A2S7   1988   333.7'2'0922[B]   87-30210
ISBN 0-8032-4161-5
ISBN 0-8032-9156-6 (pbk.)

For Peder, Rick, Beret, Kare, Rob, and Kendra

Contents

Preface

Human alteration of the environment is inevitable. It has gone on since earliest people learned to use fire. But only in the latest century of our short tenure on the planet has most of the serious damage to air, soil, water, plants, and animals taken place, and only very recently has it reached crisis proportions.

In recent decades a few dedicated conservationists have aroused a growing number of concerned citizens in support of a more enlightened land policy. It is my hope that the story of their efforts, both triumphs and defeats, will promote a better understanding of the rise of conservation in the United States and perhaps encourage others to follow in their footsteps.

Robin W. Winks, Thomas R. Cox, Donald C. Swain, Susan L. Flader, and Horace M. Albright all provided helpful criticism of portions of an earlier, shorter version of this book: *The Conservationists* (Menlo Park, Calif.: Addison-Wesley Publishing Co., 1971). The first six chapters of the earlier book have been revised and four new chapters have been added. A selected annotated bibliography (excluding major publications cited in the text) provides a guide to the sources I found most useful. Notes at the end of the book are limited to citations for quotations.

A sabbatical leave from San Diego State University allowed me to complete the manuscript. I am indebted to David Brower and Barry Commoner for assisting in my research for and commenting on the chapters about them. Linda J. Lear offered useful suggestions for the chapter on Harold Ickes, and Shirley A. Briggs and Paul Brooks helped with my chapter on Rachel Carson. I also wish to thank the many people who helped me locate illustrations, and Anthony Santangelo for the title. I am especially grateful to my wife, Karlan, who read every draft perceptively and offered numerous useful ideas for improvement.

Introduction

On an overcast November day in 1620, the Pilgrims ended their hazardous crossing of the Atlantic and stepped ashore. To them it seemed "but a hideous and desolate wilderness, full of wild beasts and wild men."[1] Dedicated to placing the land in God's service, they established a foothold on the American continent.

Although many early settlers thought they had come to virgin territory, the Indians had inhabited the eastern seaboard for more than ten thousand years. Native Americans in northern New England depended primarily on hunting and gathering; others farther south had developed productive agriculture, growing corn and beans. They used fire to clear the land of undergrowth for fields and to open it for game such as deer, turkeys, and quail. Their repeated use of the same village sites resulted in the depletion of soil fertility in neighboring fields and of local firewood, but these problems proved temporary. The Indians understood their environment well, used a variety of food sources through the changing seasons, and treated the land with care and respect. As a result they maintained a stable way of life century after century.

Except for the limited areas the European settlers found under Indian cultivation, they considered the land vacant and available to those who could put it to productive use—for agriculture and for commercial profit. They did not honor the Indians' communal approach to land use or their sense of obligation to pass the land undamaged to future generations. Instead, Europeans introduced the concept of private property and treated land increasingly as a commodity to be bought and sold in the market. New Englanders used Genesis 1:28 to justify their claim to the land, noting that the Lord directed man to multiply and to subdue the earth. They brought a burgeoning market economy that drew the Indians into increasing economic dependency. And, most serious, the colonists transmitted diseases to which the Indians had no immunity; entire villages were decimated, and the Indians could no longer maintain their long-established relationship to the land.

The growing economy in New England, short on capital and labor and dependent on exploiting the natural environment, left a legacy of waste. Farmers girdled trees or felled them with an ax, and great quantities of wood fueled inefficient fireplaces. Domesticated grazing animals multiplied rapidly, depleting the limited pastureland and forcing expansion into the interior. Plowed lands sustained increasing soil erosion. By the end of the colonial period, many species of plants, grasses, and animals had disappeared.

Farther south, profligate use of the land had become increasingly common. Thomas Jefferson noted of his fellow Virginian tobacco planters, "The indifferent state of agriculture among us does not proceed from a want of knowledge merely; it is from our having such quantities of land to waste as we please."[2] As one field became infertile or lost topsoil through erosion, the farmer had only to move to a field yet untouched.

After the colonies gained their independence, the seven states that claimed lands west of the Appalachians ceded their titles to the federal government. This act created a "public domain" and the need for a governmental policy for its control, distribution, and use. With few exceptions, the land incorporated into the Union as a result of the Louisiana Purchase in 1803 and later acquisitions became part of this public domain, if only temporarily.

Under the Land Ordinance of 1785, Congress had devised a scheme for surveying this land and selling it to private citizens. At first Congress regarded the land primarily as a source of revenue, and it was the land speculators, not the general public, who profited. Increasingly, in the nineteenth century, individual farmers acquired land as both land prices and the terms under which it could be purchased were liberalized. Finally, during the Civil War, Congress passed the Homestead Act, which gave 160 acres to each farmer who made the tract his home and cultivated it for five years. Congress also provided extensive land grants to promote railroad construction and used land to foster education and to reward veterans of American wars.

Many of these land laws ran counter to the interests of westerners, who resented interference from Washington and desired larger acreages than the law allowed. Lumbermen, ranchers, miners, and others devised ways to circumvent existing regulations. For example, when Congress passed the Swamp Land Act in 1850, permitting states to acquire title to marshy and swampy land, it hoped that the states would develop the land. For a small bribe, however, government land-office inspectors often rated good timberland as "swamp and overflow," and the state then sold this land to private parties.

Timber interests and land speculators took advantage of the Homestead Act of 1862 by hiring "dummy" entrants. These hirelings claimed the 160 acres fraudulently and promptly transferred them to their employers. Often the "farm" was actually prized timberland.

Much of the land legislation passed after the Civil War was similarly abused. The Timber and Stone Act of 1878 provided that a farmer could acquire 160 acres of timbered or stony land, at $2.50 an acre, for his personal use. Often, however, a company paid someone a small fee and the expenses incidental to purchasing a piece of timberland, and this "agent" then transferred the deed to the company.

The abundance of cheap land was only one of many factors that contributed to rapid economic growth. Supportive government policies—tariffs, subsidies, patents, and the like—provided an inviting climate for investment, and a near absence of governmental regulation gave enterprise a free hand. Improved transportation and communication opened markets and encouraged regional specialization. Laws of incorporation allowed businesses to enjoy financial liquidity through the sale of stock and limited liability for each investor. Corporations soon dominated the production and distribution of manufactured goods across the country, and the names of major companies—such as Proctor and Gamble, Eastman Kodak, and Pillsbury Flour—became household words.

In the meantime, engineering societies had proliferated, the National Academy of Sciences had been chartered, and scientific research had achieved a state of organization and success heretofore unimagined. Thomas Edison's laboratory gave way to the mammoth laboratory of the General Electric company, and Henry Ford's assembly line techniques allowed for mass production. Technological breakthroughs—the Bessemer process for producing steel, the electric dynamo, the internal-combustion engine—helped transform American life and with it the American environment.

The wasteful use of natural resources had increased in the latter half of the nineteenth century with the growth of industry, the rise of large cities, and the construction of transcontinental railroads. From New England to Oregon, loggers used strip-and-run methods. Hydraulic miners washed away hillsides and flooded valleys, while drillers depleted oil and natural gas deposits. Hunters and sportsmen decimated wildlife, and farmers, plowing under the grasslands, set the stage for the Dust Bowl disaster of the 1930s.

Not all the men who laid waste the land were land raiders, despoilers who saw no reason to use the land with care. Many were honest, hardworking settlers who did not foresee the destructive consequences of their actions. Most families, however, simply followed a course of expediency as the best path to success. And as long as the government's land policy was to promote private ownership with unfettered rights to use the land as one pleased, it seemed unlikely that many individuals would practice restraint and good husbandry.

Nevertheless, a few perceptive settlers had voiced concern for conservation soon after the first trees had been felled and the land plowed. Colonial legislatures and towns passed a number of statutes protecting forests from wasteful use, controlling the use of fire to clear land, draining marshes, clearing watercourses, protecting beaches, and regulating hunting and fishing. Nearly all these measures had a utilitarian purpose—to make the land more productive and profitable. At the same time, colonists recognized the dangers of shortages caused by local overuse, and their conservation efforts foreshadowed the later control and planning of resource development.

During most of the nineteenth century, as vast tracts of land became available to development, the early concern for conservation largely disappeared. Yet even in these years a few writers and scientists—like Henry David Thoreau, Frederick Law Olmsted, and George Perkins Marsh—promoted the idea of conservation. These three, all easterners, realized what could happen in areas where population, urbanization, and industry were all expanding. Each in his own way protested the waste of resources, the spread of ugliness, the irresponsible use of the land.

Thoreau demonstrated the value of living simply and close to nature, Olmsted helped initiate urban parks and planning, and Marsh revealed the severity of human alteration of the land.

After the Civil War, when private citizens encountered growing shortages of wildlife and forests, they experimented with the commercial propagation of fish and planting of trees. Congress, in response, established a Commission on Fish and Fisheries and passed the Timber Culture Act, which posed no threat to private profit, for they simply encouraged production. In the 1870s and 1880s sportsmen's clubs and periodicals proved popular and citizens' conservation organizations multiplied. These groups sought to protect resources such as dwindling wildlife and to provide opportunities for outdoor recreation.

Such concern by citizens provided an impetus for the growth of federally directed, scientifically conducted resource management in the United States. John Wesley Powell, for example, as chief of the Geological Survey in the 1880s, attempted to introduce enlightened land policies to the drier lands of the West. It was not until the first decade of the twentieth century, however, that Theodore Roosevelt and his chief forester, Gifford Pinchot, organized an effective conservation movement. In the 1930s a second conservation movement arose under the guidance of Franklin Delano Roosevelt and his secretary of the interior, Harold Ickes. With the support of Congress, it fostered programs to encourage economic recovery from the Great Depression and to restore the land to productivity. More recently, in the 1960s, a third wave of conservation activity, spurred by such scientists as Rachel Carson and Barry Commoner, encountered a new set of problems unleashed by the introduction of dangerous chemicals into the environment.

At the same time that Americans recognized the need to manage their resources scientifically, they also came to the defense of wilderness and rapidly disappearing scenic areas. John

Muir popularized the gospel of wilderness preservation at the turn of the century, and Stephen Mather organized the National Park Service. In later years, Aldo Leopold encouraged an ethical attitude toward the land, and David Brower sought to protect the Grand Canyon.

Throughout the rise of conservation in the United States, individuals helped awaken Americans to the plight of the natural environment. The development of a more enlightened attitude toward the land can be traced through the lives of a few farsighted men and women who pointed the way.

*Henry David Thoreau (Courtesy of the Concord
Free Public Library, Concord, Massachusetts)*

Chapter 1: The Forerunners:
Thoreau, Olmsted, Marsh

HENRY DAVID THOREAU

In the spring of 1845 a struggling young writer built a small cabin on the shores of Walden Pond near Concord, Massachusetts. The forest attracted him because he wished to learn what it had to teach. Here Henry David Thoreau spent twenty-six months, for him the most satisfying time of his life. Several years later he completed *Walden,* a description of the place and a reflection on his experiment in simple living in the woods. The influence of this book, which helped create a new interest in the world of nature, was to be felt by generations to come.

Born in modest circumstances in 1817, Thoreau grew up in Concord, the lively intellectual center of New England transcendentalism. Led by Ralph Waldo Emerson, the transcendentalists questioned the materialistic goals of the majority of Americans and sought harmony and beauty through an appreciation of nature.

At the age of sixteen Thoreau left Concord for Harvard College. There he did well enough to be selected at the end of his senior year to give one of the commencement speeches. Boldly he attacked the "commercial spirit" that prevailed in the land and expressed a number of ideas sharply at odds with those of most Americans. He even suggested a reversal of the old formula of six days of work and one of rest; it was the six days, he said, that should be free to allow people to discover the "revelations of nature."

After graduating, Thoreau returned home to his family in Concord, where he found a teaching position. Unorthodox in his ideas and practices, he rebelled against the corporal punishment he was ordered to dispense and found himself unemployed in the midst of a depression. Next he worked in his father's pencil-manufacturing business and then joined his brother in opening a successful private school. Here he introduced his students to weekly nature walks, a most unusual innovation. Shortly after his brother's death in 1842 he stopped teaching to return to the family business, but he spent little time in this or any other trade or profession.

In 1837, his first year back from Harvard, Thoreau had gained access to Emerson's library, and a friendship had begun to develop between them. On Emerson's suggestion, Thoreau began a journal in which he recorded his thoughts and experiences. In time he moved into Emerson's home, earning his keep as a handyman. Emerson's essay *Nature* impressed Thoreau, particularly the idea that each person should "enjoy an original relation to the universe." Emerson, however, failed to recognize the extent of waste and destruction caused by land development in America. He shared, apparently, the common American optimism that sound policies would somehow prevail in the long run.

Thoreau grew restless under Emerson's roof and went to Staten Island to tutor the children of Emerson's brother. The move, advised by Emerson, was meant to give him ready access to publishers who might buy material from his journal, but Thoreau never gave the plan a chance. After a visit to the great metropolis, he remarked, "I walked through New York yesterday—and met no real and living person."[1] This life seemed the opposite of what he wanted. Homesick, he returned to Concord.

In 1845, at age twenty-seven, Thoreau decided to move to Walden Pond. It was a voluntary withdrawal to a way of life in which he believed—and it gave him freedom to write. Here he finished his first book, *A Week on the Concord and Merrimack Rivers,* and wrote extensively in his journal.

His two years at Walden revealed the practical benefits of the simple life; he no longer talked about it—he lived it. Proudly he recorded that his solid little cabin, built on property owned by Emerson, cost a total of $28.12, excluding labor. That amount was far below the cost of the average home, which even then put most families in debt for years. Thoreau's grocery bill for the first eight months averaged 27¢ per week, a testimony to the advantages of cultivating a large garden and living frugally. When a neighboring woodchuck persisted in eating his bean shoots, he trapped it, scolded it roundly, and set it free at a good distance. In spite of such competition, his garden flourished and he turned a small profit. Reducing his agricultural pursuits to a minimum and accepting occasional odd jobs, Thoreau calculated that he could survive on six weeks of work a year. Free time could be devoted to more important pursuits, such as walking in the woods and putting his thoughts in order.

Although he enjoyed the stillness of the woods and the chance to study nature quietly at Walden Pond, Thoreau was not the total recluse sometimes pictured. He welcomed friends, particularly children, who came to visit, and he often walked the short distance into town for a good meal with his family. On the other hand, he grew tired of strangers who insisted on accompanying him on his nature walks. "They do not consider that the wood-path and the boat are my studio," he complained, "where I maintain a sacred solitude and cannot admit promiscuous company."[2]

Thoreau believed that most people missed the joy of living because of their everlasting scramble for possessions and their slavery to inessentials: "I see young men, my townsmen, whose misfortune it is to have inherited farms, houses, barns, cattle, and farming tools; for these are more easily acquired than got rid of. Better if they had been born in the open pasture and suckled by a wolf, that they might have seen with clearer eyes what field they were called to labor in."[3]

Thoreau sympathized with nature and criticized human society for destroying it. Life in New England was too complex and utilitarian to suit him. Above all else he prized the unspoiled world of woods and animals:

When I consider that the nobler animals have been exterminated here,— the cougar, panther, lynx, wolverene, wolf, bear, moose, deer, the beaver, the turkey, etc., etc.,—I cannot but feel as if I lived in a tamed, and, as it were, emasculated country. . . . I take infinite pains to know all the phenomena of the spring, for instance, thinking that I have here the entire poem, and then, to my chagrin, I hear that it is but an imperfect copy that I possess and have read, that my ancestors have torn out many of the first leaves and grandest passages, and mutilated it in many places. I should not like to think that some demigod had come before me and picked out some of the best of the stars. I wish to know an entire heaven and an entire earth.[4]

Thoreau worried increasingly about the spread of a technological society bent on material progress that threatened a simpler, more just society. A growing number of factories and dams intruded along the banks of once free-flowing streams, and wild animals disappeared in the face of railroads and burgeoning communities. Referring to American settlers, he said, "For one that comes with a pencil to sketch or sing, a thousand come with an ax or rifle."[5]

Yet he had little regard for the possible benefits of government action to control growth. In any case, the government would have made no moves toward conservation until the public was better informed and organized political efforts could be made to save the woods and wildlife. A nonconformist like Thoreau, even if he had fully understood the need, could hardly have been expected to organize opposition to development.

In reaction to the nineteenth-century quest for material possessions, Thoreau advocated reduced consumption and the "inward wealth" that resulted from self-sufficiency. He praised the farmer who made his own tools and the craftsman who built his own house. And he warned against earning more than was needed and the acquisition of expensive tastes. "A man may acquire a taste for wine or brandy, and so lose his taste for water," he noted, "but should we not pity him?"[6] The accumulation and protection of wealth could lead to the loss of personal integrity and freedom, dependence on vested interests, and submission to established authority.

Thoreau's unconventional behavior and occasionally prickly personality offended some people of Concord. He refused to attend the local church, unwilling to support an institution he found wanting. Ever an uncompromising individualist, he once spent a night in jail for refusing to pay his poll tax to a government that supported slavery and a war against Mexico. When his neighbors inquired about his purpose, Thoreau delivered a lecture on the relation of the individual to the state. He argued that in times of conflict, people should follow their own conscience, not the dictates of an immoral government. He desired a state that respected everyone, even those who might choose not to support it financially. His lecture, published in an obscure magazine in 1849, later appeared as "Civil Disobedience," an essay that became the manual on passive resistance for Gandhi, Martin Luther King, Jr., and many other dissenters of the twentieth century.

During his brief time at Walden Pond, Thoreau's retreat

stirred little interest. There was in fact nothing outstanding about it except that surprisingly few people had ever done anything like it before (or have since) and recorded their feelings and experiences in so telling a way. For Thoreau himself, the experience was a success, and to him that was all that mattered. As he put it, "I learned this, at least, by my experiment: that if one advances confidently in the direction of his dreams, and endeavors to live the life which he has imagined, he will meet with a success unexpected in common hours."[7]

Although he believed that his experiment was relevant to the lives of others, Thoreau was skeptical about his chances of getting his account published. When his first book, *A Week on the Concord and Merrimack Rivers,* finally appeared in 1849 in an edition of one thousand copies, it sold poorly. "I have now a library of nearly nine hundred volumes," he commented ruefully, "over seven hundred of which I wrote myself."[8] The publication of *Walden,* delayed until 1854, proved more successful; two thousand copies sold before it went out of print. Today *Walden* is the most frequently reprinted pre–Civil War book in America, appearing in nearly two hundred editions.

Thoreau spent the remainder of his years in more conventional pursuits in town; but for him nothing ever equaled his life at Walden Pond. Local farmers often called on him to survey their properties, a vocation that he could never reconcile with the development it fostered. From time to time he gave public lectures, and he also continued to contribute to the family business.

Toward the end of his life, Thoreau believed that each Massachusetts township "should have a park, or rather a primitive forest, of five hundred or a thousand acres, where a stick should never be cut for fuel, a common possession forever, for instruction and recreation."[9] Fourteen years before Congress set aside Yellowstone National Park (the first national park) in 1872, he

14

favored "preserves" for the protection of animals for people's "inspiration."

He had discarded his own gun before going to Walden Pond, feeling that no humane person "past the thoughtless age of boyhood" would "wantonly murder any creature which holds its life by the same tenure that he does."[10] He did fish, however. Once while cooking a day's catch he accidentally set fire to the nearby woods, destroying a reported three hundred acres and drawing the wrath of the local newspaper.

On rare occasions Thoreau killed animals for scientific study. Yet he did so with remorse, for he believed that more could be learned from living than from dead animals. He believed that each person's innate knowledge transcended the knowledge acquired through observation. In particular, the ability to distinguish right from wrong rested on a person's inner voice, or conscience. It was this inner voice that Thoreau followed throughout his life.

Contrary to the Calvinist view that nature opened the door to people's inherent sinfulness, Thoreau thought that nature brought out the best in people and provided an opportunity for them to move closer to the Divine Being. Nature reflected spiritual truths, and wilderness provided inspiration and beauty. Because people have souls, Thoreau believed, they could transcend their physical existence—a transcendence most likely to be sparked by a personal experience in a natural environment.

Thoreau devoted increasing time to the observation of natural phenomena, in spite of the limitations he saw in science as a discipline. Had he lived longer, he would perhaps have written a natural history of the Concord region, a project urged by his friends. He did lecture and complete an article on the succession of forest trees, his most important scientific contribution. After careful investigation, he determined why certain species survived while others failed under changing environmental conditions. His persistence in counting tree rings on a bitterly cold December day in 1860 led to his final illness. He died in 1862 at the age of forty-four.

Thoreau's major contribution to conservation was in offering a new attitude toward nature. His example encouraged other individualists to live according to their convictions. As he stated in his conclusion to *Walden*: "Why should we be in such desperate haste to succeed and in such desperate enterprises? If a man does not keep pace with his companions, perhaps it is because he hears a different drummer. Let him step to the music which he hears, however measured or far away."[11]

FREDERICK LAW OLMSTED

Three years after the publication of *Walden*, Frederick Law Olmsted, another easterner, began his first important job—under unfavorable circumstances. Sinking deep in mud and sweltering in the hot afternoon sun, the newly appointed superintendent of what was to become New York City's Central Park wished he had left his coat at home. The proposed park, which he inspected that summer day in 1857, had little to offer except its location. A few rocks and barren pastures appeared between low, swampy areas that were "steeped in the overflow and mush of pigsties, slaughter houses, and bone-boiling works."[12] Fortunately for New York City and for the future of many American cities, Frederick Law Olmsted had vision and determination. Central Park became the first of America's great city parks, and Olmsted laid the groundwork for city planning and landscape architecture in the United States.

Olmsted was born in 1822 in Hartford, Connecticut. Although his father was a wealthy merchant, Frederick had a difficult youth. His mother died when he was six, and he was first placed in the care of a Congregational minister and then enrolled in a succession of schools. The accepted memorization-

*Frederick Law Olmstead (Courtesy of The
New York Historical Society, New York City)*

and-rote method of learning proved much less valuable to his education than his own extensive reading and the long vacation trips he took with his father to New York, New England, and Canada. At the age of fifteen he was nearly blinded by sumac poisoning and had to give up the idea of a college education and a career in one of the learned professions.

While recuperating in the countryside for the next three years, he mastered the rudiments of surveying. In this rural environment he gained a deep and abiding appreciation for the outdoors. Yet one of his favorite pastimes during his convalescence was drawing plans for hypothetical cities and towns. He was a restless youth who found it hard to spend more than a short while on any one project. In 1843, after a brief try at store clerking, he shipped out for China as an apprentice seaman on the sailing ship *Ronaldson*. To Olmsted it was a miserable, wet year on the high seas, and he decided that the sailor's life was not for him.

It was now 1844 and Olmsted was twenty-two years old. At this point he gave up his earlier ambition of becoming an engineer, a merchant, or a sea captain and decided instead to be a scientific farmer. For the first time in his life he had some meaningful direction. Here was an occupation that would aid society, carry out the aims of science, and provide more of the outdoor life that so appealed to him. Eventually, in 1848, he settled on Staten Island on a 130-acre farm that his father had financed for him. Even with his administrative skill and frugal living, he had to rely on the continued financial generosity of his father to improve the property. He beautified the buildings and grounds imaginatively and soon had an attractive farm. Neighbors began to seek his advice about their own architectural problems, and he found himself spending more and more time designing and improving the farms nearby.

Olmsted's importation of French pear trees for his own farm led him into the nursery business; for six years he lived the life of a gentleman farmer, giving advice on the placing of the trees he sold, on the improvement of farming methods, and on farm design. In 1850 he interrupted this rural life with an extensive trip to Europe. The English landscape, particularly the city parks in Liverpool and London, made a lasting impression on him. When he returned he took up a new pursuit—writing—and completed a volume entitled *Walks and Talks of an American Farmer in England.*

Before long he was writing perceptively and engagingly of his travels through the slave states of the South. Believing in the importance of community, education, and free labor in a democratic society, he pointed out the misuse of people and land in the South. His newspaper and magazine articles were received enthusiastically in the North, and almost overnight he became a literary success. As a result he became a partner in a New York publishing firm in 1855 and for a time edited *Putnam's Monthly Magazine.* Two years later the firm went bankrupt and Olmsted found himself jobless and indebted. His farm had run down in his absence, and he needed capital. At this unhappy moment, he heard that New York was seeking to hire a superintendent for the development of a rural plot of land on Manhattan Island—what was to become Central Park—not far north of the boundary of New York City.

The idea for the park dated back at least to 1844, when the poet William Cullen Bryant proposed its establishment. The need for more open space and green areas for recreation had long been recognized, but nothing had been done about it; in fact, the city's open space had dwindled to a few scattered acres. Bryant had reminded the community that forty years earlier every city worker had been able to get into the countryside in half an hour. Now, however, Manhattan was in danger of losing its last opportunity to acquire recreational land that would be readily accessible to its inhabitants.

Perhaps Bryant's idea for a large urban park came from the

scenic cemeteries, such as Mount Auburn Cemetery near Boston, that had become popular across the country. At Mount Auburn, tombs, temples, and the natural landscape had been blended to serve not only as a cemetery but also as a parklike retreat. A natural next step was to propose the development of large parks solely for recreation within the cities themselves.

Andrew Jackson Downing, a landscape architect who antedated Olmsted, had called attention to the fact that the public parks and gardens of France and other European countries, which all classes of citizens enjoyed, had no counterparts in America. Feeling strongly that America should emulate Europe, Downing advocated public city parks large enough to accommodate everyone. In response, the state of New York enacted legislation in 1851 authorizing the first acquisition of land (the tract on Manhattan) for a park. For several years, however, party politics and indecision blocked any move to develop the park. Finally the project got underway, and it was at this point that the unemployed Olmsted eagerly sought and narrowly won his appointment as superintendent of New York City's park.

According to the author-scholar Lewis Mumford, the "park" that Olmsted was to develop was "a monstrosity, a challenge, an affront."[13] Only a few squatters' shacks occupied high ground above a swamp. Olmsted's idea was to provide the lower classes of New York City with "a specimen of God's handiwork that shall be to them, inexpensively, what a month or two in the White Mountains, or the Adirondacks is . . . to those in easier circumstances."[14] He believed the naming of the park to have been a "wise forecast of the future," for "twenty years hence, the town will have enclosed the Central Park."[15] Eventually, an area two and a half miles long and half a mile wide (over eight hundred acres) was transformed into a series of lakes, meadows, and wooded hills in the middle of America's greatest metropolis that millions of New Yorkers have since enjoyed.

Olmsted's first major opportunity to demonstrate his talents

Bird's-eye view of Central Park (Lithograph by John Bachmann; courtesy of The New York Historical Society, New York City)

as a landscape architect came late in 1857 when the park commissioners decided to hold a competition for a new design for the park. He joined with Calvert Vaux, a young English architect, and together they won first prize over more than thirty competitors. Recognizing the potential of Central Park, Olmsted stated, "It is of great importance as the first real park made in this country—a democratic development of the highest significance & on the success of which, in my opinion, much of the progress of art & esthetic culture in this country is dependent."[16]

As the park superintendent in the next few years, Olmsted assumed the difficult and often frustrating job of carrying out this plan. Armies of job seekers hounded him daily for work, and local politicians criticized the project and tried to promote a plan they preferred. One commissioner won support in the local press for the construction of a grand avenue to run straight across the park—an addition that would have spoiled the whole effect Olmsted and Vaux were seeking. Despite the obstacles, however, the original project proceeded efficiently and rapidly as Olmsted directed architects, gardeners, engineers, and a work force that on some days numbered over thirty-five hundred people. By 1861 most of the planting and major landscaping had been completed.

Central Park became, in Olmsted's eyes, a grand experiment aimed at uplifting the character and condition of all urban dwellers, particularly the lower classes who he insisted should have ready access to the park. He believed that public interest in new parks was evidence of a healthy instinct to counteract deterioration in the rapidly growing cities and that beauty and appropriateness in landscape design encouraged morality, good health, and a well-ordered, peaceful domestic life.

Because Olmsted and Vaux wanted the park to be a haven from the usual noise and agitation of urban life, they sought to eliminate dangerous and disturbing traffic. Four sunken crossroads, ingeniously and almost unnoticeably hidden behind careful plantings, allowed traffic to cross the long park at intervals. Today the landscape of Central Park seems so natural that one can hardly believe it is the result of two men's imagination.

Brilliant, restrained, critical—Olmsted was never easy to get along with, and he had grown restive from the constant interference with his work. When the Civil War broke out in 1861, he took a leave of absence from his Central Park job to become secretary general of the United States Sanitary Commission, forerunner of the Red Cross. The medical services provided for Union troops at the beginning of the war were unspeakably poor, but Olmsted's imagination, foresight, and organizational ability contributed greatly to their improvement.

After two years at this post, however, he was restless again and looking for something else to do. Having married his brother's widow and accepted responsibility for her three children, he faced growing financial pressures. Thus, when he received a lucrative offer from California to manage the Mariposa mining estate (formerly owned by the explorer John C. Frémont) for ten thousand dollars a year, he saw a chance to settle his longstanding debts and accepted the offer after securing a guarantee of absolute administrative control. He viewed the development of the estate as a golden opportunity to convert a barbarous frontier into a civilized community.

But the richest gold-bearing ore of the Mariposa mine had already been depleted, and even under Olmsted's management the property was beyond financial recovery. Fortunately, he was able to continue his work in landscape architecture in the San Francisco Bay area. Following a trip in the Sierra Nevada in 1864, he welcomed and may have aided congressional action to place Yosemite Valley under the protection of the state of California. The valley was to be a park "for public use, resort and recreation" and "inalienable for all time." This legislation, passed eight years before the creation of Yellowstone National Park, was a first step toward the establishment of national parks in the United States.

Olmsted was appointed by the governor to head a board of commissioners to manage the Yosemite Valley parkland. The next year Olmsted set forth a justification and philosophic base for setting aside future parks, the first statement of its kind in the United States. In this report he listed the two primary reasons for the congressional action establishing Yosemite as a park: the first was the direct financial advantage of attracting travelers; the second, and much more important, was contained in the following statement: "It is the main duty of government, if it is not the sole duty of government, to provide means of protection for all its citizens in the pursuit of happiness against the obstacles, otherwise insurmountable, which the selfishness of individuals or combinations of individuals is liable to interpose to that pursuit."[17]

Olmsted recognized the importance of outdoor recreation and sight-seeing for "the health and vigor of men" and especially for their intellect. Because the outstanding scenic areas in America were falling rapidly into the hands of the wealthy few who could enjoy the luxury of private estates, Olmsted argued that the government should take action to protect them. The land, he believed, should remain accessible to the majority of citizens, particularly to people of modest or poor means, who could not afford estates of their own.

He also believed that the government had an obligation to manage parkland once it had been set aside. He recommended, in fact, that it be treated as a museum of natural history. As he explained: "In permitting the sacrifice of anything that would be of the slightest value to future visitors to the convenience, bad taste, playfulness, carelessness, or wanton destructiveness of present visitors, we probably yield in each case the interest of uncounted millions to the selfishness of a few individuals."[18] With characteristic foresight he predicted that one day great crowds of people would inundate America's scenic areas. Just forty years earlier, one small inn had accommodated all the visitors to the White Mountains of New Hampshire; by the 1860s, six grand hotels could not handle the influx. Although Olmsted wanted parkland to be made available to the people, he insisted that all man-made features, such as roads, be kept "within the narrowest practicable limits."

Unfortunately, his report on the Yosemite parkland went largely unnoticed and then mysteriously disappeared, perhaps because others wanted the state to spend its money elsewhere.

24

In any event, when the impending collapse of the Mariposa mining estate terminated his job as manager in 1865, Olmsted returned to New York to complete the development of Central Park and to create parks in other places. Financially solvent at last, he spent the next thirty years pursuing his chosen profession, landscape architecture.

Olmsted introduced this profession into the United States and provided a model for both its techniques and its standards. Before his career ended, he contributed to the design and development of seventeen major parks (including the famed Prospect Park in Brooklyn and Franklin Park in Boston), numerous suburban developments and parkways, and such grounds as those of Stanford University and the nation's Capitol. In each case he let the unique features of the site direct his decisions and thus applied an appropriate style.

One of Olmsted's most interesting commissions was to design a model suburban village, to be called Riverside, nine miles south of Chicago. For once he had a free hand to develop a master plan without interference from politicians, real estate speculators, or anyone else. He based his plan on the theme of "rural effect and domestic seclusion." Curving streets with intermittent clumps of trees provided a refreshing contrast to the usual American town with its "constantly repeated right angles, straight lines, and flat surfaces."[19]

Regrettably, most of Olmsted's plans were eventually compromised in favor of short-run economy or expediency, and a few designs were discarded entirely. For instance, Olmsted and the civil engineer, John Croes, collaborated to design a rapid transit system and road network for upper Manhattan and the Bronx. Their imaginative system would have been inexpensive and safe for travel and would have conformed to the beauty of the natural topography. Yet city politicians blocked the proposal and substituted an ugly elevated railway that in time had to be replaced by an expensive subway system.

Olmsted's restless mind continued to lead him into new and absorbing activities. He helped plan Boston's magnificent Arnold Arboretum, which served as a forestry laboratory. And he and his friend Charles Eliot Norton played leading roles in petitioning the United States and Canadian governments to protect the scenic Niagara Falls from the eager businessmen and industrialists who wished to use the falls for their own profit; only with difficulty were they able to block the demand for waterpower development. In 1885 Olmsted was also instrumental in establishing the Adirondacks as a state forest preserve. In addition, he spent several years developing Biltmore—George Vanderbilt's estate in North Carolina—into a model planned community. Gifford Pinchot, later the nation's first chief forester, credited Olmsted for making Biltmore the "nest egg for practical Forestry in the United States."[20]

Although Olmsted's reputation rested on the aesthetic appeal of the landscapes he designed, he was much more than a maker of parks, for he saw the parks, parkways, campuses, suburban communities, and other grounds he designed as vehicles for social transformation. He wished to alleviate the social ills of an increasingly urban and industrialized society by providing environments that would foster a "healthy, virtuous and respectable life"—landscapes that nurtured people's sense of beauty, order, and respect for others.

In 1895, after a long and illustrious career, Olmsted retired. Through his appreciation of aesthetic values, his administrative ability, his foresight, and his desire to be socially useful, he left a legacy of landscape architecture apparent in America today. Lewis Mumford, a leading twentieth-century advocate of Olmsted's ideas, said of him and his followers: "They renewed the city's contact with the land. They humanized and subdued the feral landscape. Above all, they made their contemporaries conscious of air, sunlight, vegetation, growth. If we still defile the possibilities of the land, it is not for lack of better example."[21]

GEORGE PERKINS MARSH

On a day in 1863 when Frederick Law Olmsted was administering medical relief to soldiers wounded in the Civil War, George Perkins Marsh, the United States minister to Italy, quietly contemplated the Alps, which seemed to lie at his fingertips across the terrace of the medieval castle where he lived. On his desk lay the nearly completed manuscript of a work he had started three years earlier. *Man and Nature; or, Physical Geography as Modified by Human Action*, would come to be regarded as his greatest achievement, and decades later Lewis Mumford would cite it as the "fountainhead of the conservation movement."[22]

Such an extraordinary work could have been composed only by someone with Marsh's wide interests and keen intellect, his ability to synthesize, and his understanding of the interrelatedness of diverse fields of knowledge. He left his mark on all the intellectual fields he entered. His biographer, David Lowenthal, said of him:

Lawyer, editor, farmer, manufacturer, congressman, diplomat par excellence, *Marsh was the broadest American scholar of his day. He was at home in twenty languages, became the country's foremost authority on both Scandinavian and English linguistics, made important contributions to comparative philology, helped to found and foster the Smithsonian Institution, served as arbiter of public taste in art and architecture, established principles for railroad regulation, provided new insights into the nature of the history of man and of the earth.*[23]

Marsh's greatest contribution sprang from his understanding of ecology. Aware as few people were of the impact of humans

George Perkins Marsh (Courtesy of the Library of Congress)

on the environment, he called insistently for a more enlightened husbandry of the land. *Man and Nature,* which he completed in his sixty-second year, grew out of a lifetime of experience, observation, and contemplation.

Marsh was born in 1801 in the small Vermont town of
Woodstock, near the Connecticut River. His father, Charles
Marsh, was a pillar of the community and a stern disciplinarian
who reared his son as a Calvinist, a conservative, and a gentleman. The elder's swift retribution for failure contributed to
George's incentive to master Reese's *Encyclopedia*—the volumes
of which were so heavy that the boy could hardly lift them—by
the age of five. Although the lonely, largely indoor life of his
early childhood left much to be desired—he read too much and
played too little—Marsh showed even then the passion for
knowledge and the prodigious memory that never left him.
After mastering the *Encyclopedia* he began the serious study of
Greek and Latin.

At the age of eight George developed a visual disability that
prevented him from reading for four years. It was then that he
discovered the joy of the out-of-doors. In no time he was exploring the flora and fauna of the Vermont frontier as avidly as
he had read his books. In later years he referred to himself as
"forest-born" and recalled that "the bubbling brook, the trees,
the flowers, the wild animals were to me persons, not things."[24]
His father taught him the names of the trees and the features
of the land, and characteristically, he never forgot them.

Marsh's formal education added little to what he already
knew. He entered Dartmouth at the age of fifteen to study the
usual curriculum of classical languages, Scripture, and the works
of the accepted philosophers. Natural science, then considered
a threat to religion and morality, was not offered.

After graduating at the head of his class, Marsh taught Greek
and Latin for a while, then became an attorney. For the next
thirty-five years his official residence was Burlington, Vermont,

but in all that time he never quite decided what he wanted to do, vacillating from unsuccessful business ventures to politics and from politics to scholarship. Neither business nor politics ever satisfied him, and scholarship, his true love, provided no income. His lack of success in business was not for want of trying, however; he "bred sheep, ran a woolen mill, built roads and bridges, sold lumber, edited a newspaper, developed a marble quarry, speculated in real estate."[25] Finally, inherited wealth provided him with the income to build a superlative library and to study art, music, history, and languages.

In 1840 Marsh was elected to Congress. His Whig platform called for a protective tariff, sound currency, and reform. Taking little interest in the House debates, he concentrated instead on the work of the committees and became particularly interested in the question of how to dispose of James Smithson's bequest to the government of a large sum of money that was to be used for "the increase and diffusion of knowledge among men." Practical westerners in the House favored agricultural schools and other programs of immediate value, but Marsh, John Quincy Adams, and a few other intellectuals wanted to establish a large national museum and library for research. In the House debate that followed, Marsh made the finest speech of his political career, appealing to national pride by noting that the founding fathers of the Republic had almost all been scholars.

Marsh and his supporters won, and the result was the Smithsonian Institution, whose interest in climate laid the foundation for the United States Weather Bureau and whose publication of scientific papers has contributed to the growth and spread of knowledge. Marsh's protégé, the naturalist Spencer Baird, served on the staff of the Smithsonian for nearly forty years, ten of them as its director.

In 1849 Marsh's support of Zachary Taylor won him an appointment as minister to Turkey. Although hampered by a pauper's salary, he made an effective ambassador. Besides performing his official duties, he collected specimens for the Smithsonian and on an eight-month trek traveled extensively through Egypt, thence to Palestine, and back to Constantinople. Marsh recorded all that he observed, not only what he saw as a tourist but also the measurements of temperature, rainfall, and altitude, the rate and volume of the flow of streams, and a myriad of other natural phenomena—all of this just to satisfy his avid curiosity.

After returning to Washington in 1854, he turned down numerous jobs, including a Harvard history professorship, because of the low salaries offered. Instead, he returned to dabbling in such diverse activities as inventing glass instruments, quarrying marble, and lecturing. One lecture that was particularly well received addressed the topic of introducing camels into the American West. Marsh had been impressed by the hardiness and speed of the camels he observed on his Near Eastern travels. Chiefly as a result of his lectures at the Smithsonian, the army began to import a large number of camels to the Southwest in 1856, but with the disruption caused by the Civil War and the expansion of the railroads, they soon became only a curiosity.

In 1857, in response to mounting concern over the rapid decline of fish in the state of Vermont, Marsh submitted to the Vermont legislature a report on the artificial propagation of fish. Overfishing, pollution of streams from sawdust and factory wastes, and the construction of dams across streams had clearly taken their toll. Marsh, however, emphasized causes that were more obscure—particularly the deterioration of Vermont's forest and farmlands. Increasing floods in the wet season altered the course of streams and covered spawning grounds with silt, and reduced stream flow and rising water temperature accompanied the dry season.

Because Marsh saw the decline in the fish population as a "condition of advanced civilization" and believed that Americans would habitually oppose restrictive fish and game laws, he did not look to the government to solve the problem by itself. The government could help reduce illegal and excessive fishing practices and protect property used for fish propagation, but ultimately, to provide a stable habitat for fish in Vermont's streams, individual landowners had to protect forest and farmland from abuse. Marsh called for a reliance on the "enterprise and ingenuity of private citizens," counting on the spread of scientific knowledge and the pursuit of economic self-interest to encourage the establishment of fish hatcheries.[26] Typically, he approached the problem with a utilitarian bias, asking what economic benefits could be obtained.

Unfortunately, Marsh's financial condition fell to new depths. His marble quarry a failure and the camel experiment unsuccessful, he accepted a post as Vermont railroad commissioner and later assumed an English professorship at Columbia University. Finally came the break of a lifetime: President Lincoln appointed him to the coveted position of minister to Italy. He set sail for Europe shortly after the firing on Fort Sumter in 1861, and Italy remained his home until his death in 1882.

At the time he undertook the writing of *Man and Nature*, Marsh was described as "a tall, homely man with a full beard and sideburns. Sixty, he looked forty-five, his face unlined and his hair ungrizzled. He had been gaining steadily, and now weighed 230 pounds. But his square, solid physique had held up remarkably well; he could without difficulty work fourteen hours in his office and library, or climb hills all day for weeks."[27] He thrived in the pleasant Italian climate and took small excursions into the Alps as time allowed, climbing the peaks and studying the glaciers, which fascinated him.

Marsh began his book with the intention of exciting the layman's interest in "man's efforts to replenish the earth and subdue it." He took issue with earlier students of nature, including Thomas Jefferson, who regarded the changes humans wrought in nature as beneficial and desirable. Marsh noted that "it is certain that man has done much to mould the form of the earth's surface," but he questioned the wisdom of many of the changes. In *Man and Nature*, he asked to what degree man can "permanently modify and ameliorate" the earth's surface and the climate on which his material welfare depends, how far he can "compensate, arrest, or retard the deterioration which many of his agricultural and industrial processes tend to produce," and how far he can "restore fertility and salubrity to soils which his follies or his crimes have made barren or pestilential."[28]

Marsh's direct observations and personal experiences had convinced him of humankind's overall destructiveness. Years earlier he had stated that "every middle-aged man who revisits his birth-place after a few years of absence, looks upon another landscape than that which formed the theatre of his youthful toils and pleasures."[29] He had seen drastic changes in the woodlands of Vermont since the early days when his father first taught him the names of the trees and the importance of the watersheds. Nowhere in the country were the forests cut faster or was the topsoil eroded more quickly than in Vermont's Green Mountains. His own town of Burlington, which had been a great exporter of timber, became a major importer within twenty years.

Living for four years in Turkey and traveling about the Mediterranean had also made an indelible impression on Marsh's mind. Everywhere he went, destruction of the forests, overgrazing, and careless farming had left the land in ruins. As his biographer explained: "For Marsh each area pointed a moral: the sterile sands of the Sahara, the desolate pock-marked Adriatic Karst, the malarial Roman Campagna, the rock-strewn valleys of Provence and Dauphiné. Long ago fertile and populous, these regions now stood barren and deserted, monuments to human improvidence."[30]

Marsh had noted that recent floods and landslides in Europe were the direct results of forest despoliation in the Alps. But here at least were a few French scientists and engineers who were studying the differences in runoff, soil moisture, and stream flow between forested areas and bare ground, and Italian foresters were recommending national control of forest resources. Europeans, it seemed, were learning to manage their land.

Marsh's studies had taught him that nature was remarkably stable if people did not interfere. Over the centuries a balance in nature had been maintained, but human meddling had upset this balance in ways that were seldom intended. Marsh noted the following example:

Not many years ago, the pines on thousands of acres of land in North Carolina, were destroyed by insects not known to have ever done serious injury to that tree before. In such cases as this and others of the like sort, there is good reason to believe that man is the indirect cause of an evil for which he pays so heavy a penalty. Insects increase whenever the birds which feed upon them disappear. Hence, in the wanton destruction of the robin and other insectivorous birds . . . the featherless biped, man, is not only exchanging the vocal orchestra which greets the rising sun for the drowsy beetle's evening drone, and depriving his groves and his fields of their fairest ornament, but he is waging a treacherous warfare on his natural allies.[31]

Marsh discussed many such ecological situations that revealed the unique influence of humans on the world about them. For instance, beaver hats increased so rapidly in popularity that the beaver seemed destined for extinction. But no! In the nick of time a Parisian manufacturer invented silk hats, and beavers soon increased in number and returned to their important roles as dam builders and marsh-pond producers. Thus, Marsh observed that "the caprice of Parisian fashion . . . may sensibly affect the physical geography of a distant continent."[32] He stated:

Man has too long forgotten that the earth was given to him for usufruct alone, not for consumption, still less for profligate waste. . . . The earth is fast becoming an unfit home for its noblest inhabitant, and another era of equal human crime and human improvidence . . . would reduce it to such a condition of impoverished productiveness, of shattered surface, of climatic excess, as to threaten the depravation, barbarism, and perhaps even extinction of the species.[33]

Marsh did not believe that humans were part of nature but rather that their very power of destructiveness placed them apart from and above it. As he explained, "Man is everywhere a disturbing agent. Wherever he plants his foot, the harmonies of nature are turned to discords."[34] No other living creature killed in such vast quantities what it could not consume; no other species indulged in such unrestrained destruction of life for a few pelts, skins, or tusks, for oil or plumage, or indeed "just for the fun of it." The changes made by humans, moreover, could not be counteracted by any natural force. People themselves could lessen the impact of the changes they wrought, but they rarely bothered to do so. Marsh questioned earlier authorities who claimed that people's actions toward nature differed in degree but not in kind from those of wild animals. He asked his contemporaries to open their eyes and look at the evidence. Wild animals, he pointed out in one example, were never responsible for sudden changes, whereas humans often felled complete stands of trees in the space of a few days:

When the forest is gone, the great reservoir of moisture stored up in its vegetable mould is evaporated, and returns only in deluges of rain to wash away the parched dust into which that mould has been converted. The well-wooded and humid hills are turned to ridges of dry rock, which encumbers the low grounds and chokes the watercourses with its debris, and . . . the whole earth, unless rescued by human art from the physical degradation to which it tends, becomes an assemblage of bald moun-

tains, of barren, turfless hills, and of swampy and malarious plains.
There are parts of Asia Minor, of Northern Africa, of Greece, and even
of Alpine Europe, where the operation of causes set in action by man has
brought the face of the earth to a desolation almost as complete as that
of the moon.[35]

Marsh saw no easy solution to the problems he described, but science and morality were his sources of hope for the future. Because additional knowledge was needed desperately, he called for extensive "geological, hydrographical, and topographical surveys." Americans, he said, could learn a great deal from the advances made in Europe, especially in silviculture (the management of forests). He criticized the individual states in the nation for permitting such a rapid transfer of the original public domain to the hands of private citizens, for he did not believe that government would, or indeed could, move quickly or decisively enough to stem the tide of destruction. Instead of government intervention he urged "enlightened self-interest" from private business and individuals. He believed that if people wanted to, they could affect their environment beneficially as well as harmfully.

In April 1863, in the pleasant surroundings of his borrowed castle south of Turin, Italy, Marsh finished the manuscript for his book. The project had taken longer than he had expected; after all, his diplomatic duties consumed much of his time, and he was constantly reading, adding new material, and revising what he had written. Further problems with the publisher delayed the book's appearance until the following year.

More than a thousand copies of *Man and Nature* sold in the first few months after its publication, and many scientists at home and abroad commended it. A reviewer in the *Nation* called it "one of the most useful and suggestive books ever published." Europeans not only praised the book but adopted many of Marsh's ideas. Americans, unfortunately, continued by and large to waste their country's resources in blissful ignorance. A few land speculators used the book as their authority for stating, quite inaccurately, that the afforestation recommended by Marsh would permanently increase the precipitation of rain in the arid West.

But a few citizens took Marsh's warnings seriously. The danger of a timber famine led to a reversal of traditional attitudes. In 1873 a group of scientists sent to Congress a memorial on the importance of forestry, thereby laying the foundation for a policy of forest preservation and management. Many years later, Gifford Pinchot (chief forester under Theodore Roosevelt) referred to *Man and Nature* as "epoch making."[36] The book went through many printings, one of them in 1907, just before the conservation movement of Pinchot and Theodore Roosevelt reached its peak.

Marsh's book may also have advanced the movement to preserve parkland, for in the second edition (1874) he wrote: "It is desirable that some large and easily accessible region of American soil should remain as far as possible in its primitive condition, at once a museum for the instruction of the students, a garden for the recreation of the lovers of nature, and an asylum where indigenous trees . . . plants . . . beasts may dwell and perpetuate their kind."[37]

Over the years *Man and Nature* fell from public notice, but in the 1930s, when floods and soil erosion ravaged the land, it was rediscovered. The work is in fact so relevant today that an international symposium on "Man's Role in Changing the Face of the Earth" met at Princeton in 1955 to discuss the issues Marsh had raised over ninety years before. In 1965 Harvard University Press published a new edition of *Man and Nature*, and Secretary of the Interior Stewart Udall referred to Marsh's work and to that of such men as Thoreau and Olmsted as the "beginning of land wisdom in this country."[38]

Marsh's message remains unmistakable. The welfare of every

generation depends on how earlier generations have treated the soil, water, plants, and animals. Land once abused by people does not return to its natural state; it remains impoverished. To avoid such destruction, humans must first learn how they affect the environment and then how they may control it for their own well-being.

Chapter 2: John Wesley Powell

Six weary men in two battered boats emerged from the lower end of the Grand Canyon—the first party to navigate the Colorado River throughout the canyon's length. A resolute young scientist, red-bearded and with only one arm, had piloted the party down the river and now led it back to civilization. The year was 1869; the young scientist, John Wesley Powell.

This man, conqueror of the treacherous Colorado, soon faced an even greater challenge—convincing Congress and the American people of the need for the planned development of the arid region of the United States. Powell hoped that an orderly settlement of the western frontier would replace the pursuit of individual short-term gain. From his ideas and his fight to implement them rose a land- and resource-use program based on government-sponsored scientific investigation.

EARLY LIFE AND EXPEDITIONS

The first thirty-five years of Powell's life furnished no clue that he would become the most politically powerful American scientist of his time. Born in 1834, he spent his early years on the midwestern frontier. He was only five when his father, an itinerant Methodist minister, led the family west from New York to Ohio. The boy's days were filled with the experiences common to life in small towns and on rural farms. In his education he had the advantages of living close to the land and the disadvantages of being far from the cultural life of the city. His abolitionist father read the Bible aloud at home and encouraged his son to study for the ministry, but Wes did not want to follow in his father's footsteps.

When town bullies threw stones at the young boy because of his father's abolitionist stance, he found refuge with George Crookham, a neighboring farmer. Crookham first turned Wes's attention to natural history, as they discussed topics ranging from geology and botany to ethnology, philosophy, and literature. A self-taught scientist, Crookham gladly shared his library, his private museum, and his rich background with the intent neighbor boy. Together they took field trips, exploring the wonders of nature and collecting fossils, shells, flowers, and other specimens.

At the age of eighteen and armed with only his homespun education, Powell obtained a teaching position in a one-room school in Wisconsin; his wages were fourteen dollars a month. During the next few years he alternated between teaching school and attending local colleges in Illinois. Disenchanted with college—no science courses were offered and he knew more than most of his professors—he took longer and longer field trips, traveling the waters and bordering lands of the Mississippi and Ohio rivers. At the age of twenty-seven and with considerable experience under his belt, Powell was elected as the first secretary of the State Natural History Society of Illinois.

But shortly thereafter the Civil War broke out and he joined the Illinois Volunteer Infantry. Though small in stature (he was five feet six inches tall), he brought the same intelligence and dedication to military service that he brought to his other ventures. Powell soon rose to the rank of major, a title he carried the rest of his life. Through his military experience he learned about government bureaucracy and met important people—including General Grant—who later befriended him. He even managed on occasion to pursue his scientific interests; during the siege of Vicksburg, for example, Powell was searching the trenches for fossils. Although he lost his right arm from a wound received in the battle of Shiloh, he returned to active duty. It was 1865 before he finally returned to academic life as a professor of natural history.

Powell soon won a grant from the Illinois legislature for a museum for his Illinois Natural History Society. His next success—and his first in uniting politics and science—came with his appointment as museum curator. He then launched scientific expeditions to the west to collect specimens for the museum.

Starting on a shoestring budget in 1867, Powell gained Grant's support in purchasing army rations at cost and acquired a loan of scientific equipment from the Smithsonian in exchange for data acquired from topographical measurements. By the time he headed west with three students and seven amateur naturalists to the Rocky Mountains of Colorado, Powell had eleven hundred dollars in his pocket to meet all the expenses. Such enterprise became a Powell trademark.

This successful trip only whetted his appetite. Thus, he launched the Colorado Scientific Exploring Expedition to explore the Green and Colorado rivers from the present state of Wyoming through Utah and part of Colorado and into Arizona. Here was a challenge indeed: an area up to five hundred miles long and two hundred miles wide that was still largely a blank on the scientific maps in Washington. This vast unknown had given rise to legends of immense canyons and wild cataracts and to the belief that no person could enter the river and emerge alive. Undaunted, Powell thought of the knowledge to be gained.

Following a successful trip into the Colorado Rockies, Powell recruited several volunteers, most of them hardy mountain men who could take danger and hardship in stride and who responded enthusiastically to the opportunity for adventure. The voyagers departed from Green River, Wyoming, on May 24, 1869. After several weeks of hazardous river running, they plunged into the 217-mile-long depths of what Powell named the Grand Canyon in what became the state of Arizona. He vividly described his feelings as the small party pushed off from the shore:

We are now ready to start on our way down the Great Unknown. Our boats, tied to a common stake, are chafing each other, as they are tossed by the fretful river. . . . The flour has been resifted through the mosquito net sieve; the spoiled bacon has been dried, and the worst of it boiled; the few pounds of dried apples have been spread in the sun, and reshrunken to their normal bulk; the sugar has all melted, and gone on its way down the river; but we have a large sack of coffee. . . .

We are three quarters of a mile in the depths of the earth, and the great river shrinks into insignificance, as it dashes its angry waves against the walls and cliffs, that rise to the world above; they are but puny ripples, and we but pigmies, running up and down the sands, or lost among the boulders.

We have an unknown distance yet to run; an unknown river yet to explore. What falls there are, we know not; what rocks beset the channel, we know not; what walls rise over the river, we know not. The men talk as cheerfully as ever; jests are bandied about freely this morning; but to me the cheer is somber and jests are ghastly.[1]

Powell's uneasiness was well founded. Temperatures of 115 degrees during the day alternated with drenching rains at night. The men labored incessantly—portaging, pulling the boats with

Powell's second Colorado River expedition, 1871
(Smithsonian Institution Photograph No. 56332)

ropes, or running the battered and leaking crafts down the rushing torrent, where each new rapid seemed worse than the last. In places the impenetrable cliffs blocked any escape from the river and the men had to plunge blindly toward an unknown fate.

With food running short, fear rising, and their leader evidently willing to take any risk to continue his exploration, three of the men decided to leave the river and take their chances on climbing the cliffs to the plateau far above. Powell, too, looked hesitantly at the seemingly impassable rapids ahead, but decided to go on, and so the remaining six men in two boats swept through the last rapids and emerged from the canyon. Their three friends, so close to safety, scaled the canyon wall only to be killed by Shivwit Indian arrows; apparently they were mistaken for miners who had abused Indian women.

The major returned to the East a national celebrity. Although he had collected only a small amount of scientific data, Powell seized the opportunity to publicize his work. He regarded the Grand Canyon expedition as only one step in attaining a knowledge of the entire Rocky Mountain region. His greatest reward came when Congress finally agreed to support his work, at least for one year, by appropriating ten thousand dollars for a United States geographical and geological survey in the Rocky Mountain region. Thus Powell began over twenty years of service for the cause of government-sponsored science and for the orderly settlement and conservation of the lands of the arid West.

THE POWELL SURVEY

Powell's survey was limited at first because he had yet to make any major scientific accomplishments. His earlier expeditions had been reconnaissance trips for the work that lay ahead, and although a second voyage down the Colorado River in 1871 produced more scientific data than the first, Powell delegated much of his authority and turned increasingly to other interests, principally, his study of the Indians of the Colorado plateau.

Powell sharply criticized the Bureau of Indian Affairs and local Indian agents for graft, waste, and disregard for the Indians' well-being. By learning the languages and respecting the customs of the tribes he visited (he remained fascinated with ethnology throughout his life), Powell gained their trust; he could travel freely among this people whose way of life would soon be obliterated by the advance of civilization.

Until the end of the 1870s, members of the major's survey party traveled the mountains, mesas, and canyons of the Colorado plateau, concentrating on what he called the Plateau Province—an essentially unknown area stretching from south-

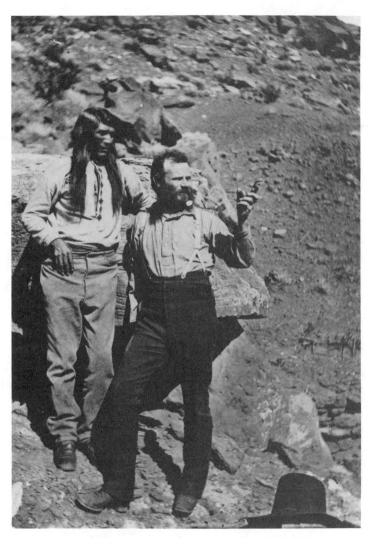

*Powell and Tau-gu, chief of the Paiutes
(Smithsonian Institution Photograph No. 1636)*

eastern Utah and western Colorado into northern Arizona and the northwestern corner of New Mexico. Powell's job was to unravel the mystery of the plateau country and to replace myth and ignorance with knowledge.

This he accomplished to a remarkable degree, thanks in part to his skill in delegating responsibility to the most able of his assistants—men like Grove Karl Gilbert, Clarence Dutton, and Almon Thompson. Throughout his career Powell attracted competent people, shared his ideas fully with them, and provided them with opportunities to develop their own talents. His survey made important contributions to the study of topography and led especially to an understanding of the processes of erosion that had created the extraordinary formations in the canyon country.

More difficult than completing the survey itself was overcoming people's false ideas about the arid West—ideas Powell was never able to dispel. In the first half of the nineteenth century, many Americans believed that a Great American Desert—a region of uninterrupted desolation—lay between the Mississippi River and the Rocky Mountains, although descriptions of the exact location and extent of this desert varied with the source and over time. This image of an uninhabitable desert had originated in the reports of government explorations, beginning with Zebulon Pike's report in 1810, and had been popularized by pioneers who crossed the plains in the heat of summer. The myth of an implacable desert barrier gained its broadest acceptance just before the Civil War.

But as the war ended, farmers turned their eyes westward, dreaming of an agricultural paradise in the unsettled lands made available by the Homestead Act. Encouraged by expansionists, who believed in "manifest destiny," and by the triumphant Republican party, they pushed from eastern Kansas and Nebraska into the higher and drier subhumid plains, where the annual rainfall was less than twenty inches and where agriculture became less and less dependable. People who had never been west of the Mississippi—dime novelists, artists, eastern politicians—helped to create a romanticized picture of the West. As a result the American public abandoned the myth of the Great American Desert for a second myth: to the west lay a garden land where farms would flourish under eastern methods of cultivation.

Wishful thinking led to the spread of the idea that rainfall was becoming increasingly abundant in the West. As fate would have it, a series of wet years followed the Civil War at the very time that farmers were beginning to advance from the well-watered lands of the Midwest into the semiarid plains. Thus, "Rain follows the plough" became the slogan of a utopian optimism that saw the arid West as a land of milk and honey with ample water for irrigation—an area of dependable climate and rich soil that awaited the arrival of civilization.

In fact, this romanticized version of a western garden land resulted in untold human waste and suffering, the despoliation of the land and its resources, and the gross political and economic mismanagement of a region covering roughly two-fifths of the United States. Only limited areas could be cultivated, whether by irrigating or by using dry farming techniques. None of the public land acts that supposedly opened the frontier to settlement provided pioneers with even a fifty percent chance of success in the arid West. Few families could afford to go west to homestead, and even if they began with a sizable claim, the chances were that in the end they would return to the East, broken by drought, blizzards, grasshoppers, or some combination of plagues. In effect, the land laws often led to human heartbreak, abandoned or tenant-operated farms, speculation, fraud, the monopolization of large areas, and the destruction of semiarid grasslands laid bare by the plow to the merciless winds.

Powell accepted the job of separating fact from fiction, and although his survey team made progress he had continual difficulty retaining government support. His was the fourth western survey authorized by Congress in the 1870s. It was also the smallest and least experienced. The more prestigious surveys were led by Clarence King and Lieutenant George Wheeler under the War Department and by Dr. Ferdinand Hayden under the Department of the Interior, and the competition between these government bureaus and the survey leaders was heavy. Though short in funds, Powell's survey established an enviable record, and his painstaking work was at last to unravel the mysteries of the arid West.

As early as 1874 Powell began to publicize his conclusions and to suggest land reforms. In one of his reports to Congress he declared, "All of the region of country west of the 100th or 99th meridian, except a little in California, Oregon, and Washington Territory, is arid, and . . . no part of it can be redeemed for agriculture, except by irrigation."[2] Although Powell failed to recognize the future importance of dry farming, his generalization still applied to most of the West. He concluded that areas for possible economic development would have to be identified by coordinated surveys of the public domain.

Powell's reports ran counter to generally accepted thought and met with little enthusiasm. The small area his surveyors had studied showed little promise of providing either mineral or agricultural wealth, and his slow, methodical research resulted in few publications. To make matters worse, a quarrelsome rivalry broke out between Hayden and Wheeler, and Congress investigated every survey, suspecting corruption and waste, two features of bureaucracy that were all too common in the United States during the post–Civil War period. Powell, blameless in this respect, had no patience for such pettiness and corruption. His plea for reform went unheeded, however, particularly within the General Land Office, which had a tarnished reputation.

Powell's opportunity came with the appointment of Carl Schurz, a reform-minded secretary of the interior, to President Rutherford Hayes's cabinet. On April 1, 1878, Powell presented Schurz with his *Report on the Lands of the Arid Regions of the West,* a prophetic document that the historian Bernard DeVoto considered as basic as *The Federalist* and one of the most revolutionary books on land use ever written by an American. The proposals in *Arid Lands,* as Powell's report was called, went far beyond coordinating the work of the various geographical surveys; it attacked the basic philosophy and the whole body of law upon which the American West was being developed. Powell noted that the hundredth meridian formed a rough boundary between the humid East and the arid West and that even a sub-humid area east of this line suffered from recurring drought. West of the line lay roughly forty percent of the United States, the arid region whose future depended on irrigation.

The arid lands could be divided, Powell said, into three main categories: irrigable lands in the lowlands, forestlands high on mountain slopes, and pasturelands in between. He paid little attention to the forestlands, stressing only the need to prevent forest fires. He himself had once set fire to the trunk of a pine tree to keep warm and then watched as the wind swept the flames for "scores of miles." Curiously, he did not recognize that the demand for lumber would lead to exploitation of forests, even in the arid lands. Neither did he foresee the need for state or national forests, fearing that graft would result if public officials managed the public lands from afar. He also believed that the coal lands were "inexhaustible," and he largely ignored questions of mineral development.

He did recognize, however, that the eastern farming practice of individual farmers operating small, separate holdings would not work in the arid West. While an individual might be able to divert water from a nearby spring or creek, he could not build a major dam or canal by himself. Such a task depended on community cooperation, such as that demonstrated by the Mormons in Utah and by a few irrigation colonies in southern California.

Powell proposed that a bill be submitted to Congress with the following provisions: (1) any nine or more persons qualified to homestead could form an irrigation district, acquire title to irrigable lands, and regulate their district's land and water as long as they complied with the general law; (2) all lands of 320 acres or more for which there was accessible water would be classed as irrigable lands; (3) no person would be allotted more than eighty acres; and (4) rights to water would be inhered in the land and could not be forfeited unless the land was not used for a five-year period. Through legislation of this sort, Powell hoped to prevent a monopolizing of the land by a few individuals who might gain control of vital water supplies.

In a proposal for a second bill he outlined provisions for "pasturage districts" for cattle and sheep raising. In these districts, ranchers with little or no irrigable land could settle on individual tracts no smaller than 2,560 acres each. Powell considered this acreage minimal for a cattle ranch meant to support a single family. He argued that water was the key to successful settlement and that the settlers themselves, in organized bodies, should decide on an equitable division of the scarce water supply through a "wise system of parceling the lands."

He also proposed that each cattle ranch include twenty acres of irrigable land on which to grow a garden and feed for the stock. To apportion the limited water equitably among the members of an irrigation or pasturage district would require a new system of land division entirely different from the checkerboard system of township and range then used by the General Land Office. According to Powell, the division of the land should conform to its topography and water supply, not to an arbitrarily drawn square of 160 acres. And instead of having the graft-ridden General Land Office conduct the surveys, he wanted the work to be done by the Coast and Geodetic Survey, a scientific agency.

Powell's *Arid Lands* shocked many Americans. He threatened the land speculators, both large and small, who were manipulating the law for private gain; he attacked the whole system of land surveys; and he proposed revolutionary land laws. But his social and economic ideas seemed even more radical, for they challenged the experience of generations of eastern frontier farmers, who had lived in a land of ample rainfall. He wanted the individual yeoman farmer to be replaced by cooperative farmers' associations. When *Arid Lands* was published, Powell stood almost alone in understanding that the arid region was neither desert nor garden. It was, in fact, a fertile land; though lacking water, it could nevertheless support small numbers of farmers who were willing to adapt to it.

To present his report was one thing; to have it accepted and implemented was quite another. Still, Powell had a few influential supporters, including Othniel C. Marsh, a paleontologist at Yale and president of the National Academy of Sciences, a group of eminent American scientists. Marsh could hold his own in the political battles of Washington, and he and Powell had a mutual opponent—Hayden. Another supporter, this one within Congress, was Representative Abram Hewitt of New York, who tacked on to an appropriation bill a clause commissioning the National Academy of Sciences to consider the problem of the western land surveys and to suggest a plan of reorganization. As a result, the academy undertook a study of the entire public-lands problem. Powell could hardly have wished for better fortune. Marsh sympathized with his ideas, and special interests in Congress could not meddle behind the closed doors of the academy.

Powell seized his opportunity, circulating copies of *Arid Lands* and testifying before a committee of the academy. His efforts were rewarded when, late in 1878, the academy issued a report to Congress recommending that the Interior Department authorize two surveys: a coast and interior survey for mapping and topography and a geological survey of "the geological structure and economical resources of the public domain." The new surveys would take the place of those conducted by Hayden, Wheeler, and Powell (King had already finished his work), and a commission would study and codify "present laws relating to the survey and disposition of the public domain."[3] In essence, the academy agreed with Powell that civilian scientists under the Department of the Interior could best handle the development of the western public lands and that a consolidated survey would prove more efficient.

Although Congress defeated a proposal for reform of the land laws, it did consolidate the remaining surveys into a single Geological Survey under the Department of the Interior. Powell helped to have Clarence King appointed as the first director of the survey, and he himself took charge of the newly created Bureau of Ethnology. During the nineteen years he managed this bureau, Powell broadened the country's knowledge of the American Indian.

CHIEF OF THE GEOLOGICAL SURVEY

When King resigned his position in 1881, Powell acceded to the directorship of the Geological Survey, a position he held for over a decade. Handling his new administrative responsibilities creatively and skillfully, he now sat at the head of government science in the United States. The Bureau of Ethnology answered only to the Smithsonian Institution, and the Geological Survey received a yearly sum from Congress, which Powell dispensed as he pleased.

Powell defined the role of both his bureaus in the broadest

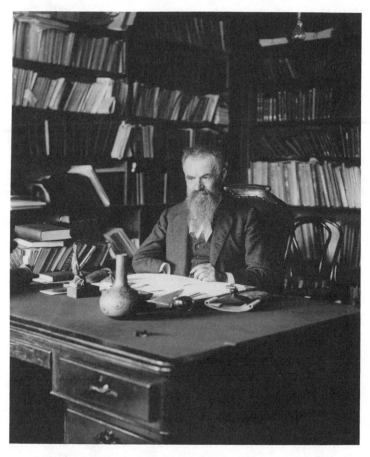

John Wesley Powell (Smithsonian Institution Photograph No. 64-A-13-A)

possible terms. Whereas King had considered the Geological
Survey to be primarily an adviser to the mining industry, Powell
thought it should be involved with all the earth sciences, for he
saw the great potential of government-sponsored research to aid
people of all classes. Geologic mapping, for example, would
benefit miners, and topographic and hydrologic mapping would
help farmers. Under Powell's leadership, the main project of the
Geological Survey became a national topographic map, which

would take years to complete. Though he recognized the value of research, he stressed the utilitarian value of applying knowledge to the development of natural resources. It was in this spirit that he tackled his new responsibilities and opportunities.

The growth of government-sponsored science in the 1880s intensified the debate over the proper domain of government, and Powell received increasing criticism. Small farmers feared that the government would close much of the public domain while the land awaited classification, and small cattlemen objected to Powell's proposal for 2,560-acre ranches, fearing that associations of large landowners would crowd them out. Other Americans complained, with some justification, that Powell neglected the timber, mineral, and mercantile potential of the arid lands. And many speculators and boosters felt threatened by Powell's ideas and proposals. Western legislators still feared his *Arid Lands* and watched his actions with suspicion, yet a joint congressional committee, which in 1884 investigated the old question of the propriety of scientific research, continued to support him and his idea of publicly financed science.

In the winter of 1886 blizzards and subzero temperatures swept down from Canada across the broad, unbroken plains, and the great cattle kingdom that had dominated the open range for twenty years came to an end. Overgrazing had so reduced the available grass that either blizzard or drought could bring ruin, and drought followed the hard winter. The greatest damage occurred in the subhumid eastern fringe of the dry lands, where agriculture had been most intense. Crops withered beneath the dry sky.

Powell understood what was happening. Eastern ideas and institutions had been imposed on a dry country. As conditions grew worse the farmers began to appeal to the government for help, and the Major finally had an opportunity to implement the recommendations in *Arid Lands,* written more than ten years before.

Because variations in yearly precipitation left settlement and economic progress in doubt, public sentiment in the West favored irrigation. Thus, Senator William Stewart of Nevada and other legislators from the arid region called on the Geological Survey to designate and survey irrigable lands and reservoir and canal sites. Powell drafted a bill for an irrigation survey and explained to a Senate committee his intent to use topographic mapping to locate irrigable lands. The bill, with Senator Stewart's support, became law in October 1888.

Powell and Stewart both thought that surveys of irrigable lands should be made at once, for each year's delay allowed further encroachments by speculators and settlers. Powell believed that topographic mapping could best identify the boundaries of irrigation districts and that hydrologic surveys and engineering studies could locate specific sites for reservoirs and canals. After the survey was completed, cooperative associations of farmers in each district would be responsible for constructing and managing their own irrigation system.

But many people were uncertain about what would happen once irrigable lands and reservoir and canal sites were determined. Would the government guarantee water rights to the settlers? Would it build the expensive dams and distribute the water? If not, who would? Would an irrigation survey merely gather information, or would it be an important step toward rewriting the land laws and establishing a new system of land development and ownership in the arid West?

In response to those who called on the federal government to control development in the West, Powell answered bluntly, "Hands off! Furnish the people with institutions of justice, and let them do the work for themselves."[4] He recommended that each community finance, build, and control its own irrigation works, but knew that land had no value without water and that the federal government would have to establish an equitable division of water between the states. Then each state would settle water disputes between irrigation districts, and the people of each district would divide the water equitably among themselves.

Powell rejected federal control of the forests and grasslands upon which the water supply of each irrigation district depended. He argued that the people who directly used a watershed would best protect it because their livelihood was involved. Powell assumed that the people of each district would have a common interest and therefore would cooperate. Besides, federal agencies had a well-deserved reputation for graft and corruption.

When he took action to implement his ideas, Powell met immediate opposition; his irrigation survey rested on explosive issues. Many congressmen attacked topographic mapping as unauthorized and unnecessary, accusing Powell of misappropriating funds intended for locating reservoir sites. Powell's desire for comprehensive and systematic surveys and economic planning for the resources of the arid lands provoked Stewart and others who favored rapid development. He also made tactical errors, calling advocates of an artesian water supply unrealistic and omitting the Pacific Coast states as well as Kansas, Nebraska, and the Dakotas from his initial surveys.

More serious, Powell supported a ruling by the attorney general upholding a clause in the Irrigation Survey Act of 1888 that prevented people from entering onto, occupying, or selling land that the Geological Survey thought could be irrigated. Powell warned that rich speculators and large companies were gaining control of the water and land and that such action would thwart his plans for the comprehensive, scientific development of irrigation districts. Some senators, however, called Powell's proposed communities "un-American" and "utopian" and blamed him for hindering progress.

In spite of limited funds Powell hurried on with his survey, hopeful that opening some areas to irrigation would meet the needs of prospective farmers and reduce the criticism of his opponents. When the first reservoir sites were designated, however, local residents feared for their own land titles and plans. Moreover, the hopelessly tangled water rights made accepting the Irrigation Survey's findings all but impossible. The major could only indicate how the water and land could be used most economically and beneficially. The legal question of ownership and control had to be left to the courts, and some of the disputes have yet to be settled.

In the summer of 1889 Powell joined a Senate Irrigation Committee that was touring the West. In a speech, he proposed that the new state of Montana use hydrographic basins, instead of the traditional, artificially created political divisions, as the guide for establishing their counties. These natural basins would form political and economic units for controlling water and the interdependent resources of timber, grass, and arable land.

The summer tour produced little except a growing antipathy between Powell and Stewart, who continued to promote rapid development. A crowning blow to Stewart came in April 1890, when the General Land Office commissioner ordered that no title patents be issued for land claims filed after October 2, 1888—the date of the creation of the Irrigation Survey. This decree officially closed the public domain, at least until Powell notified the president that he had surveyed a specific tract. To his enemies the major had become a despot blocking progress.

DEFEAT AND LEGACY

Hard as Powell fought for the continuation of the Irrigation Survey and for his general plan, the tide began to turn against him. His position was vulnerable, partly because of the successful spread of dry farming. In addition, ironically, his advocacy of large ranches in arid areas aroused antimonopolists who feared the growth of large estates. Many others, including miners and loggers, simply preferred the existing land-disposal system, which allowed ready access to and uncontrolled development of the nation's resources.

Stewart helped lead the attack at a Senate committee hearing. How had Powell gained such power? Who had said that the West was arid? Why was topographic mapping necessary before selecting reservoir sites? Why not leave the development of the West to westerners? The major replied patiently to each question, but his critics would not accept his answers.

In reply to a blunt question asking if he really approved of the implications of government control of the water in the great western rivers, he said, "I think it would be almost a criminal act to go on as we are doing now, and allow thousands and hundreds of thousands of people to establish homes where they can not maintain themselves."[5] Powell believed that there were two choices: to allow uncontrolled settlement to continue, with its profit for some and tragedy for others, or to institute planned, controlled settlement and thus avoid the waste of human effort and the destruction of natural resources.

Powell wanted the development of the arid West to conform to his own thinking, and he made the mistake of pushing far ahead of both popular thinking and congressional support. In 1890 the concept of the yeoman farmer independently building his own garden in the broad expanses of the West still dominated, and Powell failed to rally the support needed to sustain his views. Congress reopened the public domain to settlement and reduced the Irrigation Survey to impotency, its only job that of mapping reservoir sites.

Powell next fought a losing battle to defend the work and budget of the Geological Survey. Defeated, he remained director of the Survey for two years before retiring in 1894 to his Bureau of Ethnology. For the time being, the government's role in pursuing scientific knowledge and applying it to land policy was greatly reduced.

Although he met with much defeat, John Wesley Powell helped to lay the foundation for the American conservation movement. He recognized that the federal government had a responsibility to acquire a knowledge of western lands and to use this information for the welfare of all Americans. He helped to establish the Geological Survey and the Bureau of Ethnology and influenced the next leaders of conservation, including W J McGee, who has been credited as the "scientific brains" of Theodore Roosevelt's conservation program, and Frederick H. Newell, who became the first head of the Bureau of Reclamation. The bureau, established in 1902—the year of Powell's death—was built on the groundwork that he had laid, and his ideas and policies influenced such legislation as the Taylor Grazing Act of 1934, which belatedly closed the public domain to most homesteading and established locally administered grazing districts. Most important, he helped to build Washington into one of the great scientific centers of the world, and the Geological Survey became the model for the Forest Service, the Reclamation Service, the National Park Service, and all other federal agencies that have promoted conservation ever since.

Gifford Pinchot (Courtesy of the Library of Congress)

Chapter 3: Gifford Pinchot

President Theodore Roosevelt mounted the rostrum in the east room of the White House to address the distinguished audience. Before him sat the members of his cabinet, Supreme Court justices, governors from thirty-eight states and territories, and many eminent citizens, including William Jennings Bryan and Andrew Carnegie. At the close of his address the president stated: "In the past we have admitted the right of the individual to injure the future of the Republic for his own present profit. The time has come for a change. As a people we have the right and the duty . . . to protect ourselves and our children against the wasteful development of our natural resources."[1]

At Roosevelt's side stood Gifford Pinchot, a tall, slender man with a thick, drooping mustache, sharp, prominent features, and piercing eyes. The chief forester seemed to tower over the stocky president, but despite their physical differences, these two men made a remarkable team. They had planned and called into session the Governors' Conference on the Conservation of Natural Resources. The date—May 13, 1908—marked a high point in the crusade for conservation, the movement for the scientific management and use of the nation's resources under the regulation of the federal government.

Roosevelt acknowledged his indebtedness to the true leader of the conservation movement:

Gifford Pinchot is the man to whom the nation owes most for what has been accomplished as regards the preservation of the natural resources of our country. He led, and indeed during its most vital period embodied, the fight for the preservation through use of our forests. He played one of the leading parts in the effort to make the National Government the chief instrument in developing the irrigation of the arid West. He was the foremost leader in the great struggle to coördinate all our social and governmental forces in the effort to secure the adoption of a rational and farseeing policy for securing the conservation of all our natural resources. . . . I believe it is but just to say that among the many, many public officials who under my administration rendered literally invaluable service to the people of the United States, he, on the whole, stood first.[2]

EARLY LIFE AND EDUCATION

Gifford Pinchot came from a background seemingly worlds apart from his eventual post as the first American forester. Born in 1865 to wealth and social prominence, he grew up amid the tall buildings of New York City and at his family's country estate. The key influence on his future career choice was his father, James Pinchot, one of the few Americans in the latter half of the nineteenth century who worried about the depletion of the nation's forest. During the family's extended trips abroad he had been impressed by the Europeans' management of their forests, and he urged his son to enter the profession of forestry, even though such a career was new in America.

Gifford's education followed the usual pattern for a boy of his social and economic advantages: private schools in New York City, tutors in Europe, the Phillips Exeter Academy in New Hampshire, and Yale University. When Pinchot entered college in 1885, neither Yale nor any other college or university in the United States offered a forestry major. Although his conservative classmates urged him to pursue a conventional profession, he left for Europe in 1889 to talk with experts in forestry and to buy books. By good fortune he met Sir Dietrich Brandis, a German forester of world renown. The two formed an immediate friendship and the elderly man advised young Pinchot to enter the French Forest School in Nancy. Rarely has a student learned more in so short a time. But Pinchot, impatient with lectures, also traveled widely in Europe, inspecting woodlands and talking to local foresters whenever he could get one to answer his questions.

After thirteen months of intensive study and in spite of Brandis's advice that he stay for two more years, Pinchot returned home. He felt that European problems and the methods used to solve them did not fully apply to the United States, with its more democratic institutions and its vast forests. Besides, he had never been west of the Appalachian Mountains, and his ignorance of his own land bothered him.

The young man returned from Europe with the conviction that trees were a crop that could be harvested without destroying the forest, in other words, that proper management could result in sustained yield. He questioned the idea generally accepted in the United States that a forest had either to be cut and destroyed or to be preserved. Instead, he believed that proper methods would permit both commercially profitable logging and protection of the forest. In addition, he thought that good forestry depended on government control of private cutting. In Switzerland, for example, he had seen how the government controlled logging that might otherwise have caused slides on the steep mountainsides.

Pinchot realized that to gain acceptance of his concept of forest management he would have to prove it profitable and practical. To this end he enthusiastically accepted an offer to supervise George W. Vanderbilt's Biltmore—a five-thousand-acre forested estate in North Carolina. One feature of the Biltmore experiment, which had been initiated by Frederick Law Olmsted, was to retrain the local lumbermen to log selectively. Some mature trees would be left for seed, and young trees would be protected. Three years later Pinchot had achieved reasonable success, and with characteristic restlessness he looked for a new challenge.

Believing in the value of publicity, he prepared an exhibit for the Chicago World's Fair in 1893 and wrote a pamphlet entitled *Biltmore Forest*. In this, the first of his many publications, Pinchot foreshadowed his ultimate conservation philosophy by stating the three general objects of forest management at Biltmore:

The first is profitable production, which will give the Forest direct utility. If this were absent, the existence of the Forest would be justified only as it lends beauty and interest to the Estate. Second, a nearly constant annual yield, which will give steady occupation to a trained force, allow a permanent organization, and make regular operations possible. Third, an improvement in the present very mediocre condition of the Forest, without which its future would be nearly hopeless.[3]

He felt that above all, the work at Biltmore would be "useful in defining and helping to solve the problems with which American forestry must deal, and in awakening an interest in those practical details upon which its success in the future must so largely depend."[4]

The next year, 1894, marked a momentous decision in Pinchot's career. Presented with a choice between an uncertain future in forestry and a lucrative position in his wealthy grandfather's business, he committed himself to forestry. He said later, "No man can make his life what it ought to be by living it merely on a business basis. There are things higher than business."[5]

The destruction of America's forests had continued unabated for generations. Trees fell left and right from fire, disease, and the lumberman's ax. Consequently, watersheds deteriorated, silt filled waterways, and floods devastated towns and country. Forestlands in the public domain continued to pass into private hands under a land-law system based on private development of the nation's resources. Americans still held the illusory notion that forests were inexhaustible.

Steps toward forest protection had been taken in the 1870s with the formation of the American Forestry Association and a decade later with the establishment of the Division of Forestry under the Department of Agriculture, but Congress made no important move in that direction until 1891. In that year an act concerning the public lands carried an unnoticed rider that gave the president the authority to set aside certain forestlands as "public reservations."[6]

Had its true importance been realized at the time, the measure would certainly have been defeated by western congressmen, for shortly after its passage President Benjamin Harrison withdrew over thirteen million acres of timberland—the first land reserved for national forests—from the public domain. These tracts were placed under the protection of the General Land Office of the Department of the Interior. Congress provided no program for their management, however, and they remained open to fire, overgrazing, and other dangers.

Pinchot and a few other like-minded Americans urged the National Academy of Sciences to study the reserves and forests on the public lands and to make recommendations on their care to Congress. The result was the establishment of a forestry commission, with Dr. Charles S. Sargent of Harvard University as chairman and Pinchot as secretary. Though both of these strong-willed men wished to prevent the exploitation of the nation's forests, they did not agree on the best way to do it. Sargent, a botanist, favored preservation of the forests by the military; Pinchot, however, wanted the forest reserves to be used under the management of trained foresters; to Pinchot this was conservation. At this time the originally synonymous terms *preservation* and *conservation* took on different meanings.

Although the two viewpoints split the commission, its report presented a compromise. It expressed Pinchot's opinion that forests should be managed scientifically, especially because forest planning would involve the lives of several generations of people. In spite of their differences, both factions within the commission united to encourage President Grover Cleveland to more than double the size of the forest reserves. Westerners, who had successfully destroyed Powell's Irrigation Survey a few years earlier, rose in bitter protest against this new government encroachment on what they considered to be their domain. A compromise in 1897 included an amendment that provided the secretary of the interior with broad authority to regulate the occupancy and use of the reserves. This amendment opened the door for the economic use of government forests and for a professional forest service; in short, it provided the legal basis for federal management of national forests.

The ink had hardly dried on the compromise measure when Pinchot accepted an invitation to become "special forest agent" for the secretary of the interior. Writing his own instructions, Pinchot set out to inspect the disputed forest reserves, recommend boundary changes, and propose an organization for the forest service that he so wanted to see created. It made no sense to him that the Department of the Interior had jurisdiction over the forests, because the Department of Agriculture employed the only professional foresters.

The next year, 1898, Pinchot received an offer to head the Division of Forestry in the Agriculture Department. The division he inherited consisted of a two-room office, a small staff, and an equally small budget. Soon he and the Department of the Interior developed a cooperative arrangement in which his foresters gained increasing influence in the management of the forest reserves. They also offered technical information to owners of private forest tracts. Some of the largest lumber companies, including Weyerhaeuser, readily accepted advice on forest fire prevention, the use of waste materials, reforestation, and other practices that increased profits. This advisory function proved so successful that by 1901 the division had grown into the Bureau of Forestry. No one since Powell had managed to build a scientific government agency so quickly.

Although only thirty-two, Pinchot proved an able administrator. He was self-confident and opinionated and expected adherence to his views. Those sufficiently dedicated to weather years of hard work at low pay earned his loyal support and advancement in the ranks, and the result was a team spirit that has rarely been matched. He selected highly competent people as his immediate subordinates, including Henry S. Graves (an old Yale friend) and Overton Price (whom he made second in command of forestry administration). Yale men continued to dominate the bureau after the Pinchot family money helped the university open the first graduate school of American forestry.

Pinchot also proved to be a shrewd manipulator of public opinion. Through a stream of press releases and speeches and with his active lobbying in Congress, he carried his crusade for "practical forestry" before Congress and the American people. But he still had the General Land Office's inefficient control of the forest reserves to cope with. Composed of political appointees, most of them lawyers, and sensitive to the criticism of professional foresters, the General Land Office jealously guarded its jurisdiction over the federal forests. Pinchot could act only in an advisory capacity. But then, with the accession of Theodore Roosevelt to the presidency after William McKinley's assassination, new hope arose.

Before he came to depend on Pinchot to implement his policies on natural resources, the new president was already an ardent conservationist. An amateur naturalist, he had spent the summers of his youth in the country, collecting specimens such as shells, eggs, and insects. Like Pinchot, he was an avid outdoorsman and took special pride in his physical endurance and his skill in the woods. As a student at Harvard he had cultivated his serious interest in natural science, and although he eventually turned to politics, Roosevelt never lost his enthusiasm for the great outdoors. He took a turn at cattle ranching in the Badlands of Dakota Territory and wrote several books on hunting, ranching, nature study, and the history of the West.

Roosevelt's partnership with Pinchot began on a wintry day in 1899; Roosevelt was then the governor of New York, and Pinchot stopped off in Albany to discuss forestry with him. Before getting down to business, however, Pinchot, the taller man, managed to knock the stocky Roosevelt "off his very solid pins" in a boxing match. From then on the two had a mutual respect. Less than two years later Pinchot and Frederick H. Newell of the Geological Survey called on Roosevelt just before the new president moved into the White House. The two pleaded their case for forestry and reclamation, and Roosevelt responded immediately by asking them to draft their proposals for inclusion in his first message to Congress.

The president's speech reflected his own interest in conservation as well as the ideas of Pinchot, Newell, and Powell: "In the arid region it is water, not land, which measures production. The western half of the United States would sustain a population greater than that of our whole country today if the waters that now run to waste were saved and used for irrigation. The forest and water problems are perhaps the most vital internal questions of the United States."[7]

Theodore Roosevelt (in top hat) and Gifford Pinchot travel down the Mississippi River with the Inland Waterways Commission, 1907. (Courtesy of the Library of Congress)

Pinchot had an inside track in the president's "tennis cabinet," for they both enjoyed games and frequently played tennis, rode horseback, and took long walks together. Pinchot took pride in matching Roosevelt's brisk pace on their strenuous hikes. Once, while following the Potomac River back to the White

House in a driving rain, the two found their way blocked by a canal. Rather than retreating, they placed their valuables in their hats, swam the canal, and continued on their way. Pinchot even introduced the president to a new kind of exercise: wood-chopping.

The warm relationship fostered by these frequent activities gave Pinchot a decided edge in pushing his conservation program against other proposals. In fact, the president never took action on an important conservation issue without first consulting his chief forester.

With Roosevelt's strong support a reclamation act became law in June 1902. It provided for government construction of irrigation projects to be paid for by the water users. The Reclamation Service, applying Powell's earlier work, became primarily an engineering agency for reclaiming the arid lands of the West.

To get control of the forest reserves Pinchot had to overcome the opposition of western legislators and landowners, who feared increasing restrictions by the federal government. He won the favor of stockmen and lumbermen primarily by arguing that under his control the reserves would be opened to use and by opposing the formation of parks and game reserves that would prevent commercial use of the land. The climax came in 1905, when Pinchot organized a meeting of the American Forest Congress, made up of politically influential miners, lumbermen, railroad men, and representatives of irrigation and grazing interests. The meeting proved to be an effective propaganda mechanism for influencing Congress, which approved a transfer bill.

THE FOREST SERVICE

Overnight the Transfer Act gave Pinchot control of eighty-six million acres of forestland. To protect the reserves, soon re-

named national forests, the forest rangers of the newly chris-
tened Forest Service gained the authority to arrest persons who
transgressed its rules. Pinchot composed the principles upon
which the Forest Service was to administer its new responsibilities:

*In the administration of the forest reserves it must be clearly borne in
mind that all land is to be devoted to its most productive use for the permanent good of the whole people and not for the temporary benefit of
individuals or companies. All the resources of the forest reserves are for
use, and this use must be brought about in a thoroughly prompt and
business-like manner, under such restrictions only as will insure the permanence of these resources.*[8]

Pinchot interpreted his powers as broadly as possible, with
Roosevelt's full support. The chief forester stated: "I hold it to
be the first duty of a public officer to obey the law. But I hold it
to be his second duty, and a close second, to do everything the
law will let him do for the public good, and not merely what the
law compels or directs him to do."[9]

In this spirit Pinchot assumed the job of managing the national forests. To control overgrazing, which posed a threat to
watersheds in the West, he instituted a system of permits and
fees. The new system won the support of many influential cattlemen who had battled sheepherders and homesteaders and
could see advantages in having a long-term protection of the
range. They preferred the Forest Service's policy to that of the
Department of the Interior, which they feared might prohibit
grazing altogether.

Timber cutting received increasing attention every year.
Under Forest Service policy, national forests were to be used to
meet local timber needs but not to threaten the profits of the
logging industry. Thus, timber sales from national forests continued to account for a small percentage of the nation's total
production. Not until after World War II did the Forest Service

Cutover land (Photograph by Lloyd F. Ryan; courtesy of the National Agricultural Library, Forest Service Photo Collection)

foster large-scale logging operations, including clear-cutting and other controversial procedures.

Grazing and timber cutting were only two of several issues, and Pinchot saw clearly that the proper development of the West demanded a comprehensive land-management program under federal control. Such a program depended in part on revising the federal land laws, which gave land away to "land grabbers" and prevented it from being wisely developed. Pinchot noted, "The possibilities of a wiser system of land laws grow to almost boundless dimensions."[10] In 1903 Roosevelt had appointed the Public Lands Commission—of which Pinchot and Newell were members—to investigate the problem. In time the commission recommended extensive reforms, but except for making a few minor changes, Congress ignored its advice.

Pinchot favored public control of the nation's resources because he believed that this control would ensure the rational, scientific use of the land. The classification of the land according to its most valuable use, initiated by Powell, was furthered under Roosevelt's administration, but two important questions were still unanswered: who should be permitted to use the land's resources, and under what conditions should they be allowed to do so?

Pinchot answered the second question by requiring people to obtain a permit, to pay a fee, and to use the resource promptly. In answer to the question of entitlement, Pinchot established rough guidelines intended to maximize the benefits for the greatest number of people. For example, domestic water users had priority over irrigationists in the national forests, and homesteaders had preference over stockmen on agricultural lands. Pinchot consistently favored the development of resources and resisted proposals to set land aside in parks.

His views gained new support in 1907 when Roosevelt appointed James R. Garfield (son of the former president) as secretary of the interior. Garfield's attitude toward conservation closely paralleled Pinchot's, and this agreement virtually guaranteed cooperation between the two departments. Pinchot now seemed to have an open field for his plan of scientific land management.

Congress, however, remained an obstacle. The growth of the Pinchot-Roosevelt conservation program met with increasing opposition from conservatives who disliked the expansion of government power and from speculators and entrepreneurs who wanted to exploit the minerals, forests, grasslands, and water without restriction. They protested each time Roosevelt set aside additional national forests, for Pinchot's system of land management was thereby extended. In 1907 a hostile Congress rebelled against the president by amending an agricultural appropriation bill to stipulate that only Congress could create future national forests in six western states.

Because the Department of Agriculture's funds for the coming year depended on passage of the bill, the anti-Roosevelt group confidently expected the president to sign it. Threatened but far from defeated, Pinchot hurried to the White House to discuss the problem with Roosevelt. Together they concocted a plan that put their opposition in shock. Working far into the night, the Forest Service staff defined extensive areas that could be set aside as new national forests in the six states. Then, just before signing the appropriation bill, Roosevelt proclaimed twenty-one new forests comprising sixteen million acres. Outwitted, the opposition could only rage in protest.

The efficiency of the Forest Service and the staff's devotion to its chief forester only compounded the complaints against the agency. When Pinchot succeeded in placing his bureau under civil service laws in 1904, he incurred the resentment of many congressmen who wished to use Forest Service jobs for patronage. The decentralization of authority allowed rangers in the field to make local decisions, and the *Use Book,* a pocket-sized manual distributed to every ranger, encouraged uniform standards. As the new regulations brought a higher level of competency into the service, Pinchot promoted the most able of his staff on a nonpolitical basis. Critics who earlier had complained of the low caliber of government forest-reserve officials now complained that they were too efficient. Pinchot's bureau became a model of departmental reform.

A large measure of the Forest Service's success in the face of growing opposition stemmed from Pinchot's adroit use of publicity. From the time of his campaign to gain control of the national forests, he had continually promoted his program in letters, leaflets, circulars, and news releases. These news releases, carried in thirty to fifty million copies of newspapers each month, were particularly effective. In addition, an extensive mailing list carried the forestry message repeatedly to influential leaders across the country.

Although the Forest Service was successful, in 1907 the responsibility for the government's overall management of resources remained divided among a variety of conflicting agencies. As Pinchot explained: "There were three separate Government organizations which dealt with mineral resources, four or five concerned with streams, half a dozen with authority over forests, and a dozen or so with supervision over wild life, soils, soil erosion, and other questions of the land."[11] Pinchot pondered the problem:

Suddenly the idea flashed through my head that there was a unity in this complication—that the relation of one resource to another was not the end of the story. Here were no longer a lot of different, independent, and often antagonistic questions, each on its own separate little island, as we had been in the habit of thinking. In place of them, here was one single question with many parts. Seen in this new light, all these separate questions fitted into and made up the one great central problem of the use of the earth for the good of man.[12]

THE CONSERVATION MOVEMENT

From Pinchot's perspective, forestry was integrally tied to the irrigation of dry lands, to the efficient use of minerals, to the control of waterpower development, to the regulation of grazing, and to all problems of resource conservation. He believed that the nation needed a single, unified policy to make natural resources available to its people as efficiently and rationally as possible. In his attempts to sell this idea he used the term *con-*

servation, and Roosevelt quickly adopted the conservation movement as an important part of his program.

Pinchot identified the conservation movement with three principle goals: (1) to develop America's natural resources and make the fullest use of them for the present generation, (2) to prevent waste (from forest fires, for example), and (3) to develop and preserve the country's natural resources "for the benefit of the many, and not merely for the profit of a few."[13] Although the interpretation and implementation of the principles of conservation led to bitter controversy, these broad goals gave the movement wide appeal.

Pinchot emerged as the driving force behind the conservation movement, but he regarded W J McGee as its brains. McGee had spent many years with Powell in the Bureau of Ethnology and resembled him in many ways. He was born in the Midwest, had worked on a farm, and was a self-taught scientist. In the late 1870s he had carried out an extensive topographic and geologic survey in Iowa, and he later became a member of the Geological Survey. Like Powell, he had broad interests that ranged from philosophy and anthropology to the practical issue of resource development.

McGee urged the president to appoint a commission to promote the new concept of conservation, and Roosevelt responded vigorously by appointing the Inland Waterways Commission. Pinchot, McGee, and Newell served on the commission, and McGee, elected as secretary, wrote the all-important report. Operating without funds, the commission followed the president's directive to prepare a "comprehensive plan for the improvement and control of the river systems of the United States."

The commission's report reflected the new emphasis on a multiple-purpose approach by including considerations of flood control, irrigation, water transportation, hydroelectric development, and soil conservation. Each river system, it said, should be treated as a unit, regardless of political boundaries—an idea implemented much later under the Tennessee Valley Authority. Roosevelt stressed the need for an integrated policy under a single agency that could be held accountable to Congress alone. In addition, he warned against the monopolistic control of hydroelectric dam sites by waterpower companies, a problem with which Pinchot had long been familiar.

Under Pinchot's direction and aided by McGee, the commission developed plans to gather all the governors for a conference on conservation. The forester worked long months preparing for this Conference on the Conservation of Natural Resources, for it provided his best opportunity to extend his crusade for conservation and to stem the mounting opposition. Because Congress would not appropriate any money for the meeting, Pinchot paid for many of the expenses out of his own pocket.

Never had so many American scientific leaders and government officials been brought together. Pinchot and McGee took primary responsibility for selecting the speakers, and they also wrote many of the speeches. The conservation of natural resources, labeled by Roosevelt "the most weighty question now before the people of the United States," became momentarily the leading topic of conversation throughout the country.

Roosevelt promptly appointed the National Conservation Commission to make an inventory of the country's natural resources. As might have been expected, he placed Pinchot in the key position of chairman of the commission's executive committee, and the chief forester's friends held other strategic positions. Although Congress refused to provide funding, the commission succeeded in collecting an extensive inventory of the nation's natural resources from federal and state agencies. Organizing this material into four categories of resources— water, forest, land, and mineral—the commission recorded the supply, rate of use, and date of probable exhaustion of the country's natural wealth.

Pinchot arranged to have the commission's findings publicized by presenting them before a second conference of governors in December 1908. The three-volume report revealed that most of the public domain had passed into private hands. The commission's recommendations, reflecting the conservation policy of Pinchot and the Roosevelt administration, expressed a need for the following: (1) a careful reclassification of the remaining public lands, (2) the repeal of outmoded land laws, (3) stricter forest-fire control, (4) a reforestation program, (5) the control of grazing outside the national forests, (6) the leasing of federal coal lands, and (7) the prevention of soil erosion. Additionally, the commission recommended that new national forests be set aside in the eastern United States, particularly because the logging industry cut trees much faster than they could grow.

The governors supported the commission's work by calling for the continuation of its investigations and by encouraging the establishment of similar state organizations. Within a short time forty-one states had organized conservation commissions, which in turn made their own recommendations. On the surface, at least briefly, it seemed that the federal government and states would cooperate on conservation issues, but special interests balked at attempts to implement the recommendations.

Furthermore, Congress had never supported the Governors' Conference or any of the commissions Roosevelt had created. Many congressional leaders resented the president's expanding the power of the executive branch and were exasperated by Pinchot's continued influence and by the whole conservation movement. Thus, the opposition rallied behind an amendment providing that no congressional funds could be used directly or indirectly to support any federal commission not specifically established by Congress. Without funds, Pinchot and his colleagues could no longer devote time to the National Conservation Commission, and it quickly died.

As Roosevelt's term drew to a close he tried to spread the

conservation crusade beyond the boundaries of the United States. In February 1909, delegates from Canada, Mexico, and Newfoundland met in Washington, D.C., to discuss the principles of Pinchot's conservation program. This North American Conservation Conference recognized the need for international cooperation and recommended a world conference on resource use and conservation. Roosevelt sent invitations to fifty-eight nations for this proposed event, but the plans ended when his successor, William Howard Taft, moved into the White House.

In spite of the national publicity for conservation and although scientists in federal bureaus had led in the formulation of conservation policy, Congress increasingly blocked conservation legislation after 1907. Many congressmen opposed the idea that the executive branch should act as steward of the land and self-proclaimed protector of the public welfare. In retaliation they tightened funds and questioned the president's right to take any action not specifically authorized by law.

When the Governors' Conference failed to push Congress into supporting conservation, Pinchot tried to arouse the American people, arguing that they had a duty to guarantee future generations the same opportunity for happiness that they had had. According to his pessimistic predictions in *The Fight for Conservation* (1910), timber would last only thirty years at the present cutting rate, and coal would be gone in two hundred years. In addition, high-grade iron ore deposits were dwindling, and the Mississippi River carried away an estimated 400 million tons of the country's richest topsoil every year. Silt had settled in streams, making them less navigable than they had been fifty years earlier, and overgrazed western grasslands could sustain only half the stock they had nourished originally. Yet Pinchot noted that Americans were remarkably optimistic:

This hopefulness of the American is, however, as short-sighted as it is intense. As a rule, it does not look ahead beyond the next decade or score

*of years, and fails wholly to reckon with the real fortune of the Nation.
. . . The planned and orderly development and conservation of our natural resources is the first duty of the United States. It is the only form of
insurance that will certainly protect us against the disasters that lack of
foresight has in the past repeatedly brought down on nations since passed
away.*[14]

While carrying his crusade to the American people, Pinchot
hastened to strengthen his policy as much as possible during the
last weeks of Roosevelt's administration. Although the president had handpicked William Howard Taft as his successor and
although rumors circulated that Pinchot might be made a
member of his cabinet, the ambitious chief forester had growing doubts. Earlier, Roosevelt had passed him over for secretary of the interior in favor of Garfield on the political grounds
that a westerner was needed for the job; and the nation's farmers blocked any chance of his heading the Department of Agriculture.

THE BALLINGER-PINCHOT CONTROVERSY

Pinchot's doubts about his future intensified when the presi-
dent-elect, addressing a conservation conference in Washington D.C., publicly set aside a speech that Pinchot and his colleagues had prepared for him. His uneasiness changed to alarm
when Taft announced that Garfield, Pinchot's close friend,
would be replaced as secretary of the interior by Richard A.
Ballinger, who had served briefly as head of the General Land
Office two years earlier. It was now obvious that although Pinchot would be retained as chief forester, the new president
planned to chart his own course in conservation.

Pinchot already knew Ballinger. With their divergent views
on conservation, the two had clashed immediately. Ballinger,
who favored independent entrepreneurs in the West, opposed

Pinchot's notion of active governmental control of resources and his lease-and-fee system.

Both Ballinger and President Taft, strict interpreters of the Constitution, found fault with Pinchot's methods. They believed that the executive branch should take no action without specific authorization from Congress. Therefore, they disapproved of the various conservation commissions that Roosevelt had created without congressional approval.

While Ballinger worked to overthrow Pinchot's policies, relations between the Department of the Interior and the Forest Service deteriorated. Pinchot had enjoyed a direct working partnership with Garfield, but now he had to operate through established channels. Cooperative arrangements, such as the one whereby the Forest Service managed Indian reservation forestlands, came to an end. Ballinger insisted that legal questions involving disputed land claims within the national forests be handled by the General Land Office's lawyers, who were under his control. More serious, he undercut the implementation of Pinchot's comprehensive federal land-management plan.

The growing antagonism between the two men became an increasingly serious problem for Taft. Pinchot's prior success and control of conservation policies had rested on his direct access to the White House and his relationship with the president. Now the White House doors were closed to him. Taft became more and more impatient with the chief forester's personal pleas for support and his criticism of the secretary of the interior. Taft wanted a quiet Forest Service and instructed that its publicity be restricted. Instead, Pinchot brought his cause to the public's attention by organizing the National Conservation Association. The stage was set for a showdown.

The conflict between Pinchot and Ballinger finally centered on a question involving land use in Alaska. Each accused the other of establishing policies that benefitted special interests. Pinchot complained directly to Taft that Ballinger had assisted a group of thirty-three persons, known as the Cunningham claimants, in illegally gaining title to valuable coal lands. With the aid of evidence collected by Louis Glavis, a General Land Office agent, Pinchot argued that the Cunningham group had knowingly conspired to transfer their title to a large corporate syndicate headed by magnates J. P. Morgan and Daniel Guggenheim. The fact that Ballinger had served as legal counsel for the Cunningham claimants in the summer of 1908 added to Pinchot's suspicions.

As the conflict broke into the open, Taft came to Ballinger's defense and Glavis was fired. In the end a joint committee of twelve congressmen investigated the Ballinger-Pinchot controversy. Although most of the committee members were Taft supporters, Pinchot realized that he might still win his point by presenting his case to the public. The basic issue was the government's role in the management of resources, but Pinchot focused on the emotionally charged moral issue of whether great financial interests should be allowed to monopolize the nation's resources to the detriment of the public welfare.

Taft tried to end the dispute quietly but failed to mediate a settlement. He did not want to be forced to fire Pinchot, for such an action would inevitably alienate the Roosevelt wing of the Republican party. But the chief forester—irascible and self-righteous—finally left him no choice. Pinchot celebrated his dismissal, believing that he had promoted the conservation movement in which he so strongly believed.

The congressional investigating committee split on the question, the majority defending Ballinger but the minority criticizing him for not acting in the public interest. Though Pinchot lost officially, public opinion favored him, especially after Ballinger supporters misdated an important document. Ballinger soon resigned, partly because he had defended himself so weakly and partly because Taft had failed to support many of his recommendations.

Pinchot felt that he had won after all, for Henry Graves, his old Yale friend and forestry associate, replaced him as chief forester in 1910. Furthermore, Taft appointed Walter L. Fisher, who shared Pinchot's views on conservation, as the new secretary of the interior. The investigating committee, although exonerating Ballinger, supported Pinchot's position by recommending that the government lease the disputed Alaskan coal lands at a fair price.

At last Pinchot felt vindicated, but the conservation movement that he had helped launch had overextended itself and splintered. Neither Congress nor the Taft administration supported Pinchot's proposals for a unified system of resource management. Instead, individual resource users pursued their separate interests in traditional ways through the agencies in the federal bureaucracy that were most sympathetic to their goals. And the government departments and bureaus jealously guarded their own spheres of influence and jurisdiction.

As a private citizen, Pinchot continued to champion the "wise use" of resources, by which he meant the efficient commercial development of forest resources. Advocating sustained-yield practices, he did not sympathize with the rising national interest in wilderness preservation and outdoor recreation. Though he failed to block the creation of the National Park Service in 1916, he helped prevent the transfer of the Forest Service to the Department of the Interior in the 1930s. Pinchot's emphasis on utilitarian conservation had been important to the conservation movement of the early twentieth century, but it became increasingly out of tune with the national concern for environmental quality in the decades that followed World War II.

For the rest of his long life Pinchot promoted conservation, which he regarded as the "greatest good of the greatest number for the longest time."[15] He fostered scientific forestry through research, education, forestry journals and magazines, and such organizations as the Society of American Foresters. In addition, he implemented many of his forestry policies in Pennsylvania, where he served two terms as governor (1923–27 and 1931–35). His primary legacy remained the concept of the regulated use of resources—"to make the forest produce the largest amount of whatever crop or service will be most useful, and keep on producing it for generation after generation of men and tree."[16]

Chapter 4: John Muir

As the storm moved rapidly into the northern Sierra Nevada, the slender, bearded naturalist pushed deeper into the woods to enjoy its "music and motion." The tallest and sturdiest trees rocked in the gale. About midday it occurred to the intrepid traveler "that it would be a fine thing to climb one of the trees to obtain a wider outlook and get [his] ear close to the Aeolian music of its topmost needles."

Selecting one of the largest trees, he climbed up to where the "slender tops fairly flapped and swished in the passionate torrent" and he "clung with muscles firm braced, like a bobolink on a reed." From this vantage point he looked "over the piny hills and dales as over fields of waving grain, and felt the light running in ripples and broad swelling undulations across the valleys from ridge to ridge, as the shining foliage was stirred by corresponding waves of air." For hours he swayed in the wind, his senses tuned to the storm: "The fragrance of the woods was less marked than that produced during warm rain, when so many balsamic buds and leaves are steeped like tea; but, from the chafing of resiny branches against each other, and the incessant attrition of myriads of needles, the gale was spiced to a very tonic degree."[1]

John Muir saw harmony and order in even the wildest storm, for he believed nature to be God's work. He is best remembered for his poetic sensitivity to nature and his leadership in preserving the land, particularly places of great scenic beauty.

EARLY LIFE

Muir's childhood could have left him bitter and unresponsive to the world about him. He was born in Scotland in 1838, the third of eight children, and reared by his father, Daniel, according to religious beliefs so severe that they were almost sadistic. The boy did well just to survive his early years. His formal education, a brief affair, began early when on his third birthday he started elementary school. The methods were spartan. As Muir later put it, "the whole education system was founded on leather." There were whippings at school, there were endless whippings at home from his father, and between times the young boys tested each other's fortitude by thrashing each other unmercifully.

But the harsh treatment got results. John soon found "that there was a close connection between the skin and the memory, and that irritating the skin excited the memory to any required degree."[2] Thus he learned to recite the New Testament and several grammars by heart. As a brief letup from this stern discipline, he occasionally had the good fortune to walk the countryside with his grandfather. It was on these hikes along the rocky shore of the North Sea that he first experienced the joys of nature.

In 1849 the Muir family endured a six-week voyage across the Atlantic to the United States, where they passed through the Erie Canal and then crossed the Great Lakes. After a stay in Milwaukee they finally settled in a Scottish community on the frontier of Wisconsin to begin a hard life in the New World much like the one they had left in the Old. Only sixty miles to the south another boy, John Wesley Powell, was growing up in a similar atmosphere of hard work and against the same formidable odds. Muir's young life consisted of backbreaking labor: "We were all made slaves through the vice of over-industry. . . . We were called in the morning at four o'clock and seldom got to bed before nine, making a broiling, seething day of seventeen hours long loaded with heavy work, while I was only a small stunted boy."[3] Believing that pain and fortitude paved the road to heaven, Daniel Muir forced his children to maintain a regimen that would have been hard on grown men.

John found some retreat in the neighboring wilderness. Whenever he could, he stole away to enjoy the lakes and woods that bordered the family farm. Here he observed the wide variety of birds and animals that frequented the area as the seasons changed. He even hunted now and then, although he came to abhor the practice in later years.

As the oldest son, John assumed the responsibility of looking after his brothers and sisters. Frequently he used his command of the Bible as the one device by which he could win concessions from his reluctant father. When Daniel decided that the family should be vegetarians, John reminded him that God had fed Elijah meat as well as bread and vegetables. And when all books except the Bible were banned in the household, John pointed out that his father couldn't read the Holy Book without his glasses, thereby justifying the study of optics—and the necessity to have a book on the subject.

At best there was little time for study, but from time to time young Muir managed to borrow a few books from a sympathetic neighbor. He had to hide them until he could sneak into the cellar, where he read them by candlelight. And once in a while after the family's evening worship, John could spend a few precious minutes with his books. Daniel was annoyed by his son's reading, but he allowed him to read in the morning providing he was ready for his duties at daybreak. Rising at one o'clock, John relished several hours of freedom—and his disgruntled father had to keep the promise he had given.

INVENTOR, STUDENT, VAGABOND

Although Muir rebelled against his father's religion, he carried the Bible and his own conception of God's universe wherever he went for the rest of his life. But it was his inventive genius that prompted him to leave home. In addition to reading, he also whittled during those freezing, predawn hours of his "liberty," and with his knife and the tools he devised he invented an amazing variety of mechanisms. These included a sensitive thermometer that recorded the warmth of a person who approached it within four feet, clocks, doorlocks, barometers, a self-setting windmill, and an automatic device for feeding the horses at any hour.

Encouraged by a neighbor, Muir took three of his inventions to the state fair in Madison, where he won a fifteen-dollar prize, local fame, and a job in a machine shop. His overriding ambition, however, was to enter the University of Wisconsin. He had seen it from the fairgrounds, and so he went to present himself for admission. Muir described the situation:

With fear and trembling, overladen with ignorance, I called on Professor Stirling, the Dean of the Faculty, who was then Acting President, presented my case, and told him how far I had got on with my studies at home, and that I hadn't been to school since leaving Scotland at the age of eleven years, excepting one short term of a couple of months at a district school, because I could not be spared from the farm work.[4]

The university let him matriculate, and here he spent nearly three years, living on no more than a dollar a week for milk, bread, and lodging. But Muir took advantage of his inventiveness: he made a bed that flipped him on his feet early in the morning, and after a brief period during which he dressed, his mechanical desk raised and opened the first book to be read, then raised and lowered other books at an established rate for the rest of the day.

New worlds of knowledge began to open to Muir through his studies. One of his professors, Ezra Carr, introduced him to chemistry and geology, and Muir soon converted his dormitory room into a chemistry laboratory. His classics professor, James Butler, encouraged him to record his observations in a notebook and to use the metaphors that came to him so easily. When a fellow student aroused his curiosity about plants, Muir quickly acquired Wood's *Botany* and delighted in nature walks in the surrounding countryside. While at the University of Wisconsin he also became acquainted with the writings of the German naturalist and geographer Alexander von Humboldt, the Swiss-American geologist Louis Agassiz, and other prominent scientists.

More than anyone else at the university, Carr's wife, Jeanne, had a lasting influence on Muir. As his mentor and confidante, she shared her broad intellectual interests with him. She also acted as a bridge between the reclusive John Muir and the outside world, introducing him to people and books. Later she maintained a supportive correspondence, encouraging and influencing the development of his philosophy of nature. In return he shared his ideas and later struggles as an author with her.

Muir was by conviction a pacifist, and he identified himself more as a Scotchman than as an American. Fearful of being drafted into the Civil War, he went to Canada in 1864 and spent a year studying plants there. Then, using his inventive skills, he worked in factories in Canada and Indiana before an industrial accident nearly blinded him.

Disenchanted with his life among machines and lacking a

plan for his life, in 1867 he left on a thousand-mile hike to the Gulf of Mexico, "botanizing" along the way. As he said, he left "the Wisconsin University for the University of the Wilderness." This long trek was to be a turning point in his thinking and in his life. For the next forty-seven years he remained a traveler and a student of nature; to him, the wilderness was always to hold more than civilization, which "drives its victims in flocks, repressing the growth of individuality."[5]

Muir began the journey that eventually took him to California planning to travel by the "leafiest, wildest, and least trodden way" he could find. He carried only a plant press, a small bag of personal belongings, and three books—the New Testament, Robert Burns's *Poems,* and Milton's *Paradise Lost.*

When he reached Florida and encountered malarial swamps occupied by alligators, he realized how easily he could perish; the alligators proved better adapted than he to that environment. He regarded alligators and snakes as "part of God's family" and believed they were cared for with the same "tenderness and love as is bestowed on angels in heaven or saints on earth."[6] Yet the humans Muir observed did not act in harmony and cooperation with other living things. In this conflict between nature (especially plants and animals) and humankind, Muir sided with nature. He remarked, "If a war of races should occur between the wild beasts and Lord Man I would be tempted to sympathize with the bears."[7] He attacked the orthodox Christian idea that the earth had been made for humans and that its resources had value only as commodities for their use. Rather, Muir regarded all living things as equally important parts of the universe: "The world, we are told, was made especially for man—a presumption not supported by all the facts. A numerous class of men are painfully astonished whenever they find anything, living or dead, in all God's universe, which they cannot eat or render in some way what they call useful to themselves."[8]

These people, Muir believed, created a God in their own image: "He [God] is regarded as a civilized, law-abiding gentleman in favor either of a republican form of government or of a limited monarchy; believes in the literature and language of England; is a warm supporter of the English constitution and Sunday schools and missionary societies; and is as purely a manufactured article as any puppet of a half-penny theatre."[9]

Muir concluded that Nature (God) had made humans, animals, and plants for the "happiness of each one of them" and not for the happiness and use of humans alone. He explained, "The universe would be incomplete without man; but it would also be incomplete without the smallest transmicroscopic creature that dwells beyond our conceitful eyes and knowledge."[10]

These were the thoughts in Muir's mind when his trek led him on board a ship bound for California. Small wonder that when he landed on the docks at San Francisco he asked directions "to anywhere that is wild." Following someone's advice to take the Oakland ferry, he crossed the bay and was soon hiking toward the Sierra Nevada, joyful at the prospect of returning to the wilderness.

Muir was just thirty years old in the spring of 1868 when he gathered his few belongings and headed for the mountains. Nearly six feet tall, he stood straight as an arrow; clear blue eyes shone through a tangle of beard and hair, which he rarely bothered to comb. For a year he wandered through the foothill country of California, herding sheep and doing other odd jobs. But by the fall of 1869 he had settled in Yosemite Valley, and there he lived intermittently for several years. The nomadic Muir had found his wilderness in the Sierra—a range of mountains he described as "so gloriously colored, and so radiant, it seemed not clothed with light, but wholly composed of it, like the wall of some celestial city."[11] In this wilderness he experienced an "unconditional surrender to Nature"[12] and became increasingly aware that the wild things he loved stood in peril of their lives.

YOSEMITE VALLEY

Yosemite Valley had been granted to California in 1864 for "public use, resort and recreation" and was to be held "inalienable for all times." It was in fact the first area in the country specifically set aside to be *preserved* for all future generations. As such, it marked the real beginning of the national park system, even though Yellowstone, created in 1872, was the first officially designated national park. Yosemite did not achieve this status until 1890, and the valley actually remained under state control until 1906.

For a time Muir worked sawing timber for James M. Hutchings, who owned a hotel opposite Yosemite Falls. Muir sawed only fallen timber, however, for he accepted the job on the condition that no living trees would be cut. As the number of tourists grew, he spent an increasing amount of his time guiding visitors. In 1869 alone, over a thousand visitors braved the hard trip into Yosemite, some of them after crossing the country on the newly completed transcontinental railroad. Many were sent to Muir by Ezra and Jeanne Carr, his old friends from Wisconsin who had since moved to California.

Muir, however, personally invited his most famous guest, Ralph Waldo Emerson, to whom he wrote, "It will cost you nothing save the time and very little of that for you will be mostly in Eternity."[13] This meeting with Emerson he later called one of the two high points of his life; the other was the discovery of a rare flower in a Canadian swamp. Although he admired the Transcendentalists, he thought them too removed from the Sierra wilderness. "Even open-eyed Thoreau," Muir observed, "would perhaps have done well had he extended his walks west-

Muir in Yosemite (Courtesy of the Sierra Club Colby Library)

ward to see what God had to show in the lofty sunset mountains."[14]

Whenever possible, Muir traveled into the higher mountains of the Sierra, where he took special notice of the small glaciers, observing their movement and correctly deducing that they were remnants of a past glacial age when advancing ice had carved the sides of Yosemite Valley. This glacial theory was in conflict with the accepted explanation that the valley had been created by a cataclysmic event, and Muir's friends urged him to share his thoughts through publication. Though skeptical of the value of such an effort and reluctant to make it, he completed an article entitled "Yosemite Glaciers." The *New York Tribune* purchased it immediately and published it in December 1871. This publication launched Muir's writing career. From then on, however, he was to concentrate more and more on botany and less and less on geology.

Between 1872 and 1875 Muir traveled widely throughout the Sierra, climbing numerous peaks and becoming increasingly aware of civilization's threat to his wilderness home:

Incredible numbers of sheep are driven to the mountain pastures every summer, and in order to make easy paths and to improve the pastures, running fires are set everywhere to burn off the old logs and underbrush . . . . They sweep through nearly the entire forest belt of the range from one extremity to the other. . . . Whether our loose-jointed Government is really able or willing to do anything in the matter remains to be seen.[15]

Muir expressed outrage at loggers who dynamited the giant sequoias, the world's largest trees, remnants of which were then cut by the mills that everywhere fringed the timber belt. He described one mill as "booming and moaning like a bad ghost."

He had written several articles "to entice people to look at Nature's loveliness,"[16] and he now took up the battle to protect the Sierra. Early in 1876 he presented his first lecture on the need for conservation to the Literary Institute of Sacramento. He was ill with fright but made his point. A newspaper article described him as "at once the most inartistic and refreshing, the most unconventional and positive lecturer we have yet had in Sacramento."[17]

Two weeks later the *Sacramento Record-Union* published his article "God's First Temples," in which Muir used pragmatic, economic arguments to support forest preservation. He noted that the farmers dependent on irrigation in California's great Central Valley could not survive without the protection of their timbered watershed in the Sierra. In another article he recommended the creation of a "Commission of Forestry" and a ban on "running fires, sheep and the axe" above six or seven thousand feet in elevation.[18] His appeal to the state legislature to revise inadequate state laws, particularly for the protection of the giant sequoias, went unheeded.

Muir realized that sporadic lectures and newspaper stories by themselves would not reach the mass American audience that had to be aroused if the wilderness was to be protected. Thus, he turned increasingly to *Harper's Monthly* and *Scribner's Monthly,* both of which had national circulation. *Scribner's* soon became the *Century Magazine* and attained a circulation of over 200,000. Muir wrote about the mountains of California and their beauty, and his numerous articles helped create a new understanding and appreciation of the aesthetic value of the wilderness. Eventually this understanding led to practical support for having scenic areas set aside as parks.

Although Muir continued to demonstrate his passionate concern for the wilderness, he also recognized his loneliness. For several years Jeanne Carr had played matchmaker between Muir and Louie Strentzel, the only child of a wealthy and well-established California family. Swayed by the prospects of a secure home, children, and a place to store his botanical specimens, Muir married her in 1880. At the age of forty-two he settled down to family life in a valley near Martinez, a small town at the mouth of the Sacramento River. During the next two years he developed his horticultural skills and became a successful fruit farmer.

In the summer of 1888, after several years in "civilization," Muir began making frequent trips to the mountains to immerse himself again in the wilderness. From then on he applied himself to the "real work" of his life: writing and working for the preservation of wilderness. In particular he focused on the plight of his beloved Yosemite.

The Yosemite Valley had remained under the control of the State Board of Commissioners, which had unfortunately disregarded or lost a report prepared by Frederick Law Olmsted that incorporated the principles that later became those of the National Park Service. The commission, strongly influenced by the Southern Pacific Railroad (which then controlled politics in California), had allowed some commercial development of the Yosemite Valley floor, including plowing, orchard planting, timber cutting, grazing, and fencing. Muir, naturally, was adamant in his opposition to the destruction of any of the valley's natural beauty; he had attacked the "vulgar, mercenary improvement" of Yosemite as early as 1872 in a letter to the *New York Tribune.*

In the summer of 1889 Robert Underwood Johnson, associate editor of *Century Magazine,* met Muir in San Francisco and traveled with him to Yosemite. Here the two decided to work to establish a large national park that would include all of the high mountain country surrounding the valley. While Johnson lobbied for the park in Washington, Muir wrote two articles for *Century Magazine* and several letters to influential people. By the following June he had left for Alaska to recover from an illness; as he explained, "No lowland microbe could stand such a trip."[19] In 1890, shortly after he returned, completely cured, Congress created Yosemite National Park but excluded the valley, which still remained under state control. At the same time, farther south in the Sierra, two other parks, Sequoia and General Grant, were established as a result of the efforts of a few local citizens.

The future of Yosemite Valley remained uncertain, and Muir directed much of his energy toward getting it transferred from the state to the federal government. To help rally public support for the overall preservation of scenic lands in the Sierra,

Muir instructing members of the Sierra Club (Courtesy, The Bancroft Library)

Muir and twenty-six others gathered in San Francisco in 1892 to found the Sierra Club. Muir was chosen by unanimous consent to be its first president. Enthusiasm ran high, especially when John Wesley Powell came to a meeting and told about his exploration of the Colorado River. The club's primary and immediate purpose, however, was to act as guardian of the Sierra Nevada.

With his first book, *The Mountains of California* (published in

1894), and with a steady stream of articles in national magazines, Muir continued to carry his message to the American people: "The tendency nowadays to wander in wildernesses is delightful to see. Thousands of tired, nerve-shaken, over-civilized people are beginning to find out that going to the mountains is going home; that wilderness is a necessity; and that mountain parks and reservations are useful not only as fountains of timber and irrigating rivers, but as fountains of life."[20]

He wrote of his anxiety over the continued threat to the all-too-limited wilderness that had been set aside in the forest reserves and parks of the West:

The forty million acres of these reserves are in the main unspoiled as yet, though sadly wasted and threatened on their more open margins by the axe and fire of the lumberman and prospector, and by hoofed locusts [sheep], which, like the winged ones, devour every leaf within reach, while the shepherds and owners set fires with the intention of making a blade of grass grow in the place of every tree, but with the result of killing both the grass and the trees.[21]

CONFLICT WITH PINCHOT

Muir and the Sierra Club welcomed the National Academy of Sciences' Forest Commission when it reached the West Coast in the course of its investigation of the American forests. Muir had declined membership on the commission, wishing to be free to act as an adviser, but he was an unofficial member and served as the commission's guide on a tour of the western forests in the summer of 1896.

Muir traveled with some of the members of the commission from Chicago to the Black Hills, on to the Bighorn Mountains of Wyoming, and across the Bitterroot Mountains to Montana. Here Gifford Pinchot joined them, and they all continued west to the Pacific Coast states and into the Southwest. Everywhere they observed the results of the misuse of government land laws: bare hills, blackened stumps, sparse grasslands, and land seized for commercial advantage by railroads, corporations, and private individuals.

Muir, Pinchot, and Charles Sargent (chairman of the commission) shared the conviction that a system of forest protection and management was sorely needed, but Muir sided with Sargent against Pinchot in favoring immediate army protection for the forest reserves. The commission compromised and in its report recommended military control until a corps of professional foresters could take charge.

At this time Muir and Pinchot had a mutual respect. When they reached the Grand Canyon, the two decided to brave freezing temperatures to camp on the south rim. Pinchot later related, "Muir was a storyteller in a million. We made our beds of cedar boughs in a thick stand that kept the wind away, and there we talked till midnight. It was such an evening as I have never had before or since."[22]

For the time being, both men were fighting for the careful management of the new reserves that President Cleveland had set aside on the basis of the commission's report. Muir led the battle with a forceful article, "The American Forests," which was published by the *Atlantic Monthly*. He began, "The forests of America, however slighted by man, must have been a great delight to God; for they were the best he ever planted."[23] Muir recounted the long story of destructiveness in the United States. It galled him that other civilized countries had long since taken farsighted steps to care for their forests and that the United States was just beginning to do so:

So far our government has done nothing effective with its forests, though the best in the world, but is like a rich and foolish spendthrift who has inherited a magnificent estate in perfect order, and then has left his fields and meadows, forests and parks, to be sold and plundered and wasted

at will, depending on their inexhaustible abundance. Now it is plain that
the forests are not inexhaustible, and that quick measures must be taken
if ruin is to be avoided.[24]

To a large extent Muir agreed with Pinchot's criticism of the
General Land Office's management of the forests, although he
thought Congress was also to blame by not having provided adequate funds and personnel. He told of how a lumber company
in the coastal redwood country hired the whole crew of every
vessel that called at port: each man was instructed to file a claim
on 160 acres and then deed the land to the company, and in exchange was paid fifty dollars and all expenses. To counter these
deceptive acquisitions, Muir called "for the government to begin a rational [equitable] administration of its forests."[25] Part of
the nation's forests, he thought, should be preserved in their
natural state as parks, and part should be managed forests as
Pinchot had recommended. He felt that time was running out
and that it had been amply demonstrated that local laws and
regulations were not protecting the forests successfully. In eloquent terms he warned:

Any fool can destroy trees. They cannot run away; and if they could,
they would still be destroyed,—chased and hunted down as long as fun
or a dollar could be got out of their bark hides, branching horns, or mag-
nificent bole backbones. . . . Through all the wonderful, eventful cen-
turies since Christ's time—and long before that—God has cared for these
trees, saved them from drought, disease, avalanches, and a thousand
straining, leveling tempests and floods; but he cannot save them from
fools,—only Uncle Sam can do that.[26]

Muir and Pinchot's friendship was short-lived. Muir's first
biographer, Linnie Marsh Wolfe, recounts that a split between
the two occurred when Muir returned in 1897 from one of his
trips to Alaska. He read in a morning newspaper that Pinchot
had stated that sheep grazing in the forest reserves did little if

any harm. He could hardly believe what he read, knowing what sheep had done to the Sierra. Pinchot had been appointed as a special forestry agent, and if this was what he really thought, he might recommend a policy that would threaten the beauty of the forests.

It was inevitable that the men clash, for they held opposing philosophies of conservation. Their major disagreement centered on the question of whether providing opportunity for recreation and for the enjoyment of scenic beauty constituted a legitimate use of the land. Muir contended that it did, and that the government should therefore protect wilderness in parks. Pinchot measured the usefulness of resources in terms of practicality and economics. Thus, he rejected the idea of national parks and opposed any kind of land preservation that would interfere with the commercial use of resources. In brief, Muir was a *preservationist*, whereas Pinchot favored regulated use, or what he called *conservation*.

In another *Atlantic Monthly* article Muir attacked Pinchot's utilitarian approach, and the *Atlantic*'s circulation jumped. Such strongly persuasive articles caused Muir's reputation as the leading spokesman for wilderness preservation to be spread across the country.

Muir's position has often been misunderstood because of his outspoken defense of unspoiled wilderness. What is forgotten is that Muir accepted the construction of roads into limited areas of the Sierra so that people unable or unwilling to walk could also enjoy nature. Apparently he believed that tourism would enhance public interest in the protection of the Sierra. Certainly he did not foresee that automobiles would later be bumper-to-bumper in Yosemite Valley. Of course, Muir did not oppose the wise use of resources for the benefit of people, and in this regard he agreed with Pinchot. But he insisted on the additional need to preserve outstanding scenic areas. As he explained it:

The United States government has always been proud of the welcome it has extended to good men of every nation, seeking freedom and homes and bread. . . . The ground will be glad to feed them, and the pines will come down from the mountains for their homes as willingly as the cedars came from Lebanon for Solomon's temple. . . . Mere destroyers, however, tree-killers, wool and mutton men, spreading death and confusion in the fairest groves and gardens ever planted,—let the government hasten to cast them out and make an end of them.[27]

Muir's efforts were at least partially rewarded when the House of Representatives voted down a Senate proposal that would have abolished the disputed forest reserves created by President Cleveland in 1897. In addition, his Sierra Club had blocked the efforts of stockmen and lumbermen to reduce Yosemite National Park to half its original size. Yet these successful defensive actions were holding operations at best and did not ensure the preservation of the wild areas that Muir wanted protected.

ROOSEVELT AND THE RECESSION OF YOSEMITE VALLEY

When Roosevelt became president in 1901, he solicited advice on the state of the nation's natural resources from various men throughout the country, Muir among them. Muir responded with valuable information and the recommendation that the management of the forest reserves be placed in the hands of a forestry bureau under the Department of Agriculture. He and his fellow preservationists were heartened by the president's public statements.

In 1903 Muir was to tour the forests of Japan, Russia, and Manchuria with Sargent. He had made all his plans when he received a letter from Roosevelt in which the president asked him to be his guide on a four-day visit to Yosemite. Muir left the decision up to Sargent, saying, "An influential man from Washington wants to make a trip to the Sierra with me, and I might be able to do some forest good in talking freely around the campfire."[28] Sargent was more than willing to change his plans.

The meeting took place in May. Roosevelt had planned to get away from people and politics by camping out under the stars, but when his stage arrived at the Mariposa Grove of giant sequoias, the president found that his valise had been sent on to a hotel where state politicians and the park commissioners were waiting for him and a banquet had been planned. According to a reporter, Roosevelt's "jaws snapped together like a coyote, and the flow of language made even the drivers listen with admiring attention. It put an end to all monkeying with the President's luggage."[29]

For the next three days and nights, he and Muir traveled together in Yosemite, spending long hours in conversation around the campfire. Muir did most of the talking; he explained in his colorful way the dangers that were besetting America's wilderness and suggested a variety of remedies. At one point the president mentioned his hunting activities, and Muir reportedly replied, "Mr. Roosevelt, when are you going to get beyond the boyishness of killing things? . . . Are you not getting far enough along to leave that off?"[30] The next morning, much to their delight, they found themselves covered with four inches of snow. Roosevelt had such a good time that he again declined to attend an elaborate banquet so that he could spend one last evening in the woods with Muir.

Although Muir incurred the lasting enmity of the park commissioners and frustrated politicians, who blamed him for monopolizing the president's time, there is no doubt that he made a deep and favorable impression on Roosevelt. When the president addressed a crowd in Sacramento after leaving Yosemite, he carried Muir's message with him:

Lying out at night under those giant sequoias was lying in a temple built by no hand of man, a temple grander than any human architect could by any possibility build, and I hope for the preservation of the groves of giant trees simply because it would be a shame to our civilization to let them disappear. They are monuments in themselves. . . . We are not building this country of ours for a day. It is to last through the ages.[31]

In the next few years Roosevelt more than tripled the square miles reserved in national forests, doubled the number of national parks, and established seventeen national monuments, including the Grand Canyon.

Muir had also gained the president's support for returning Yosemite Valley to the federal government. His inability to accomplish this goal had been a long, festering problem for Muir during the 1890s. But after returning from his year abroad with Sargent, he and William Colby of the Sierra Club launched a campaign to win public and legislative support in California for this important change in jurisdiction.

Muir's book *Our National Parks* (1901) had helped to arouse interest. Gradually, government workers and newspaper editors began to sympathize with Muir's criticism of the state's management of Yosemite Valley. And the newly-elected governor, George Pardee, had accompanied Roosevelt to Yosemite and recognized the need to provide proper protection for the valley. There was still much opposition, however, for many people either objected to federal control or had vested interests.

Muir countered by enlisting the aid of Edward H. Harriman, president of the Southern Pacific Railroad, with whom he had traveled on an expedition to Alaska in 1899. Harriman, who wanted to help his friend and to promote his company's tourist business, swung the Southern Pacific Railroad's powerful lobby behind the bill. Fortunately, many of California's taxpayers welcomed the idea of sharing with the rest of the country the cost of maintaining Yosemite Valley. But in spite of all the points in favor of the preservationists, the recession bill in the state leg-

John Muir (Courtesy of the Sierra Club Colby Library)

islature passed by only one vote, and Congress delayed accepting control of Yosemite Valley until 1906. Even so, this marked a major, if tardy, triumph for Muir and the Sierra Club. After the struggle Muir commented: "I am now an experienced lobbyist; my political education is complete. Have attended Legislature, made speeches, explained, exhorted, persuaded every mother's son of the legislators, newspaper reporters, and everybody else who would listen to me. And now that the fight is finished and my education as a politician and lobbyist is finished, I am almost finished myself."[32]

HETCH HETCHY

But the major fight of Muir's life lay just ahead. He described the problem to President Roosevelt in an appeal for aid:

There is now under consideration, as doubtless you well know, an application of San Francisco supervisors for the use of the Hetch-Hetchy Valley and Lake Eleanor as storage reservoirs for a city water supply. This application should, I think, be denied, especially the Hetch-Hetchy part, for this Valley . . . is a counterpart of Yosemite, and one of the most sublime and beautiful and important features of the Park, and to dam and submerge it would be hardly less destructive and deplorable in its effect on the Park in general than would be the damming of Yosemite itself.[33]

Muir recognized San Francisco's need for an adequate water supply, but he insisted that there were other excellent dam sites available in the Sierra. Even the Tuolumne River, which ran through Hetch Hetchy, could be dammed farther downstream without damaging the beautiful valley. Muir realized that if Hetch Hetchy, which lay within the boundaries of the national park, could be flooded and used for commercial purposes, then no park in the country would be safe from similar commercialization. San Francisco, on the other hand, could hardly be expected to give up its attempt to acquire valuable property free of charge from the federal government. And although other reservoir sites abounded, they would have to be acquired from private parties at substantial cost.

The door to commercial utilization of parklands had been left open by an act of 1901 that authorized the secretary of the interior to grant rights of way across government reservations for any kind of water conduit. The act specifically included California's three national parks, and the mayor of San Francisco, James Phelan, had filed immediately for reservoir rights at Hetch Hetchy. The Department of the Interior rejected his application initially, but the city attorney, Franklin K. Lane, continued to work for its acceptance.

By 1905 San Francisco had gained the support of Pinchot, the chief forester, who looked at the issue from his utilitarian point of view. He believed that San Francisco should be permitted to meet its water needs from the national park, and he stated, "I will stand ready to render any assistance in my power."[34] Roosevelt sympathized with both Muir and Pinchot and for once gave only indecisive support to his chief forester. But Muir's problem was compounded by the appointment of James Garfield as secretary of the interior, for Garfield approved of San Francisco's plan to develop Hetch Hetchy and had the power to settle the matter.

The heated debate marked a final break between the preservationists, led by Muir, and the utilitarians, headed by Pinchot. In an attempt to block San Francisco, the supporters of Yosemite Park gathered all their forces, including *Century Magazine,* Frederick Law Olmsted, Jr., and J. Horace McFarland, president of the American Civic Association. Pinchot retaliated by excluding Muir, Sargent, and other leading preservationists from the list of those invited to the 1908 Governors' Conference on conservation. McFarland, however, attended as an association president and seized the opportunity to state the preservationists' case. "I would urge this august and influential assembly," he said, "to consider the essential value of one of America's greatest resources—her unmatched natural scenery."[35]

McFarland defended Muir's position and attacked America's materialism and tolerance of ugliness. To Pinchot he stated, "Hetch Hetchy valley of the Yosemite region belongs to all

America, and not to San Francisco alone." And he closed by declaring, "We have, for a century . . . stood actually, if not ostensibly, for an uglier America; let us here and now resolve . . . to stand openly and solidly for a more beautiful, and therefore a more prosperous America."[36] This forceful speech was eventually to have many repercussions, but it did little to change the Hetch Hetchy debate.

Secretary Garfield approved San Francisco's permit, granting the reservoir site and arguing that domestic water use and irrigation constituted the greatest benefit to the public. To his friend William Colby, Muir wrote wearily, "We may lose this particular fight, but truth and right must prevail at last. Anyhow we must be true to ourselves and the Lord."[37]

There was still a small measure of hope, for Congress had to approve the permit and the people of San Francisco had to accept it. The fact that the Lake Eleanor site down the river had to be developed before Hetch Hetchy could be touched would delay the sad event, and meanwhile the issue had attracted national attention. A number of prominent men across the country rallied to the cause and succeeded in blocking congressional approval in 1909.

In that year Taft became president and promptly appointed Richard Ballinger as secretary of the interior, replacing Garfield. Immediately the preservationists launched an offensive to have Garfield's permit for the Hetch Hetchy site revoked. They wanted the whole issue studied carefully by a group of competent, disinterested engineers. Muir continued to write pamphlets on the issue and guided both Taft and Ballinger on brief visits to Yosemite. These visits gave Muir a golden opportunity to defend the preservation of Hetch Hetchy, and he took full advantage of it.

The struggle went on and on from one year into the next. Walter Fisher replaced Ballinger after the latter's dispute with Pinchot, and Fisher, after making a careful tour of Hetch

Hetchy, supported the preservationists. This victory was only another holding operation, however, for San Francisco continued to press its claim. Muir came under bitter attack, and Hetch Hetchy, contrary to fact, was labeled "swampy" and a "mosquito meadow."

When the army engineers finally filed their report, they admitted that there were several other sources of water that could be used alternatively. But they nevertheless supported San Francisco, recommending Hetch Hetchy for the sole reason that it would cost the city less than the other available sites.

The dispute became more complicated in 1913 under the administration of Woodrow Wilson when Congress considered a Hetch Hetchy bill that would transfer the site to San Francisco. An amendment required the city to distribute hydroelectric power generated through the development of the valley directly to its ultimate consumers, which meant that a government agency would be selling "public power" in competition with private power companies. The latter, led by the Pacific Gas and Electric Company, tried to block the bill for their own business reasons; and Muir, on the same team for the most different of reasons, actually found himself labeled a friend of the power interests.

The death blow came to the preservationists' cause with Wilson's appointment of Franklin Lane, San Francisco's former city attorney, as secretary of the interior. Muir battled to the end, but Congress gave Hetch Hetchy to San Francisco with Wilson's blessing. In essence, the economic concept of conservation based on Pinchot's idea of beneficial use had won over Muir's preservationist philosophy. Muir's eloquent plea in defense of nature's outstanding scenic treasures had gone unheeded: "These temple destroyers, devotees of ravaging commercialism, seem to have a perfect contempt for Nature, and instead of lifting their eyes to the God of the Mountains, lift them to the Almighty Dollar. Dam Hetch Hetchy! As well dam for watertanks the people's cathedrals and churches, for no holier temple has ever been consecrated by the heart of man."[38]

A defeated Muir still saw hope for the future: "Fortunately wrong cannot last," he wrote. "Soon or late it must fall back home to Hades, while some compensating good must surely follow."[39] Muir died in 1914 and therefore did not see the inundation of Hetch Hetchy, but had he lived only two years longer he would have been pleased to see the rise of a National Park Service designed to preserve and protect all national parks.

The year before Muir died, the University of California recognized his lifework by conferring an honorary degree upon him with these simple words: "John Muir, Born in Scotland, reared in the University of Wisconsin, by final choice a Californian, Widely travelled Observer of the world we dwell in, Man of Science and of Letters, Friend and Protector of Nature, Uniquely gifted to Interpret unto others Her mind and ways."[40]

Chapter 5: Stephen Mather

Secretary of the Interior Franklin K. Lane sat reading his mail on a fall morning in 1914. One letter caught his attention. Although its content, a complaint about the national parks, was common enough, the writer's signature, Stephen T. Mather, rang a bell. Lane recalled that Mather, a fellow Californian and a graduate of the University of California at Berkeley, had worked for the *New York Sun* before making a small fortune as a borax manufacturer. It so happened that Lane needed a new assistant to help administer the national parks—someone with ability and independent means who would be willing to devote himself to public service for $2,750 a year. "Dear Steve," the secretary wrote to Mather, "if you don't like the way the national parks are being run, come on down to Washington and run them yourself."[1]

Lane's letter found Mather restless and in need of a new outlet for his boundless drive and energy. He had won all his earlier challenges, and now, at forty-seven, was intrigued with the idea of trying to bring some order into the chaotic administration of the parks. This, he thought naively, might take him a year, and he would then return to private life. In fact, the task of administering the national parks absorbed the rest of Mather's career; he served under three presidents and five secretaries of the interior. Under his able leadership the national parks came of age and Americans accepted the aesthetic enjoyment of scenic areas as a legitimate use of the land.

BUSINESS VENTURES

Mather's father, a prosperous merchant, had moved to California shortly before Stephen's birth in 1867. While growing up, young Mather threw himself into every activity with an enthusiasm he never lost—a zeal that earned him the epithet the "Eternal Freshman." His engaging smile, blue eyes, and lithe, tall figure gave him a look of distinction, and his personal warmth and fondness for people were irresistible. As one close friend remarked, "If he was out to make a convert, the subject never knew what hit him."[2]

Mather graduated from the University of California at twenty and spent the next five years as a reporter on the *New York Sun*. His future father-in-law took a dim view of the newspaper profession, however, and Mather finally joined his own father in the borax business in New York. Here and in Chicago he achieved unparalleled success as the advertising and sales-promotion manager for Francis Marion Smith's Pacific Coast Borax Company. Among other accomplishments, Mather built the legend of "Borax Smith" by promoting the publication of *Illustrated Sketches of Death Valley* (by John R. Spears), and he helped coin the famous trade slogan "20 Mule Team Borax." All of this sales and advertising experience was valuable to him later when he needed to promote the national parks. In connection with the borax business he also occasionally interviewed various congressmen about the tariff affecting the trade; this experience, too, proved useful to him.

112

In 1903 Mather entered into partnership with a friend and in the next eleven years built a modest fortune. It was during this period that he became a committed conservationist. He had followed the early fight for the recession of Yosemite Valley to the federal government, and he joined the Sierra Club and took frequent trips into the mountains. On one excursion he met John Muir, who urged his support against the inroads of loggers, miners, and others into the Sierra Nevada. Two years later, while visiting Sequoia and Yosemite national parks in 1914, he observed cattle grazing in the parks, poor roads and trails, and private landholdings in the most scenic areas. It was his irate letter of protest against such mismanagement that brought him Lane's invitation. And in January 1915 he arrived in Washington to assume his job as assistant to the secretary of the interior.

THE RISE OF A NATIONAL PARK SERVICE

In Washington Mather talked immediately with Secretary Lane, who described Mather's job to him. He learned that he would have to chart a new course, for no other country in the world except Canada had parks. The basic problem was that thirteen national parks and eighteen national monuments in the United States lacked sufficient protection and funds for management and development. Mather first needed to arouse public and congressional interest in order to obtain authorization for a bureau of national parks and adequate appropriations. The next steps would be to organize the bureau, make sure it functioned efficiently, improve and promote travel to the parks, and expand and improve the quality of the whole park network.

Mather balked only at the inevitable web of government red tape he would have to cope with. Lane helped with this problem by appointing Horace Albright, an astute young lawyer from California, to be his assistant. Mather promptly learned one disillusioning lesson when he refused to pad his initial budget request by thirty percent, as he was advised to do. "I'm a businessman," he explained indignantly. "We won't ask for a penny more than we can justify, and we'll spend it exactly the way we tell them we will."[3] Precisely as his Washington advisers had predicted, his budget was slashed.

Mather realized that Congress was not going to authorize adequate funding until the American people demanded it and that the people would not do much demanding until they had been introduced to the parks. Thus, the first task was to publicize the parks and promote American tourism. With no government funds to use, Mather reached into his own pocket to offer Robert Sterling Yard, an old friend from the *Sun,* a position as the national parks' publicity chief. Yard succumbed to Mather's persuasive charm and became one of the parks' most avid supporters.

In making the parks known across the country, this veteran newsman and editor helped immensely, particularly through several illustrated books. *National Parks Portfolio,* a fancy and expensive volume published in 1916, was underwritten by western railroads that Mather had approached for funds. The first 275,000 copies were sent gratis to the country's most important leaders of opinion, and the favorable response exceeded Mather's highest hopes.

Believing that the best way to gain support for his program was to get the congressmen themselves into the parks, Mather borrowed Robert B. Marshall, chief geographer of the Geological Survey, to organize a mountain trip into the southern Sierra Nevada for the summer of 1915. His carefully selected guests included Frederick H. Gillett, ranking Republican on the House Appropriations Committee; Gilbert Grosvenor, editor of the *National Geographic Magazine*; Ernest O. McCormick, vice president of the Southern Pacific Railroad; Emerson Hough, author and outdoors editor of the *Saturday Evening Post*; and Burton Holmes, noted world traveler and lecturer. Because it was important for his guests to enjoy themselves, Mather brought along a famous Chinese cook, Ty Sing, and had fresh fruit and vegetables hauled into the mountains daily at his own expense.

The trip took the visitors first through the Giant Forest, a prized scenic area within Sequoia National Park that remained in private hands, then through the park itself, and finally through the Kern Canyon and Mount Whitney area, which Mather wanted to have added to the park. Mather's tactics worked just as he had planned; the next year Congress appropriated 50,000 dollars to purchase the private tracts in the Giant Forest—the first authorization of this kind for any park—and the National Geographic Society contributed the remaining 20,000 dollars needed to complete the purchase.

Thus Mather's first year as assistant to the secretary of the interior drew to a close—and a year of accomplishment it had been! Many Americans had suddenly become aware of the national parks. He had stimulated broad newspaper support through personal contact with leading editors, using his past experience on the *Sun* and in promoting borax. In addition, he had gained the unstinting support of Grosvenor and of George Horace Lorimer, editor of the *Saturday Evening Post*. But all this, he knew, only scratched the surface of what had to be done.

During his first year Mather had visited most of the parks and gained a firsthand understanding of the need for roads, campgrounds, and accommodations for the public. He had also developed and clarified his ideas of what the parks should be; he saw clearly the need to protect them from commercialization, the necessity to eliminate privately owned lands within their boundaries, and the desirability of adding new parks and scenic areas to those already protected.

In the meantime, the effort to establish a bureau of national parks gathered momentum. J. Horace McFarland, who had spoken so eloquently for aesthetic conservation at the 1908

Governors' Conference, led the movement to establish a special bureau. "Nowhere in official Washington," he complained, "can an inquirer find an office of national parks or a single desk devoted solely to their management."[4] Rather, each park had a separate administration and a separate budget. Furthermore, four of the parks remained under the official control of the army, although the secretary of the interior had actual jurisdiction.

Back in 1910, McFarland and Frederick Law Olmsted, Jr., had drafted a bill for the establishment of a park bureau. Like his father, Olmsted was a great landscape architect, and he had already inspired several city park plans in Baltimore, Pittsburgh, Boston, and elsewhere. In 1911 the participants in the first National Parks Conference at Yellowstone had recognized that only a strong bureau could meet the needs of the parks, and in 1913, with the loss of Hetch Hetchy, the lack of such a bureau was more stinging than ever. Only a vigorous park service could hope to block further devastating raids on the parks, and efforts to establish such a service were redoubled.

The primary opposition came from the Forest Service, which continued to hope for the transfer of the parks to the Department of Agriculture. Although never honored, this request was understandable. The parks and national forests commonly lay side by side, many of the administrative problems were the same, and the Forest Service administrators realized that the new parks would consist largely of land currently under their jurisdiction.

But whatever the opposition, the National Park Service Act finally received President Wilson's signature late in August 1916, just in time for Albright to wire the good news to Mather, who was completing another mountain trip. As set forth in the act, the new Park Service was "to conserve the scenery and the natural and historic objects and the wild life therein and to provide for the enjoyment of the same in such manner and by such means as will leave them unimpaired for the enjoyment of fu-

Horace Albright (far left), Stephen Mather (far right) (note the special license plate on Mather's Packard automobile) (Courtesy of the National Park Service)

ture generations."[5] The act granted the secretary of the interior authority to make rules and regulations for the park as he saw fit. When Congress finally appropriated funds for the new Park Service, Mather became its first director, and Albright his assistant.

By the end of 1916, his second year in government service, Mather could report major achievements. Lassen Volcanic National Park in California and Hawaii National Park had been added to the system, and Alaska's Mount McKinley soon followed. The demand for information on the parks had multiplied so rapidly that additional educational materials were needed to teach the public the purposes and uses of these remarkable scenic areas. In greater numbers than ever before, Americans were discovering their parklands.

But Mather paid a price for his strenuous work. The incessant whirlwind of activity wore him down, and constant worry took its toll. Although a Republican, he did not want a change of administration at this crucial time and agonized over the 1916 presidential election, which gave Wilson his narrow victory. Preparations advanced for the largest national-parks conference yet to be held, but Mather, under continuous tension and badgered by his critics, suffered a breakdown. For the next eighteen months he was forced to rest, while Albright, now twenty-seven years old, assumed control.

It was Albright, working with the advice of others, who used many of Mather's ideas to develop a set of guidelines to serve as a framework for the national park system. In a letter from Secretary Lane to Mather dated May 13, 1918, these principles were set forth:

First, that the national parks must be maintained in absolutely unimpaired form for the use of future generations as well as those of our own time; second, that they are set apart for the use, observation, health, and pleasure of the people; and third, that the national interest must dictate all decisions affecting public or private enterprise in the parks.

Every activity of the Service is subordinate to the duties imposed upon it to faithfully preserve the parks for posterity in essentially their natural state. The commercial use of these reservations, except as specially authorized by law, or such as may be incidental to the accommodation and entertainment of visitors, will not be permitted under any circumstances.[6]

This statement is to this day the Park Service's primary guideline.

DEFENSE OF THE PARKS

In 1917, when the United States entered World War I, funds for park development became scarce. Even more worrisome, patriots across the country demanded that resources within the parks be developed to aid the war effort. Albright, trying to block the most damaging proposals, fought a defensive battle. To make matters worse, Lane seemed to forget some of his own conservation goals in his eagerness to aid the Allies. Albright narrowly defeated attempts to open some of the parks to extensive grazing. Fortunately, United States Food Administrator Herbert Hoover managed to block a proposal that buffalo and elk in Yellowstone be slaughtered to provide food. But mining, lumber, and power interests continued to use the war as an excuse to try to develop parklands they had long coveted.

Mather returned to work with renewed zeal, challenging the commercial threats to the parks. The loss of Hetch Hetchy still rankled, and he vowed to prevent another such disaster. The act surrendering Hetch Hetchy to San Francisco had stipulated that the city should build roads and trails and make other improvements that would open the area for recreation. But when Mather pressed for compliance with this section of the law, he got little response. Disregarding another stipulation of the law, now that the reservoir was finally completed, San Francisco sold hydroelectric power to the Pacific Gas and Electric Company instead of directly to the public. And most discouraging, the heart of the magnificent Hetch Hetchy Valley now lay under water—a sad ending to John Muir's long struggle.

The most serious proposal for new dams involved two areas in Yellowstone National Park, including beautiful Lake Yellowstone. Irrigationists in Idaho and Montana, pressing separate rival claims, gained the sympathy of Secretary Lane. In his 1919 director's report Mather protested:

Is there not some place in this great nation of ours where lakes can be preserved in their natural state; where we and all generations to follow us can enjoy the beauty and charm of mountain waters in the midst of primeval forests? The country is large enough to spare a few such lakes and beauty spots. The nation has wisely set apart a few national parks where a state of nature is to be preserved. If the lakes and forests of these parks can not be spared from the hand of commercialization, what hope

can we entertain for the preservation of any scenic features of the moun-
tains in the interest of posterity?

Yellowstone Park has been established for nearly half a century. Every
plan to exploit it for private gain has failed to receive the consideration
of Congress. Mighty railroad projects have even gone down to ever-
lasting defeat. Must all the victories of the past now become hollow mem-
ories by the granting of reservoir rights that will desecrate its biggest and
most beautiful lakes, and form the precedent for commercial exploitation
of all of its scenic resources—its waterfalls, its forests, its herds of wild
animals, its mineral waters?[7]

When his protests and delaying tactics proved ineffective,
Mather offered his resignation. At the last moment, however, and
for other reasons, Lane resigned instead. Although his successor,
John Barton Payne, supported Mather, a pending congressional
bill would have opened all existing parks to waterpower development. This bill threatened the integrity of the entire national
park system, for once the doors were open to commercial development the parks as such would disappear. Mather supported the
controlled use of public land, but he drew a definite line at the park
boundaries. In his 1920 *Report* he stated:

Good projects, bad projects, indifferent projects all must face the same fate.
The great primary principle that the national parks must be forever main-
tained in absolutely unimpaired form for present generations and posterity
has been established by Congress, and until Congress, having the ultimate
decision, by legislative mandate annuls or changes this principle, it must
be faithfully, unequivocally, and unalterably adhered to.[8]

Mather gambled that the American people would never stand
for a legislative mandate that destroyed their parks.

He called on all his friends to help him and used every possible connection to influence members of Congress in their ultimate decision. McFarland, Yard (president of the National
Parks Association), Olmsted, and many others rallied to the de-

fense of the parks. Mather held numerous dinners for key congressmen and cabinet officials—and invariably showed them park movies or slides. As a result of these efforts and with the support of the eastern press, the bill to open the parks to water development met defeat.

But almost at once a new problem materialized: a change of administration with the election of President Warren Harding. The future looked bleak, for the new secretary of the interior, Senator Albert B. Fall of New Mexico, seemed to hold the westerner's traditional attitude toward land development. Yet Fall retained Mather, much to Mather's surprise.

He was right in expecting trouble, however. One of the worst predicaments arose when Fall wanted to establish a new national park that would take the form of a horseshoe around his own ranch in New Mexico. Fall had in mind a park composed of numerous separated tracts of land where hunting, grazing, lumbering, mining, and water and power development would all be allowed. Fortunately, his proposal could not withstand the attacks of Yard, McFarland, Lorimer, and other Mather followers. By the time Fall left office in 1922 his scheme had been defeated.

But by 1922 Mather was worn out by the struggle, smarting from his critics' constant attacks and depressed by the suicide of J. Arthur Elston, his close friend and congressional supporter. He again had to withdraw from his active working life for several months. His rest was well earned, for the National Park Service was now firmly on its feet, having withstood the assault of commercial enterprise both during and immediately after the war. The worst was over.

EXPANSION OF THE PARKS

While struggling against commercialization, Mather had also been working to increase the number of parks and monuments. In accordance with Lane's guidelines, Mather sought parks with "scenery of supreme and distinctive quality or some natural features so extraordinary or unique as to be of national interest and importance." The park system "should not be lowered in standard, dignity, and prestige by the inclusion of areas which express in less than the highest terms the particular class or kind of exhibit which they represent."[9]

When he returned to work in 1918, Mather first focused on preserving the coastal redwoods of California. A few limited groves had been set aside, including Muir Woods National Monument, but the major redwood forests, which contained the world's tallest trees, lay in private hands. Mather supported the formation of an unusual organization, the Save-the-Redwoods League, whose aim was to purchase as much land as possible in the finest stretches of forest for preservation in state parks. Over the years the league has had notable success in acquiring land through contributions, many of them memorials, by private citizens.

In 1919 three new parks—Zion (in Utah), Grand Canyon (in Arizona), and Lafayette (later renamed Acadia, in Maine)—were added to those under Mather's control. The last of the three had the distinction of being the first national park in the eastern United States. The reason for the long delay in acquiring an eastern park was that so much of the land east of the Appalachians was both highly developed and privately owned. For the most part, western parks could be acquired by transferring government-owned land from one bureau to another. To create Acadia, all of the land had to be purchased by the government, a difficult and expensive task. In the end a few people purchased the land and presented it as a gift to the people of the United States.

By 1920 Mather's bureau administered nineteen national parks, and at this point Mather had no desire to add extensive new areas to the system. Instead, he wanted to expand a few of

The Three Tetons, Grand Teton National Park (United States Department of the Interior National Park Service Photograph)

the best parks to round out their boundaries, add only new areas that were of exceptional quality, and block proposals for inferior parks. In particular, he hoped to add the Grand Teton country to Yellowstone in Wyoming and the high, southern Sierra Nevada to Sequoia.

The Forest Service, however, controlled most of the scenic areas that Mather wanted to add to the park system and saw no need for change. Thus, the old "utilization versus preservation" controversy begun by Pinchot and Muir flared once more. The Forest Service feared the growing power and popularity of Mather and the Park Service, because further park enlargement would come, for the most part, at the Forest Service's expense. In defense, the Forest Service began to expand its own preservation of prized scenic areas coveted by the Park Service and to encourage public recreational use of Forest Service holdings. Soon the rivalry between the two bureaus broke into the open. As expected, the Forest Service still wanted the parks to be placed under the Department of Agriculture, whereas the Park Service thought it made more sense for the Department of the Interior to control the national forests. The results were a stalemate, suspicion, and a continuing rivalry.

The Forest Service argued that if the Park Service took charge of promoting outdoor recreation it would invite further commercialization of the parks. Mather believed that the parks belonged to the people and should be visited and enjoyed by all, but in his mind this enjoyment did not constitute commercialization. He insisted that the one real distinction between the national parks and the national forests was that the parks were to be *preserved* for all time. Both parks and forests contained outstanding recreational areas, "the first [parks] a limited group of smaller areas conserved as nature made them, the other [forests] a very large group of great areas subject to certain definite commercial uses prescribed by Congress—notably, lumbering, irrigation, and power."[10]

President Calvin Coolidge, disturbed by the heated dispute over territory between rival government bureaus, hoped that the disagreement could be settled at the Conference on Outdoor Recreation, which was held in May 1924. Although the compromises that came out of this meeting satisfied neither side, the Park Service in time gained most of what it wanted, including the Tetons and the Mount Whitney country east of Sequoia.

The only new park added during the remainder of Mather's administration was Bryce Canyon in Utah.

Meanwhile, Mather continued to stress the need for eastern parks, despite the expense and difficulty involved in acquiring them. He appointed a commission to study all the possibilities in the southern Appalachian Mountains, and the commission recommended park sites in the Great Smoky Mountains of Tennessee and in the Blue Ridge Mountains of Virginia. Congress approved of the two sites and of Mammoth Cave in Kentucky as well, but final authorization rested on the acquisition of funds. Thanks to the generosity of John D. Rockefeller, Jr., and to contributions of state funds, all three areas eventually became parks.

During these years a number of national monuments were established. Under the Antiquities Act of 1906, the president could "declare by public proclamation historic landmarks, historic and prehistoric structures, and other objects of historic or scientific interest" on the public lands.[11] Though the act was intended primarily to protect Indian archaeological sites in the Southwest, Mather used it to set aside other monuments, including Katmai, an area larger than Yellowstone, in Alaska.

Mather also contributed to the growth of state parks throughout the country. Many scenic areas had potential park value but did not seem to qualify for the national park system. And some areas, such as Lake Tahoe in California and Grand Coulee in Washington, had already been developed by private parties. Other areas resembled too closely some other park that had already been set aside; Mount Hood, for example, resembled Mount Rainier. Mather considered some attractive areas, such as the Indiana sand dunes, too difficult to acquire, and others, such as the Ouachita Mountains in Arkansas and the Wasatch Mountains in Utah, not sufficiently outstanding.

Many of these areas were worth saving, however, and Mather received continual pressure to place them under federal protection. He knew that he could undermine the whole park system by adding inferior areas, for such a move would inevitably open the door to his critics and to the demands of commercial interests. In the past, local support had succeeded in winning park status for three substandard parks—Platt (in Oklahoma), Sully Hills (in North Dakota), and Wind Cave (in South Dakota)— before the establishment of the National Park Service. Numerous proposals came before Mather, but he chose to support the expansion of state parks, which had slowly been gaining ground since the grant of Yosemite Valley to the state of California in 1864.

Some notable state parks had already been established: Niagara Falls in 1885 and Michigan's Mackinac Island and the Palisades Interstate Park of New Jersey and New York in 1895. As late as 1920, however, only twenty states had any parks, and only a few of the twenty had begun to develop organized state park systems. To promote such a development Mather organized a convention on state parks at Des Moines, Iowa, in 1921. A permanent organization, the National Conference on State Parks, resulted, adopting the slogan "A State Park Every Hundred Miles." Mather helped keep the organization solvent and gave it his active support for the rest of his life.

MATHER'S MANAGEMENT OF THE PARKS

Mather's contribution to the park system included more than protecting the parks from the threat of commercial development and adding new parklands. He also initiated the administrative system that to this day guides the public's use of the parks. Recognizing that Americans often based their impression of the National Park Service on their contact with park rangers, Mather upgraded personnel standards. He wanted capable individuals who would devote their lives to serving the

Park Service and the public, and he instilled a remarkable esprit de corps.

Mather took seriously the directive that the parks were to be set aside "for the use, observation, health, and pleasure of the people." He once said to a friend, "They belong to everybody. We've got to do what we can to see that nobody stays away because he can't afford it."[12] To this end he appealed to the railroads to lower rates, improve schedules, and cater to park visitors. One of the most useful arrangements allowed tourists to go to Yellowstone by one railroad line and leave by another without extra charge. Mather also promoted "package tours" at bargain rates, and he made railroad executives so confident of the economic advantages to be derived from tourism that they quickly invested money and time in promoting the parks.

But Mather foresaw that automobiles would dominate future travel into the parks and that many changes would therefore be needed in both roads and accommodations. Automobiles, which had first appeared before the turn of the century, increased rapidly in number, and the years of Ford's mass-produced "tin Lizzy" were just beginning. At about the same time, the "See America First" movement spread across the country. The underlying aim of this campaign was to keep the American tourist-dollar at home by publicizing the benefits of travel in the United States, particularly to the national parks.

By 1915 the automobile had replaced the horse-drawn stage in all parks, and with the end of the First World War and the practice of installment buying, cars became so commonplace that traffic congestion began to be a problem. Automobile clubs sprang up across the nation. Mather himself, who delighted in touring by car, played an instrumental role in establishing the National Park-to-Park Association, whose members hoped to see roads (unpaved, at first) constructed so that all the parks would be accessible by automobile.

With good reason, drivers complained about the deplorable

park roads. What were narrow, rutted, poorly graded sinks of dust in dry weather became impassable quagmires in the rainy season. Mather could do little to improve the situation, for despite park entrance fees as high as ten dollars (they were later substantially lowered), Congress alone could provide the necessary funds. Thus, he continued to use his most effective method of influencing Congress—bringing congressmen and their wives into the parks. When members of the House Appropriations Committee visited the Grand Canyon in 1923, Mather sent Albright to take advantage of the opportunity. Albright drove the visitors over the roughest roads, and finally, on the road to Flagstaff, the car became mired in mud. The congressmen got the message and soon approved 7.5 million dollars—more than double the total amount appropriated in preceding years—for building roads in the parks.

Mather believed that in each park a single road should lead through a representative section of the park's most scenic area. Although he wanted most of the parkland preserved in as natural a state as possible, he also wished that the old, young, infirm, and sedentary could see the parks. To realize this goal he encouraged the building of such scenic routes as Glacier National Park's dramatic Going-to-the-Sun Highway in Montana. Since then a few outstanding roads have been added, including the twelve-thousand-foot-high Trail Ridge Road in Colorado's Rocky Mountain National Park and the Blue Ridge Parkway between Shenandoah National Park in Virginia and the Great Smoky Mountains National Park on the border between North Carolina and Tennessee.

Mather also tackled the problem of inadequate accommodations in the parks. Chaotic and wasteful competition for the tourist trade damaged the parks, hurting the businesses concerned and resulting in poor service for park visitors. Mather decided that it would be best to allow a single fully qualified operator to hold a license for the concessions (hotels, transportation, and so on) in any one park. Under this system of regulated monopoly, the government approved standards of service and rates. The arrangement solved most of the earlier problems despite its shortcomings, but it ran counter to the accepted idea of free enterprise, and Mather again became the target of criticism.

The critics who gave him the most trouble were two senators, Thomas J. Walsh of Montana and Ralph H. Cameron of Arizona. Walsh wanted franchises in Yellowstone for his friends to operate, but Mather fought back, for if politics once entered the parks there would be no end to the corruption. Besides, the existing tourist camp run by Walsh's associates was substandard in all respects. In the end Walsh lost. Cameron's even more ambitious scheme was to control the Grand Canyon through mining claims to key locations. When Mather and the Supreme Court destroyed this pernicious plan, Cameron succeeded for a brief time in eliminating any congressional appropriation for Grand Canyon National Park. Then, in an attempt to embarrass Mather, he launched an investigation of the Park Service.

At the same time, Mather found himself criticized by nature lovers, who thought that his policies compromised the quality of the parks. Observing the crowds that flocked to the parks, one disgruntled wilderness advocate stated that the only difference between Yosemite Valley and Los Angeles was that the one had trees and no traffic policemen and the other had traffic policemen but no trees. These critics wanted few if any "improvements" in the parks, preferring that they be left in a state of complete wilderness. Mather sympathized but was too realistic to bar the voter and taxpayer from the parks. He knew that the strength of the national park system depended on its popularity in Congress and thus ultimately on public support.

Another of Mather's contributions resulted from his desire to make the public's visits to the parks as valuable as possible. When he heard about a nature-study program that was being conducted at Lake Tahoe in 1919, he determined to transfer the two professors in charge to Yosemite. The following year Yosemite visitors were taken on field trips and given campfire lectures for the first time. These lectures became so popular that similar programs were established in all the parks and have been a highlight of park enjoyment ever since.

Mather soon realized that the growth of this educational service needed coordination, so he appointed Ansel F. Hall as chief naturalist of the Park Service. Park rangers and interested teachers began to receive training at the Yosemite School of Field Natural History. And with the help of Rockefeller money, Hall promoted park museums, which were ultimately to become the heart of the Park Service's educational program. In addition, students, teachers, and scientists, following the example of John Wesley Powell, used the parks as laboratories for advanced study in geology, botany, zoology, and many other fields.

When Albright succeeded Mather as director of the National Park Service, this educational and scientific work was greatly expanded. For example, he implemented his belief in the importance of the history of the nation's parks by appointing a chief park historian, and he made a major contribution to the preservation of America's past by helping set up a system of national historic monuments. The most impressive of these—the Colonial National Monument in Virginia (established in 1930)—included parts of Jamestown, Williamsburg, and the Yorktown battlefield.

FORCED RETIREMENT AND LEGACY

By 1927 Mather had been in government service for twelve years. In this time he had accomplished his primary objectives and had founded a remarkably vital bureau of national parks. Part of his success could be credited to his wisdom in appointing such competent persons to key positions. Managing adroitly to

Mather (on ladder) with park superintendents at the Cliff Palace, Mesa Verde National Park, 1925 (Courtesy of the National Park Service)

avoid political pressure, he made his own selections and promotions on merit. With a corps of trained and dedicated men, he recruited his park rangers through the civil service. With pride he said: "I believe that today the National Park Service is a model bureau from the standpoint of efficiency in expenditure of public monies, adherence to the federal budget system, individual output of employees, cooperation with other government bureaus, low overhead expenses, and high morale and public spirit of personnel."[13]

Mather had accomplished for aesthetic conservation what Pinchot had achieved earlier for the cause of utilitarian conservation. In fact, the two men had much in common. Both devoted their zeal and energy to government service and gave generously of their personal wealth to promote public interest. Both built government bureaus that are functioning today in accordance with the basic policies they laid down. Now, under Mather's skillful direction, the Park Service seized the initiative in its contest with the Forest Service.

Mather's political and economic ideas fitted well with those of the presidents under whom he worked. To a surprising degree he managed to keep free of congressional or presidential control. And he had unusual success in winning the cooperation of large businesses, such as the railroads, and in procuring generous donations of land and money from private citizens. Yet he would not tolerate any action by private enterprise that marred the beauty of a park. For example, he blocked construction of a proposed cableway across the Grand Canyon, and he personally directed and watched the destruction of an unsightly sawmill that the Great Northern Railroad had delayed removing from Glacier National Park.

If Mather had a weakness, it was his failure to foresee the long-range effects that changes in the parks would have upon all the flora and fauna. He did not understand the interrelationship between living organisms and their environment. Adequate wildlife management and an effective wilderness-preservation policy had yet to be developed. But this can hardly be blamed on Mather, for the study of ecology was only in its formative years.

Mather did succeed in his dual effort to sell the idea of the parks to the American people and Congress and to preserve them from commercialization. The national park system became a model for other countries. Canada in particular followed the example of the United States in setting aside areas of outstanding scenic beauty, especially in the Rocky Mountains, where four adjoining parks—Jasper, Banff, Yoho, and Kootenay—make up one of the world's largest wildlife preserves. The United States and Canada joined in 1932 to establish the Waterton-Glacier International Peace Park, the first such preserve in the world. In fact, the beginnings that Mather made ultimately led to wide-scale international efforts to promote the establishment of national parks.

Although Mather had mentioned retirement, he looked forward to serving under Herbert Hoover. In November 1928, however, he was felled by a massive stroke and had no choice but to retire. Thus, he left the Park Service in Albright's competent hands. For a time Mather seemed to be recovering, but he died suddenly in January 1930.

Many people who make important contributions to society are not recognized in their own lifetime; Mather was an exception, appreciated by his country while he lived. Now, at his death, Congress approved and the president signed a bill for a Mather memorial only fifteen hours after a typed copy of the bill first reached the floor. Such unparalleled speed was recognition in itself. His many friends decided to remind the nation of Mather's service by placing a simple plaque in his memory in the national parks and monuments. Every year millions of Americans read its message:

HE LAID THE FOUNDATION
OF THE NATIONAL PARK SERVICE,
DEFINING AND ESTABLISHING THE POLICIES
UNDER WHICH ITS AREAS SHALL BE DEVELOPED AND
CONSERVED UNIMPAIRED FOR FUTURE GENERATIONS.
THERE WILL NEVER COME AN END TO
THE GOOD THAT HE HAS DONE.[14]

Chapter 6: Aldo Leopold

In the final section of his book *A Sand County Almanac*, the American philosopher-scientist Aldo Leopold wrote:

When god-like Odysseus returned from the wars in Troy, he hanged all on one rope a dozen slave-girls of his household whom he suspected of misbehavior during his absence.

This hanging involved no question of propriety. The girls were property. The disposal of property was then, as now, a matter of expediency, not of right and wrong.

Concepts of right and wrong were not lacking from Odysseus' Greece: witness the fidelity of his wife through the long years before at last his black-prowed galleys clove the wine-dark seas for home. The ethical structure of that day covered wives, but had not yet been extended to human chattels. During the three thousand years which have since elapsed, ethical criteria have been extended to many fields of conduct, with corresponding shrinkages in those judged by expediency alone. . . .

There is as yet no ethic dealing with man's relation to land and to the animals and plants which grow upon it. Land, like Odysseus' slave-

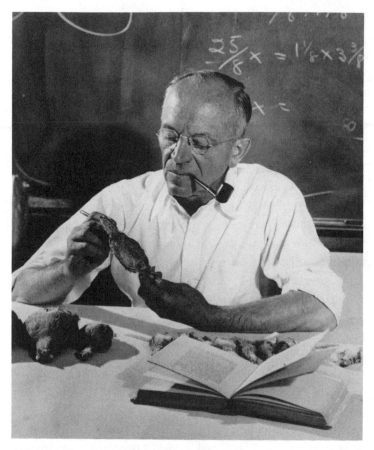

Aldo Leopold (Courtesy of the University of Wisconsin–Madison Archives)

girls, is still property. The land-relation is still strictly economic, entailing privileges but not obligations.[1]

Leopold's remarkable collection of essays was published in 1949, the year after his death, and became the bible of the environmental movement of the 1960s and 1970s. It has sold more than one million copies. The general acceptance of a "land ethic," for which Leopold pled so eloquently, remains today the most challenging goal for conservationists. Conservation cannot depend on technological advances and government controls; it must work first through changes in people's attitudes toward the world in which they live.

Born in 1887 in Burlington, Iowa, to an outdoors-loving German family, Aldo Leopold grew up in a spacious home on a bluff overlooking the Mississippi River. His maternal grandfather—architect, civic leader, and naturalist—helped establish the family business of manufacturing fine walnut desks. His father taught him the ethics of responsible recreational hunting, and his mother nurtured his aesthetic appreciation of nature.

Living on the migratory route of millions of geese and ducks, Aldo spent his boyhood exploring nearby woods and marshes, hunting, and observing wildlife. With a growing interest in ornithology and natural history, he recorded his daily observations in a journal. This became a lifelong practice. By age sixteen, when he left for the East to pursue his education, he had decided on a career as a forester.

In 1909, with a master's degree from Yale University's School of Forestry, Leopold secured a post in the Forest Service and started work in the New Mexico and Arizona territories. Here he lived for several years while territorial status gave way to statehood and both new states began to fill with people.

A misdiagnosed illness in 1913 ended his backcountry adventures and nearly cost him his life. After his recovery he traveled throughout New Mexico and Arizona making speeches and meeting with local forest officers, sportsmen, and stockmen to encourage them to organize local game-protection societies. He supported associations that worked for stricter game-law en-

136

forcement, predatory-animal control, and the creation of a system of game refuges.

Under Leopold's leadership a group of New Mexico sportsmen campaigned for a new approach to hunting that was based on the hunter's sense of responsibility for the hunted. As editor of the sportsmen's association newspaper, Leopold expressed the group's hope "that every citizen may learn to hold the lives of harmless wild creatures as a public trust for human good, against the abuse of which he stands personally responsible."[2]

In 1916 Leopold was placed in charge of coordinating the planning for recreational land use in the country's southwestern national forests, including the Grand Canyon. The Forest Service was responding to a legislative mandate to provide increased recreational facilities, and it was also responding to competition from the National Park Service. Three years later, after a brief stint promoting game conservation for the Albuquerque Chamber of Commerce, Leopold became chief of operations in the Southwest District, second in command in administering twenty million acres of national forest.

With his experience in the field, Leopold grew increasingly doubtful whether land development in the Southwest provided more benefits than liabilities. Soil erosion overshadowed profits from livestock, and much of the wilderness, intact when he first arrived, had disappeared. Leopold blamed tourism and the "good-roads movement" rather than agriculture or logging for the decimation of wilderness and wildlife. He observed, "Our remaining wild lands are wild because they are poor. But this poverty does not deter the booster from building expensive roads through them as bait for motor tourists."[3] Every small mountain community and local chamber of commerce pressed for roads, regardless of the financial cost and the impact on the land. Leopold pondered, "Who wants to stalk his buck to the music of a motor?"[4]

Though Leopold noted that Pinchot's plan for developing and safeguarding resources had been ably carried out, he questioned whether such a policy "should continue to govern in absolutely every instance, or whether the principle of highest use does not itself demand that representative portions of some forests be preserved as wilderness."[5] By "wilderness" he meant a "continuous stretch of country preserved in its natural state, open to lawful hunting and fishing, big enough to absorb a two weeks' pack trip, and kept devoid of roads, artificial trails, cottages, or other works of man."[6]

After arriving in the Southwest in 1909, Leopold had identified six roadless areas, each consisting of more than half a million acres. By 1921 only one remained, and he proposed that this area at the headwaters of the Gila River be administered by the Forest Service as a wilderness area, or "national hunting ground."[7] In 1924 the district forester complied, creating the first officially designated wilderness area in the country, a harbinger of the system established under the National Wilderness Preservation Act of 1964.

Although he had rejected several offers of promotion because he wanted to stay in the Southwest, in 1924 Leopold agreed to move to Wisconsin to become the associate director of the U. S. Forest Products Laboratory. But he was little interested in research on forest products (what to do with a tree once it had been cut down), for he wished to study the living forest.

He did play a central role in the passage of the Wisconsin Conservation Act of 1927, establishing a conservation department to look after the state's forests and wildlife. When the expected job as director of the new department failed to materialize, Leopold left the Forest Products Laboratory to pursue his own interests: wildlife and conservation.

Funded by the Sporting Arms and Ammunition Manufacturer's Institute, Leopold conducted a game survey in nine midwestern states. Between 1928 and 1930 he investigated to determine which environmental factors affected game productivity; then he presented recommendations to restore game through the management of habitat. When funds gave out in the depths of the Great Depression, he became self-employed as a forestry consultant and wrote a book entitled *Game Management*, which provided the guidelines for a new branch of science and for a new profession. Leopold himself accepted the first professorship in game management in the United States at the University of Wisconsin, and here he worked for the rest of his life as a teacher, researcher, and author.

Leopold's ideas on wildlife and wilderness had evolved over the years as he read extensively the works of early explorers and naturalists and as he gained experience in the field. One lesson proved especially painful. In an effort to increase the number of deer in the Southwest, he had encouraged the extermination of wolves and mountain lions. Many years later in Wisconsin, he received reports of uncontrolled growth in the deer population, with resulting damage to vegetation and danger to the deer themselves. In response, the Forest Service ordered the reconstruction of an abandoned wagon road into the Gila wilderness to provide easier access for hunters.

Leopold regretted his failed policy. More poignant was his recollection of the day he shot a wolf, thereby contributing to the eradication of the species in that part of the country:

We reached the old wolf in time to watch a fierce green fire dying in her eyes. I realized then, and have known ever since, that there was something new to me in those eyes—something known only to her and to the mountain. I was young then, and full of trigger-itch; I thought that because fewer wolves meant more deer, that no wolves would mean hunt-

ers' paradise. But after seeing the green fire die, I sensed that neither the wolf nor the mountain agreed with such a view.[8]

Leopold now advocated the scientific management of wildlife habitats by both public and private landholders rather than a reliance on game refuges, hunting laws, and other methods intended to protect desired species of game. As the historian Susan Flader noted, he "began to view wildlife management increasingly as a technique for restoring and maintaining diversity in the environment rather than primarily as a means of producing a shootable surplus."[9]

Wilderness also took on a new meaning for Leopold; he no longer saw it as a hunting or recreational ground but as an area for studying a healthy biotic community, including wolves and mountain lions. He joined with a few others in 1935 to found the Wilderness Society, an organization dedicated to expanding and protecting the nation's wilderness areas. He regarded the society as "one of the focal points of a new attitude—an intelligent humility toward man's place in nature."[10] In fact, Leopold contributed actively to more than one hundred professional and conservation organizations in his lifetime, balancing his research and writing with practical conservation efforts in the public arena.

He spent spare moments in the "sand counties" of Wisconsin, where John Muir had spent his boyhood. The once-forested region had been logged, swept by repeated fires, overgrazed by dairy cows, and left barren. In 1935 Leopold purchased eighty acres of the land, including a dilapidated chicken house, which he converted into a cabin. This shack served as a weekend refuge: "At daybreak I am the sole owner of all the acres I can walk over. It is not only boundaries that disappear, but also the thought of being bounded. Expanses unknown to deed or map are known to every dawn, and solitude, supposed no longer to exist in my county, extends on every hand as far as the dew can reach."[11]

Leopold admires a pine planted by his family on their sand-country farm. (Photograph by Robert A. McCabe; courtesy of the University of Wisconsin–Madison Archives)

Leopold's five children (all of whom became renowned naturalists) and his wife participated in a family effort to restore the land to ecological health. As he encouraged: "Acts of creation are ordinarily reserved for gods and poets, but humbler folk may circumvent this restriction if they know how. To plant a pine . . . one need only own a shovel. By virtue of this curious loophole in the rules, any clodhopper may say: Let there be a tree—and there will be one. If his back be strong and his shovel sharp, there may eventually be ten thousand."[12]

In reality, it took more than a strong back and sharp shovel to rejuvenate the land; it took knowledge, humility, and perseverance, for fires, plant diseases, droughts, floods, grazing animals, and vandals all took a heavy toll. To express his ideas about the land, Leopold combined vignettes of his experiences with some of his earlier essays in a book-length manuscript. But not until April 14, 1948, did a publisher agree to publish *A Sand County Almanac*, "as intimate a collaboration between a man and a landscape as has ever existed in life or in literature."[13] One week later, at the age of sixty-two, Aldo Leopold died fighting a neighbor's grass fire, his last act an attempt to protect a piece of land he so loved and valued.

A PHILOSOPHY OF CONSERVATION

Leopold's major objective in his writing and teaching was to make people aware that they belonged to a community composed of soil, water, plants, and animals—that they belonged to the land. He believed that past efforts to conserve the land had failed principally because of the mistaken attitude that people possessed the land—that it was a commodity to be treated like any other commodity. To Leopold, the future of conservation and perhaps of the human race depended on the adoption of a new attitude of respect and responsibility. If people accepted such a perspective they could live in harmony with the land, but

they needed to develop an "ecological conscience"—an awareness of the relationship between organisms (including people)
and their environment.

The premise upon which this new ethical attitude rested was
that "the individual is a member of a community of interdependent parts." The first principle of conservation was "to preserve
all the parts of the land mechanism." It was obvious to Leopold
that Americans neither understood nor appreciated the land.
In their careless, conquering hands, soil eroded, waterways filled
with sewage, and entire species of plants and animals disappeared. Leopold proposed that the human's role be changed
from "conqueror of the land-community to plain member and
citizen of it." But he realized that people could adopt a new ethical attitude only toward something they could "see, feel, understand, love, or otherwise have faith in." To explain the in-
terdependency of the many members of the "land-community,"
he used the image of the pyramid of life:

*Plants absorb energy from the sun. This energy flows through a circuit
called the biota, which may be represented by a pyramid consisting of layers. The bottom layer is the soil. A plant layer rests on the soil, an insect
layer on the plants, a bird and rodent layer on the insects, and so on up
through various animal groups to the apex layer, which consists of the
larger carnivores. . . . Proceeding upward, each successive layer de-
creases in numerical abundance. Thus, for every carnivore there are
hundreds of his prey, thousands of their prey, millions of insects, un-
countable plants. The pyramidal form of the system reflects this numerical progression from apex to base. . . . The lines of dependency for food
and other services are called food chains. Thus soil-oak-deer-Indian is
a chain that has now been largely converted to soil-corn-cow-farmer.
Each species, including ourselves, is a link in many chains.*[14]

Thus far in the history of life on earth, a remarkably stable
circuit of energy has flowed from the soil to plants, from plants
to animals, and back to the soil through death and decay. Only

gradual evolutionary change over the millenia has added successive new layers to the pyramid, making new, more complex food chains.

Leopold noted that the tools people had invented had enabled them to make rapid and violent changes in the intricate biotic pyramid, but that they had altered the food chain without understanding the possible consequences. For example, large predators such as wolves and mountain lions, at the top of the pyramid, had been largely exterminated. In addition, domestic species of plants and animals had been substituted for wild ones. Some species had completely disappeared, and still others had proliferated unduly and turned into pests. In Leopold's words, "Agricultural science is largely a race between the emergence of new pests and the emergence of new techniques for their control."[15]

Leopold agreed with Charles Darwin "that men are only fellow-voyagers with other creatures in the odyssey of evolution." If man was apart from and above the other species, it was because he had a conscience—not because of his power to exterminate other species or to manipulate the biotic community:

For one species to mourn the death of another is a new thing under the sun. The Cro-Magnon who slew the last mammoth thought only of steaks. The sportsman who shot the last pigeon thought only of his prowess. The sailor who clubbed the last auk thought of nothing at all. But we, who have lost our pigeons, mourn the loss. Had the funeral been ours, the pigeons would hardly have mourned us.[16]

The loss of the passenger pigeon saddened Leopold for two reasons: first, it had been a part of the biotic pyramid, with as much right to exist as any other species; and second, its existence made human life more worthwhile. In a poetic commentary he stated:

There will always be pigeons in books and in museums, but these are effigies and images, dead to all hardships and to all delights. Book-pi-

geons cannot dive out of a cloud to make the deer run for cover, or clap their wings in thunderous applause of mast-laden woods. Book-pigeons cannot breakfast on new-mown wheat in Minnesota, and dine on blueberries in Canada. They know no urge of seasons; they feel no kiss of sun, no lash of wind and weather. They live forever by not living at all.[17]

Leopold shared John Muir's indignation over people's arrogance toward the land, an arrogance that resulted in part from their "Abrahamic concept of land." He explained: "Abraham knew exactly what the land was for: it was to drip milk and honey into Abraham's mouth. At the present moment, the assurance with which we regard this assumption is inverse to the degree of our education."[18] Leopold was convinced, in fact, that urbanized people forgot that their welfare depended ultimately on the health of their total environment—not on industry and the local shopping center. As he remarked: "Twenty centuries of 'progress' have brought the average citizen a vote, a national anthem, a Ford, a bank account, and a high opinion of himself, but not the capacity to live in high density without befouling and denuding his environment, nor a conviction that such capacity, rather than such density, is the true test of whether he is civilized."[19]

THE IMPORTANCE OF WILDERNESS

In Leopold's opinion, two changes in the course of human existence were imminent. One was the "world-wide hybridization of culture" caused by industrialization and modern transportation; the other was the disappearance of wilderness from most of the inhabited parts of the world. Neither could be prevented entirely, but might not wilderness be preserved and enjoyed, Leopold asked, by ameliorating the effects of present changes? In twentieth-century America, only isolated fragments of the original "wild" exist outside of Alaska. Even the prairie's native long grass, which covered thousands of square miles in the days of the buffalo, is nonexistent except in scattered patches along railroad rights-of-way. Wilderness of all kinds—grasslands, forests, mountains, deserts, coastlines—is diminishing toward extinction.

When Leopold wrote of his concern, only one large area east of the Rockies had been formally reserved as a wilderness: the Quetico-Superior wilderness in Minnesota and Ontario. Yet the existence of even this one eastern wild area had been challenged continually by Americans who wanted to open the area for one reason or another. Leopold urged them to remember that to make a wild area readily accessible to public use through roads and mechanical transportation is to destroy the wilderness. Fortunately, the western United States, less populated and developed, contained large remnants of the former wilderness, particularly in land under the control of the Forest Service and Park Service.

Many different arguments have been offered in defense of wilderness. Leopold revealed his own feelings when he stated: "I am glad I shall never be young without wild country to be young in. Of what avail are forty freedoms without a blank spot on the map?"[20] And again he commented:"Wilderness areas are first of all a series of sanctuaries for the primitive arts of wilderness travel, especially canoeing and packing. I suppose some will wish to debate whether it is important to keep these primitive arts alive. I shall not debate it. Either you know it in your bones, or you are very, very old."[21] He protested against those who argued that preserving wilderness was undemocratic because few people could or would bother to use it. To compare the number who visit a golf course or a summer resort area with the number whovisit a wilderness is to miss the point, he believed. In his words: "Recreation is valuable in proportion to the intensity of its experiences, and to the degree to which it *differs from* and *contrasts with* workaday life. . . . Mechanized recreation already has seized nine-tenths of the woods and mountains; a decent respect for minorities should dedicate the other tenth to wilderness."[22]

Leopold advocated a new approach to recreational enjoyment, an approach based on the development of one's perception of natural processes—in short, nature study. "The outstanding characteristic of perception is that it entails no consumption and no dilution of any resource." Innumerable people can enjoy viewing and photographing wildlife, for example, but the pleasure of the successful hunter, the "trophy hunter," is selfish, destroying not only what is hunted but also everyone else's opportunity to enjoy it. Leopold thought that the promotion of perception was "the only truly creative part of recreational engineering." It was his contention that recreational development was "a job not of building roads into lovely country, but of building receptivity into the still unlovely human mind."[23]

Leopold's position represents that of a minority of Americans. He believed that certain values and experiences were essential to the health of the society, even if only a few people could experience them. He repudiated the idea that the mass of citizens should determine all the values and all the uses of the land. In the foreword to *A Sand County Almanac* he stated:

Like winds and sunsets, wild things were taken for granted until progress began to do away with them. Now we face the question whether a still higher "standard of living" is worth its cost in things natural, wild, and free. For us of the minority, the opportunity to see geese is more important than television, and the chance to find a pasque-flower is a right as inalienable as free speech.

These wild things, I admit, had little human value until mechanization assured us of a good breakfast, and until science disclosed the drama of where they come from and how they live. The whole conflict thus boils down to a question of degree. We of the minority see a law of diminishing returns in progress; our opponents do not.[24]

The wilderness, Leopold contended, also has practical usefulness, even if not in immediate economic terms, for land that has been subjected to human interference and control has increasing difficulty renewing itself. In short, when land has suffered erosion, floods, the invasion of rodents, and similar phenomena, it is sick. Leopold explained:

> The practices we now call conservation are, to a large extent, local alleviations of biotic pain. They are necessary, but they must not be confused with cures. The art of land doctoring is being practiced with vigor, but the science of land health is yet to be born.
>
> A science of land health needs, first of all, a base datum of normality, a picture of how healthy land maintains itself as an organism.[25]

As Leopold saw it, the best example of healthy land is wilderness. Therefore, wilderness is by far the most useful laboratory in which to discover basic cures for the maladies of the land. Furthermore, without wild areas to serve as a basis for comparison, people may eventually lose sight of what healthy land is. And because each biotic community is different, a wilderness of each type of land is needed.

Wilderness, moreover, provides the only hope of saving the large carnivores from extinction. Grizzly bears and wolves, for example, have been all but exterminated outside of Alaska. Even the national parks have proved to be too small as reserves for animals that roam long distances. When Leopold came west as a young forest ranger in 1909, grizzly bears inhabited all the major mountain ranges, and their subsequent disappearance upset him. "Relegating grizzlies to Alaska is about like relegating happiness to heaven; one may never get there," he said.[26]

Leopold understood that wilderness is a precious resource whose value will increase with its increasing scarcity. As he recognized, one of the most serious problems in wilderness preservation is that wilderness can shrink but can rarely grow. Thus, Americans, as well as people elsewhere in the world, may never have any more wilderness than they have at the present moment. In concluding his argument Leopold had this to say:

Ability to see the cultural value of wilderness boils down, in the last analysis, to a question of intellectual humility. The shallow-minded modern who has lost his rootage in the land assumes that he has already discovered what is important; it is such who prate of empires, political or economic, that will last a thousand years. It is only the scholar who appreciates that all history consists of successive excursions from a single starting-point, to which man returns again and again to organize yet another search for a durable scale of values. It is only the scholar who understands why the raw wilderness gives definition and meaning to the human enterprise.[27]

A CHALLENGE FOR THE FUTURE

Leopold believed that the conservationist's hope lay in a restoration of harmony between humans and the land and that this, in turn, depended on the adoption of a new set of values, a land ethic: "A land ethic, then, reflects the existence of an ecological conscience, and this in turn reflects a conviction of individual responsibility for the health of the land. Health is the capacity of the land for self-renewal. Conservation is our effort to understand and preserve this capacity."[28]

In Leopold's opinion, the adoption of an ecological conscience by the individual or of a land ethic by society was unlikely unless young people could acquire an understanding and appreciation of how the land community functioned. As he pointed out:

There is as yet no social stigma in the possession of a gullied farm, a wrecked forest, or a polluted stream, provided the dividends suffice to send the youngsters to college. Whatever ails the land, the government will fix it.

I think we have here the root of the problem. What conservation education must build is an ethical underpinning for land economics and a universal curiousity to understand the land mechanism. Conservation may then follow.[29]

In the hope of contributing to a better understanding of nature, Leopold continued his study of ecology and spent his last years teaching in the classroom and writing. In his teaching he questioned the wisdom of relegating all problems of land management to the government. Although he recognized the steadily increasing importance of government ownership and regulation of resources, he doubted whether the government alone could heal a sick land. Instead, he urged people to adopt a set of values that would place more responsibility on private landowners.

Leopold took a dim view of the prevailing attitude among conservationists that their behavior should consist of obeying the law, voting for other conservationists, joining a few organizations, and taking conservation measures that were economically feasible. The government, it was assumed, would do the rest. Education to promote such behavior included no ethical considerations, called for no personal obligations or sacrifices, envisaged no changes in accepted practices. As a result, the land continued to suffer, and with it the interests of the community.

It puzzled Leopold that from their churches and schools people accepted obligations free of self-interest but that they continued to treat the land like a slave:

A system of conservation based solely on economic self-interest is hopelessly lopsided. It tends to ignore, and thus eventually to eliminate, many elements in the land community that lack commercial value, but that are (as far as we know) essential to its healthy functioning. It assumes, falsely, I think, that the economic parts of the biotic clock will function without the uneconomic parts. It tends to relegate to govern-

ment many functions eventually too large, too complex, or too widely dis-persed to be performed by government.

An ethical obligation on the part of the private owner is the only vis-ible remedy for these situations.[30]

Leopold stated that Americans would have to start thinking about more than economics if the country was ever to accept a land ethic. He believed that each question regarding the land should be examined in view of what is ethically and aesthetically right. He explained, "A thing is right when it tends to preserve the integrity, stability, and beauty of the biotic community. It is wrong when it tends otherwise."[31] To Leopold the important thing was to strive toward a goal. Indeed, he left us a goal—to achieve harmony with the land—and he left us his land ethic as the way to approach that goal.

Chapter 7: Harold Ickes

The newly appointed members of the cabinet met in the Oval Room of the White House on inauguration night, March 4, 1933. The crisis facing the nation called for extraordinary action, and President Franklin Delano Roosevelt (FDR) wanted the new cabinet sworn into office without a single day's delay. In the small gathering stood Harold L. Ickes, a little-known Chicagoan and Roosevelt's unlikely choice as the new secretary of the interior.

Ickes's appointment came as a reward to midwestern independent Republicans who had rallied behind the president's campaign. It also resulted from the president's sympathy with Ickes's devotion to the cause of Progressive reform—a movement that had begun in the era of Theodore Roosevelt. The new secretary of the interior would hold that office longer than anyone before or after him—nearly thirteen years—and would establish a remarkable record as steward of the public lands and guardian of its resources.

Ickes was born on a Pennsylvania farm in 1874, and he had a difficult childhood. His hard-drinking and unsuccessful father ignored him. And although his mother, a staunch Scotch Presbyterian who took her politics as seriously as her religion, taught him the virtues of honesty and hard work, she died when he was sixteen. Fortunately, he went to live with his favorite aunt in Chicago. Encouraged by a dedicated high school teacher, he enrolled in the newly opened University of Chicago. Doggedly he pursued his studies, living in an unheated room and working long hours. In spite of his fatigue, to save ten cents a day he walked to his job teaching night school. Graduating in 1897 at the head of his class, he chose not to appear to receive his diploma because he was embarrassed by his shabby clothes. Overcoming such difficult circumstances helped to instill in him a desire for recognition and achievement, identification with the underdog, and an independent spirit.

Ickes quickly revealed a penchant for local politics. Immigrants overflowed in the streets of Chicago at the turn of the century, and "boss and machine" politics dominated the city's government. Though he was influenced by Jane Addams and other reformers, the young man also gained a grudging respect for the "bosses" who knew how to use political power effectively. Early on, he sided with independent dark-horse candidates—people with integrity and high ideals. As he explained, "Going down with a candidate that you swear by, rather than swear at, is much better for your disposition, particularly if you are dead set upon swimming against the current."[1]

After graduating, Ickes worked his way up to the position of assistant political reporter for the *Chicago Record,* where he gained expertise in urban politics, becoming "cynically wise to the selfishness and meanness of men when their appetites are involved."[2] In this job he also honed his writing skills and exhibited a combativeness that never left him. At the same time, he demonstrated notable organizational skills as a behind-the-scenes manager in several political campaigns, though he chose not to run for office himself. Ickes decided that a law practice would provide more status and clout in the political arena than would journalism, so he went on to complete a law degree (with honors) at the University of Chicago, but in the following years his practice of law was distinctly secondary to his reform activities. In 1911 he married Anna Wilmarth Thompson, and through the unhappy marriage, which lasted until his wife's death in an automobile accident in 1935, he attained wealth and social connections he had never had and was freed to focus on politics.

An active Progressive, Ickes supported Theodore Roosevelt's Bull Moose campaign in 1912. He remained a leading figure in the Progressive party in Illinois and in the national movement to revive the party long after its collapse at the onset of World War I. Following Roosevelt's death he adopted a new champion, Senator Hiram Johnson, hoping to foster his own ambition for national recognition while continuing to struggle against moneyed interests. But when Johnson lost in the 1924 Republican presidential primary election, Ickes retreated to local politics. As chairman of the People's Traction League in Chicago, he battled corruption and Samuel Insull's control of transit and utilities.

Frustrated by the policies of Republicans, he befriended reform-minded Democrats. In 1932 he accepted leadership of the western branch of the National Progressive League to support Franklin Delano Roosevelt, for he hoped to gain a position in the nation's capital. Little did he realize that fortuitous circumstances would result in his appointment as secretary of the interior in Roosevelt's cabinet. Thus, at the age of fifty-nine Ickes finally had an opportunity on the national level to exercise his administrative abilities and to advance the causes in which he believed.

CONSERVATION SINCE TEDDY ROOSEVELT AND PINCHOT

Ickes believed that conservation was among the most important responsibilities of government and regarded himself as a conservationist in the mold of Theodore Roosevelt and Gifford Pinchot. He dedicated himself to restoring the public's trust in a department tainted by the Ballinger-Pinchot controversy as well as Teapot Dome, the 1920s scandal in which Secretary of the Interior Albert B. Fall had been convicted of accepting bribes for leasing two naval oil reserves to private interests.

Unfortunately, the momentum of the conservation movement under Roosevelt and Pinchot had slowed during the difficult years of World War I and in the 1920s. President Warren G. Harding, who followed Woodrow Wilson, had largely ignored conservation in his effort to return the country to "normalcy." And the management of resources had continued to stagnate under President Calvin Coolidge, whose emphasis on economy in government had hamstrung the federal conservation program.

Despite the lack of executive leadership and the continued wasteful depletion of resources, scientific research by government bureaus had aided future management of America's resources. For example, Hugh Bennett of the Bureau of Soils (who later became head of the Soil Conservation Service under FDR) had called the nation's attention to the problem of soil erosion and gained congressional support for an experimental program to reduce erosion through controlled land use.

The increased research of the 1920s had helped lay the groundwork for the acceptance of multipurpose resource planning in the 1930s. The Boulder Canyon Project, authorized in 1928 and completed eight years later, had provided irrigation water for more than one million acres of land, generated hydroelectric power for the development of the Southwest, regulated the flow of the Colorado River, and provided water for domestic use in Southern California.

When Herbert Hoover moved into the White House in 1929, he revealed a direct personal interest in the conservation of natural resources, but he faced a personal dilemma. Although he wanted to prevent the wasteful exploitation of resources, he believed in "rugged individualism" and could not in good conscience use the full power of his office to control private business. Instead, he acted on his belief that "to sustain the spirit of responsibility of States, of municipalities, of industry and the community at large is the one safeguard against overwhelming centralization and degeneration of that independence and initiative which are the very foundations of democracy."[3] Thus, he decentralized control over conservation programs, promoted the voluntary cooperation of individuals and states with the national government, and encouraged efficiency and reduction of waste. Hoover's application of "voluntarism" to manage natural resources, however, proved no more successful than his application of "voluntarism" to stem the downward spiral of the Great Depression and rejuvenate the economy. The complexity and urgency of the nation's economic problems were too great for a solution based on voluntary cooperation.

INDIVIDUALISM AND CIVIL RIGHTS

Ickes drew a sharp distinction between "rugged individualism," which he defined as the pursuit of personal advantage without concern for others, and the principle of "the greatest good of the greatest number," which he championed. He regarded laissez-faire as a "pernicious" doctrine that allowed the wealthy few to run roughshod over the majority and to exploit the country's resources, and he believed that the liaison between business-people and politicians would inevitably jeopardize the public welfare. It made no sense to him that poverty and hunger should be permitted in a country capable of providing a decent living for all its citizens.

He blamed "rugged individualists" for the rapid deterioration of the American land and its resources. As he explained, "In the early days our forefathers could cut down a forest or exhaust the fertility of a farm and then blithely move on to a new forest and a new farm. . . . The highest concept of statesmanship was to make it possible for the eager, aggressive pioneer to possess, to despoil and then repeat the process indefinitely."[4] Shortsighted and unchecked greed, Ickes believed, resulted in "denuded forests, floods, droughts, a disappearing water table, erosion, a less stable and equable climate, a vanishing wildlife."[5] American taxpayers, he warned in 1934, would have to pay billions of dollars to purify polluted waterways, reforest timberlands, rehabilitate farmlands ravaged by erosion, and protect grasslands laid bare by overgrazing.

Ickes advocated protection of the rights of minorities and took the position that "society is no happier or stronger than its most miserable and weakest group."[6] He was particularly concerned for American Indians and desired the position of commissioner of Indian affairs before the job as secretary of the interior fell unexpectedly into his lap. As secretary he selected John Collier as the new commissioner and supported the Indian Reorganization Act of 1934, which helped launch the so-called Indian New Deal, instituting far-ranging reforms in Indian affairs. Ickes opposed the policy established under the Dawes Act (1887) that allowed the conversion of reservation lands to private property. Instead, he upheld the right of Indians to their own culture, including communal ownership of land. He discouraged boarding schools that separated Indian children from their parents, and he encouraged gainful employment on the reservation and recruited Indians to work in the Interior Department.

At a time of widespread racial segregation, Ickes employed blacks in responsible positions and opened the dining room in the Interior building to them. In a well-publicized incident in 1939, after the Daughters of the American Revolution had refused the use of their hall to the great black soprano Marian Anderson, he arranged for her to perform on the steps of the Lincoln Memorial, introducing her to a crowd of seventy-five thousand. Someone once said of Ickes, "He was the best liberal, the best Negro, the best Indian, the best Nisei and the best Jew in Washington."[7]

Ickes called for recognition of the rights of others and acceptance of "regulation made for the common good." In his book *The New Democracy,* published in 1934, he stated that the government should be responsible for universal education, protection against disease, improved medical care, decent living conditions, help for the unemployed and elderly, and many other programs, including conservation. He believed that a free press, an informed electorate, and honest public officials could prevail against privileged interests. Advocating a fairer distribution of wealth, he eagerly accepted the opportunity to head the Department of the Interior.

AS SECRETARY OF THE INTERIOR

Ickes had limited experience with the national government and was a newcomer to the Department of the Interior. When established in 1849, the department had been a grab bag of administrative units including the General Land Office (administering the disposal of the public domain), the Bureau of Indian Affairs, and both the Patent and Pension offices. Other agencies were gradually added or annexed, including Powell's Geological Survey (1879), the Reclamation Service (1902), the Bureau of Mines (1910), and Mather's National Park Service (1916). In addition, Ickes had administrative jurisdiction over education, charitable institutions, the territories of Alaska and Hawaii, and Puerto Rico and the Virgin Islands, and he had such duties as supervising government buildings in the nation's capital.

The Interior Department had acquired a reputation for corruption—for bending to pressures from private-interest groups in its management of public resources. Ickes settled quickly into his new job, determined to make his department a model of honest public service. Though some of his methods were heavy-handed, no one could deny that "Honest Harold" quickly put his house in order. Insisting on efficiency and dedication, Ickes kept close scrutiny on his employees, even eavesdropping on and monitoring the phone conversations of his subordinates. In short, he demanded loyalty to his administration and wanted to assure that no graft took place. One disgruntled congressman thought Ickes had "the soul of a meat ax and the mind of a commisar."[8] Ickes compared his experience in public life to his performance on the dance floor as a college student: "I bumped into too many other people—*sometimes* by accident."[9] Although his actions undoubtedly hurt morale, they quickly put people on their toes and left no question who was in command.

Ickes's cantankerous character became legendary. The historian Arthur M. Schlesinger, Jr., said of him:

By the evidence of the diary into which he regularly discharged his most private thoughts, he was a quivering mass, sensitive as a girl, suspicious as a moneylender. The years of battle had hardened his skin rather than his sensibility. There were softer strains within: the dry, deadpan humor; the deep concern for friendless groups like Indians; the delight in dahlias; the gourmet's fondness for good food and liquor; above all, the touching, desperate need for private affection and public reassurance.

A nagging mastoid ailment and chronic insomnia increased his internal tension. Wanting everyone to love him but trusting no one, he was convinced that mankind was engaged in an unrelenting conspiracy against him. He questioned everyone's motives, regarded disagreement as sabotage and vindictiveness (at least his own) as virtue. . . . His egotism was so massive that he remained personally unconscious of its existence. With the best will, he could not but conclude that anything which extended his power served the republic.[10]

Schlesinger also recognized the other side of the coin—that "bellicosity implied boldness; self-righteousness implied rectitude; ambition implied energy; mistrust implied vigilance." Here was an "indominable defender of the national interest."[11]

FDR supported conservation, except when he considered the political price too high—for example, when conflict arose over government control of oil policy or the reorganization of federal bureaus. A supportive Congress behind him, Roosevelt joined with Ickes, Secretary of Agriculture Henry Wallace, and others to begin to rehabilitate the land nationwide, creating new federal conservation agencies and services and directing large appropriations into new programs. During the "One Hundred Days" of the New Deal, both the Tennessee Valley Authority (TVA) and the Civilian Conservation Corps (CCC) gained congressional approval. The TVA was the most sweeping and daring application of multiple-purpose resource planning yet attempted.

THE TVA AND THE CCC

The Muscle Shoals of the Tennessee River had long attracted interest as a potential dam site. Back in 1903, Theodore Roosevelt had vetoed a bill designed to place the site in the hands of a private utility company. Some years later, during the First World War, the government began construction of a dam and

*Harold Ickes (center), with President Roosevelt (left) and
Henry Wallace, 1933 (Courtesy of UPI/Bettmann Newsphotos)*

power plant to facilitate the production of nitrates for muni-
tions. After the war ended, debate broke out over whether the
government should operate the complex or sell it to private
business. In the ensuing struggle, Senator George W. Norris of
Nebraska blocked a sale of these government resources to Henry Ford, urging federal development and control of a whole
system of dams on the Tennessee River. Congress twice approved his proposal, but President Coolidge and President
Hoover successively vetoed the bills.

When Franklin Roosevelt became president he saw that a
major river basin could be developed as a unified project. The

TVA act set up a government corporation, under a three-person board, to administer "the proper use, conservation, and development of the natural resources of the Tennessee River drainage basin." The Tennessee River drained forty thousand square miles in seven states, one of the most poverty-stricken areas in the nation. Here was a grand experiment—an opportunity to rejuvenate an area whose most readily available resources had already been consumed.

Arthur Morgan, the TVA's first director, obtained Ickes's cooperation in acquiring office space within the Interior Department, but the TVA remained administratively separate from Ickes's jurisdiction—an arrangement the secretary viewed with mixed feelings. As Public Works administrator and a long-time advocate of public power, Ickes helped municipal plants and county cooperatives in the distribution of public power generated by the TVA. He argued that private power companies had failed to provide the energy needed by the people of the impoverished Tennessee Valley and that now these companies should not be allowed to sell energy produced by the TVA for their own profit. At the same time, he complained about the TVA's independence, arguing that the organization would be better managed under his direction. Ickes feared that the TVA would become a model for independent power agencies elsewhere in the country. Roosevelt, however, paid no heed to Ickes's complaint, and the TVA retained its independence.

To this day the TVA remains controversial. Some Americans saw it as the showcase of New Deal resource management, a model to be copied at home and abroad. Others considered it a socialistic boondoggle. Whether or not the investment was worth the price, the Tennessee Valley did benefit from flood control, reforestation, soil conservation, cheap power, and the introduction of improved farming techniques.

In his presidential acceptance speech, FDR proposed another new, but less controversial, agency, which would place a

*FDR (at head of table) and Ickes (third from left) enjoy lunch at a
CCC camp in Virginia, 1933 (Courtesy of the Library of Congress)*

million men in forestry programs. The Civilian Conservation
Corps (CCC) had a dual purpose: to create jobs immediately for
unemployed young men and to restore the land to productivity.
The accomplishment of these goals depended on federal-state
cooperation and on effective coordination between several federal agencies: the Department of Labor helped recruit young
men; the U.S. Army supplied and directed CCC camps; the Office of Education provided educational programs; and the De-

partment of the Interior, the Department of Agriculture, and the Army Corps of Engineers selected and supervised projects.

Not surprisingly, rivalry between bureaus occurred. The Department of Agriculture, with jurisdiction over the Forest Service, controlled most of the projects, and Ickes balked at what he considered a subsidiary role for the Interior Department. Nevertheless, his department reaped many benefits. In particular, the young men of the CCC built campgrounds, trails, roads, telephone lines, and many other improvements in the national parks; the Bureau of Reclamation received CCC assistance in the construction of irrigation projects; several CCC camps aided the Division of Grazing in rehabilitating grasslands, controlling rodent and insect populations, and providing water in arid regions; and over eighty thousand Indians participated in projects on reservations.

By helping to restore America's resources, thousands of young men were able for the first time in his life to begin to pay their way. Although they earned only thirty dollars a month, part of which they sent home to family, they also received good food, housing, and clothing at a time when all three were desperately needed. By the end of the program in 1942, over two and a half million boys had enrolled in the CCC. The saving of human resources may have been the greatest dividend of all.

SOIL CONSERVATION, PARKS, AND RECLAMATION

The CCC alone could not hope to solve the problem of soil erosion in the western United States. While the noted soil scientist Hugh Bennett was testifying at a Senate hearing in Washington, the sun grew dim behind a great dust cloud blown east from the country's interior. Facing the senators, Bennett pointed to the dust and said, "There, gentlemen, goes part of Oklahoma now."[12] He got the money needed for his efforts to control soil erosion and restore the land to productivity in the Dust Bowl, and he led the work of Ickes's newly created Soil Conservation Service.

Many of the problems of depleted grasslands and soil erosion had been caused by continued overstocking and mismanagement. Cattlemen and sheepmen had long enjoyed unrestricted use of public range, but because of the resulting devastation, westerners had reluctantly recognized the need for some kind of control. Ickes opposed proposals to transfer these lands to state control, arguing that selfish interests would find it easier to plunder resources. Instead, he urged federal management of the remaining public domain.

Accordingly, he supported a bill introduced by Congressman Edward Taylor of Colorado authorizing the secretary of the interior to establish grazing districts and regulate land use by a permit-and-fee system. The act allowed for the closure of the public domain to homesteaders, ending the era of American history in which each pioneer could claim 160 acres of unsettled land as his own. Ickes set up the Grazing Service in an attempt to provide opportunities for small ranchers while still conserving the soil.

Ickes also took a special interest in the administration of the National Park Service. He had always enjoyed flowers and gardens, and on a two-week horseback trip through Glacier National Park in 1916 he came to appreciate wilderness as much as other areas of scenic beauty. He had known and respected Stephen Mather, a fellow Chicagoan, and he wisely asked Mather's successor, Horace Albright, to remain as director of the Park Service in 1933. Albright understood the bureaucracy in Washington, provided valuable advice on appointments, and reinforced Ickes's support for aesthetic conservation. He also helped persuade FDR to transfer historic battlefields, national monuments, and many national cemeteries to the National Park Service, and he fostered a historic preservation program within the Park Service.

Ickes faced the same dilemma encountered earlier by Mather and Albright—where to draw the line between the current use of the parks and their preservation for future generations. The Park Service promoted heavier use of the parks, in part to encourage economic recovery in surrounding communities. Ickes, however, opposed most new park roads and supported the concept of wilderness parks long before the idea gained approval from Congress. On one important issue he bowed to political pressure, reluctantly approving the construction of a tunnel within Rocky Mountain National Park to transport water from the western slope to the dry plains to the east. Fortunately, the Colorado–Big Thompson project was completed with care and left little imprint on parkland.

In spite of an acrimonious relationship between Ickes and Arno B. Cammerer, who became director of the National Park Service in 1933, the expansion of the national parks and monuments proceeded rapidly. Ickes played an instrumental role in obtaining approval for Olympic National Park (Washington) in 1938 and Kings Canyon National Park (California) in 1940. Increasingly, in the late 1930s, he argued against the development of roads and other improvements within national parks—for instance, in the Everglades of Florida—that would compromise their integrity; and he called on Congress to define and set standards for "wilderness national parks."[13] In addition, in 1943 he helped persuade Roosevelt to use the Antiquities Act of 1906 to proclaim Jackson Hole in Wyoming a national monument. Ickes also advocated the acquisition of hundreds of miles of coastal shoreline before the land fell into private hands. (Although Congress had authorized the first national seashore at Cape Hatteras in North Carolina in 1937, no land was acquired for this purpose until many years later.) And he encouraged the creation of city and state parks, having witnessed the heavy cost paid by the city of Chicago in its recovery of recreational frontage on Lake Michigan that had earlier been given to the railroad.

Though Ickes initially showed little interest in federal irrigation projects in the West—the Reclamation Fund was exhausted and agricultural surpluses were causing widespread concern—he enthusiastically supported public power. He pushed the Boulder Canyon Project, completed in 1936, hoping to establish publicly controlled hydroelectricity and basin-wide resource planning. Hoover (Boulder) Dam became a model for other New Deal projects in the West.

With the prospect of repayment from the the sale of hydroelectric power and with money from the Public Works Administration and other sources, the federal government began to build several new dams and storage reservoirs. These included the Grand Coulee Dam—part of the Columbia Basin Project in the state of Washington—which created a lake 150 miles long, stretching to the Canadian border. The Bureau of Reclamation so successfully promoted multiple-purpose river basin developments that by 1940 thirteen major storage dams were under construction.

The energy produced at federally owned dams effected the postwar transformation of Southern California and other parts of the West into industrial and agricultural centers. No less impressive were the changes that cheap electricity brought to the individual farm home. A decade after FDR's first inauguration, reclamation projects had doubled and power production had increased phenomenally. The Bureau of Reclamation had become the world's greatest producer of electric power.

Parts of the West, however, particularly on the Pacific Coast, developed too rapidly. Increased revenues led to the proliferation of dams and canals, many of which proved ill planned or unnecessary (such as the Glen Canyon Dam on the Colorado River). Furthermore, siltation, salination, and water evaporation, as well as the loss of aesthetic resources, caused people to question the wisdom of several projects. And communities sprang up and grew rapidly, the demand for raw materials soared, and the ecological health of the land suffered—results that Ickes had not envisaged.

THE PWA, NATIONAL PLANNING, AND GOVERNMENT REORGANIZATION

In addition to holding the office of secretary of the interior, Ickes served as head of the Public Works Administration (PWA), a major agency established in 1933 that made grants and loans to lesser political units and private businesses. Under Ickes, administrative overhead costs were kept under 1 percent, an enviable record.

With an initial appropriation of $3.3 billion, the single largest government appropriation up to that time, the PWA started twenty thousand construction projects in its first two years, affecting nearly every county in the nation. Ickes worked an average of fourteen hours a day, with Christmas off and "only half time on Sunday." Because opportunities for fraud and graft abounded, he oversaw nearly every detail, "refusing to sign anything that [he] had not personally read."[14]

As Ickes explained, the task of the PWA was "to build permanent and socially desirable projects that would be assets of the communities which they would serve."[15] These included such varied developments as the electrification of the Pennsylvania Railroad between Washington, D.C., and New York City, a water supply system for Denver, and a library at the University of New Mexico. The PWA financed construction of 70 percent of the nation's new schools, contributed to the completion of Hoover Dam ahead of schedule, and aided the construction of the TVA and Grand Coulee and other major dams. The agency's imprint on the national recovery and long-term economic growth was undeniable.

Even with its excellent record, Ickes's administration was sharply criticized. His demand for federal control of funds drew the ire of state officials. And when he appointed Louis R. Glavis (the same Glavis who had exposed Secretary of the Interior Ballinger in his conflict with Pinchot) to head a team investigating proposed projects, complaints of wiretapping and other overzealous methods arose. Additionally, his insistence on careful planning to eliminate boondoggles and to assure cost-effectiveness led to inevitable delays in the expenditure of funds at a time of massive unemployment. Ickes advanced with all due speed but never compromised his pledge to give the public its money's worth.

By mid-August 1934 the PWA was spending $39 million a week, but Roosevelt considered other agencies, particularly the Works Progress Administration, under Harry Hopkins, to be quicker at creating jobs. Two years later, when funding for the PWA declined, a disgruntled Ickes offered his resignation. But FDR handled Ickes deftly, as he did on more than one occasion, soothing his bruised ego and reassuring him that his services were indispensable.

Although Ickes favored a public-works program, especially in time of unemployment, he argued that the PWA had suffered from the lack of prior planning. Before stepping down as head of the PWA he proposed several useful public works for the future: superhighways from coast to coast, a water-pollution control program, forest renewal and erosion control, irrigation and hydroelectric power projects, and low-cost housing. He emphasized that such improvements, "carefully planned in advance," would provide a far better use of labor and resources than had resulted from America's happy-go-lucky attitude.

As Ickes stated in his book *The New Democracy*, the Roosevelt administration was the first to adopt as a national policy "the theory that the country as a whole, including commerce, industry and finance, ought to be developed and used for the greatest good of the greatest number."[16] But this could not be done without a thorough study of the entire country. To foster such study and planning, in 1933 FDR established a National Planning Board under Ickes. Though it was intended to stimulate economic recovery through a comprehensive public-works program, Ickes hoped the board would become a permanent institution for conservation and national planning.

With increasing criticism of New Deal policies and the advent of World War II, the board languished and died in 1943. At the time of its demise, it was studying the problems of the country's economic conversion from wartime to peacetime. The board's call for federal intervention to resolve rising social problems, particularly its plea for comprehensive social and health insurance, alienated conservatives and threatened bureaucrats in existing agencies. And Congress, influenced by the Army Corps of Engineers, preferred to continue using a piecemeal approach to resource management.

National planning never attained the potential Ickes had seen for it, nor did the Division of Power, which he had initiated in 1941 in the Department of the Interior to formulate and centralize public power policy. But he looked to government reorganization as another way to enhance national efficiency, promote the public welfare, and at the same time broaden his own administrative authority. In 1935, partly as a result of the transfer of the Soil Erosion Service from Interior to Agriculture, Ickes launched an offensive to consolidate the control of resource management. The administrative stakes were high, for conservation programs thrived in the 1930s, adding more than 18 million acres of national forests, 142 million acres of public grasslands, and several new national parks and monuments.

While Ickes coveted control of the national forests, the Forest Service had its eye on the public grazing lands.

In spite of active campaigning for his "Department of Conservation" bill, Ickes met defeat. Lobbyists for the Forest Service, especially in the West, inundated Congress with letters of protest. Gifford Pinchot accused previous Interior Department administrations of fraud, theft, and waste. He argued, "Wood is a crop. Forestry is tree farming. It belongs in the Department of Agriculture with all other farming and production from the soil."[17] Professional foresters, as well as conservation organizations such as the American Forestry Association, defended Pinchot's position, stating that the Forest Service had done a good job. And local resource users—lumbermen, farmers, and stockmen—advocated maintaining decentralized administration, for they wanted to participate in decisions affecting their livelihood, particularly in those regarding the issuance of permits and charging of fees.

When Congress finally passed the Reorganization Act in 1939, Ickes gained little except the Bureau of Fisheries and the Biological Survey, which were merged to form the Fish and Wildlife Service. Wildlife conservation had made major advances during FDR's first two terms; existing refuges had been improved and new ones added.

In 1940, political pressures from fellow Democrats dashed Ickes's hopes that the president might finally transfer the Forest Service to his control. At this point Ickes again offered his resignation, deeply disappointed at the defeat of his plan. In a handwritten note Roosevelt responded: "We—you & I, were married 'for better, for worse'—and it's too late to get a divorce & too late for you to walk out of the home—anyway. I need you! Nuff said. Affec. FDR"[18] Noting in his diary that it was "pretty difficult to do anything with a man who can write such a letter," Ickes agreed to stay.[19]

The struggle over conservation ebbed as FDR increasingly turned his attention to foreign affairs and the growing war in Europe. The president had never given his open support for a department of conservation, and Ickes had failed consistently to recognize his opposition's strength. There the matter ended.

THE WAR YEARS AND BEYOND

Ickes had been one of the first important American leaders to speak out forcefully against fascism in the 1930s, denouncing the sale of oil to Italy during its conquest of Ethiopia and strongly criticizing Franco's seizure of power in Spain. He used his department's control of helium to block the sale of it to the Nazi regime for use in Hitler's fleet of dirigibles, and he discouraged the export of oil and scrap iron to Japan, despite criticism from the State Department.

The new priorities in America during World War II brought the momentum of the New Deal conservation program to a halt. Ickes found himself on the defensive in his effort to protect national parks and wildlife refuges from loggers, miners, ranchers, and other resource users. For example, in a letter to FDR a few days before Pearl Harbor, he warned that a proposed bombing range would threaten extermination of the rare trumpeter swan. The president responded immediately with an order to the secretary of war: "Please tell Major General Adams or whoever is in charge of this business that Henry Lake, Utah, must immediately be struck from the Army planning list for any purposes. The verdict is for the Trumpeter Swan and against the Army. The Army must find a different nesting place!"[20]

For the most part Ickes's role was to help provide needed resources for the war effort, particularly now that he was the newly appointed petroleum administrator for war. Earlier he had had to grapple with the conditions that accompanied the opening of the east Texas oil fields—overproduction, wildly fluctuating prices, and rampant waste. Caught between major oil companies and independent producers and lacking the support of FDR and congressional Democrats from the oil states, Ickes had made limited progress in the 1930s in his quest to stabilize oil prices and encourage conservation. Though he had sought to broaden federal regulation of the oil industry, control remained in the hands of state governments and the industry itself. In his frustration he warned that "unless we put a stop to this wanton waste, this profligate dissipation of an indispensable natural resource, our children will feel for us the pitying contempt that we so richly deserve."[21]

Now, in 1941, Ickes became responsible for seeing that the production and distribution of oil met national wartime needs. Pragmatic and nationalistic, he put aside his enmity toward big business and worked closely with oil company representatives to assure steady production. Despite criticism from those who opposed such a grandiose scheme, he successfully administered the construction of oil pipelines from the Texas oil fields to the East Coast. An agency of the Joint Chiefs of Staff later announced, "At no time did the Services lack for oil in the proper quantities, and the proper kinds and at the proper places. . . . No Government agency . . . achieved a prouder war record."[22] Ickes contributed significantly to war production, at one time holding several administrative positions simultaneously.

He had less success in promoting America's acquisition of oil reserves overseas. Recognizing that the rate of oil production at home could not be sustained, Ickes advocated an active government policy abroad that called for the purchase of oil reserves, the construction of a Saudi Arabian oil refinery, and the completion of a pipeline from the Persian Gulf to the eastern Mediterranean. The United States military supported his proposals, but he failed to convince other policymakers; petroleum industry leaders and conservatives in Congress feared government controls, the State Department objected to Ickes's involvement in Middle East foreign policy, liberals cautioned against entanglements in that part of the world, and FDR failed to give strong support. As a result, Ickes complained, the United States had no international oil policy. In fact, the nation remained wedded to a laissez-faire oil policy dominated by the major oil companies.

At the war's end, Ickes warned that the United States lacked the oil, zinc, copper, mercury, nickel, and chromite needed for another protracted conflict. He criticized the use of the highest grade of coal for generating steam in power plants, because he believed this coal would be needed for future steel production. And he noted that the high-quality iron ore deposits of Minnesota's Mesabi Range were being depleted, moving the country toward increasing dependence on foreign supplies.

As partial solutions to shortages, Ickes suggested stockpiling scarce minerals, exploring for new deposits, and finding better methods for recycling scrap metal. He concluded that America could no longer afford its "present non-conservation policy" and proposed a long-range program that would guarantee the nation's future mineral supply. To meet the future demand for minerals, Ickes, like most others, focused on increased production rather than on a change of the consumption habits that led to an ever-larger demand.

After the war Ickes's tenure as secretary of the interior was short-lived. With FDR's death in 1945, Ickes lost his foremost booster. The new president, Harry Truman, lacked Roosevelt's concern for conservation, and when Ickes publicly criticized Truman's nomination of the California oilman Edwin Pauley as undersecretary of the navy, Truman charged insubordination. Ickes testified before a Senate committee that Pauley had offered to raise three hundred thousand dollars for the Democratic party in exchange for assurances that the federal government would not push its claim to tideland oil. Ever sensitive to possible graft in government, Ickes protested and offered a "not very courteous" letter of resignation, which Truman promptly accepted.

Thus, in 1946 Ickes entered into semiretirement, living on his farm in Maryland with his young wife, Jane Dahlman, and their two children. He lived another six years, but as his wife said, something in his spirit had died when he left office, for "he felt he could no longer be of service to the country and the world."[23] He remained an active proponent of conservation and a critic of public policy, writing a syndicated column for the *New York Post* and contributing regularly to the *New Republic*, a liberal weekly.

Even if Ickes had ignored his advancing years and held his position as secretary of the interior a while longer, there is little likelihood that he would have succeeded in furthering his environmental New Deal policies. National security and short-term economic expediency now prevailed. Whereas Ickes had regarded the Department of the Interior as a vehicle by which to aid all Americans, his successors increasingly used government to help the country's business interests.

State and local control, susceptible to the influence of local resource users, increased at the expense of federal regulation. The administration of public grasslands, for example, had passed to the Bureau of Land Management and fell increasingly to district boards controlled by large ranchers who dominated the local livestock associations. As a result, these ranchers leased the land for grazing at fees much lower than the fees for comparable private grazing land. The land was used mainly for private profit, while other uses—such as recreation and wildlife preservation—suffered. Ickes protested what he considered an abrogation of the intent of the original legislation, the Taylor Grazing Act of 1934.

Even so, the FDR-Ickes program had made important contributions to the cause of conservation. More land had been set aside for wildlife and aesthetic purposes, and reclamation and public power development had made great advances. The Roosevelt administration had successfully used conservation as a means of pump priming to encourage employment and economic recovery while at the same time providing lasting benefits for the nation by restoring the land. In addition, efforts at nationally coordinated planning, although short-lived, had helped educate many Americans about the magnitude of the problems they faced in an increasingly industrialized state. And the much-maligned Department of the Interior had gained a prestige and respectability it had never known.

The wisdom of Ickes's effort to consolidate control of natural resources under one department is still debated. Given the divergent views of conservation that exist, control by a single administrative unit would inevitably displease a large number of resource users. To Ickes, however, the return of special-interest groups to dominate resource decisions was clearly a step backward. It was left to a new breed of environmental activists in the postwar era to combat the explosive growth of environmental pollutants that accompanied America's pursuit of material abundance.

Chapter 8: Rachel Carson

Senator Abraham Ribicoff addressed the middle-aged woman who sat at the table before his committee: "You are the lady who started all this."[1] The woman was Rachel Carson, biologist and author of the controversial best-seller, *Silent Spring.* The June morning in 1963 marked the opening of Senate hearings on environmental pollution. Senator Ribicoff's words acknowledged that Carson's study of pesticides and her skill as a writer had launched the hearings as well as the environmental movement of the 1960s.

Few in the audience realized how seriously ill Carson was or how hard she had struggled during the four years she had worked on her book. When she died of cancer the following spring, Ribicoff again addressed his committee: "This gentle lady, more than any other person of her time, aroused people everywhere to be concerned with one of the most significant problems of mid-20th century life—man's contamination of his environment."[2]

*Rachel Carson (Photograph by Erich Hartmann;
courtesy of the Rachel Carson Council)*

Born in 1907 and raised in the lower Allegheny Valley of Pennsylvania, Rachel was the youngest of three children. The Carson family had little money and lived in a small house in a wooded area. Her mother, a graduate of Washington Female Seminary, introduced Rachel to the world of books and to the natural wonders of the countryside where they lived. "I can remember no time when I wasn't interested in the out-of-doors and the whole world of nature," she later recalled.[3]

At the age of ten Rachel won an award for a story submitted to *St. Nicholas*, a leading children's magazine, and this encouraged a childhood dream to be a writer. She excelled at school, continued to write, and entered Pennsylvania College for Women. A freshman theme, written at the age of eighteen, reflected her upbringing: "I love all the beautiful things of nature, and the wild creatures are my friends."[4] She was an avid reader; she had been introduced to the classics of English literature and among American authors favored Mark Twain.

Shy and having no social pretense, Carson focused on her studies. Yet in many respects she was a typical college woman, although she attended school on a very tight budget. Using family property as collateral, she had to borrow from the college to supplement a scholarship; she lacked even the thirty-five cents that many of her fellow classmates could spend for a visit to the local beauty parlor. Her interests and activities ranged widely, from the college prom to competitive field hockey and basketball.

By good fortune she met Mary Scott Skinker, a gifted and demanding teacher who became her mentor and friend. It was Skinker who in Carson's sophomore year excited her curiosity about biology and inspired her to change her major from English. This was no easy decision, for with a biology major she would have to take additional courses to graduate. More important, fellow students as well as the president of the college derided her, considering literature a more appropriate degree for a woman. Encouraged by Skinker and the two other biology majors at the college, Carson persevered, enduring long hours in the cramped, drafty laboratories on the top floor of Dilworth Hall, but enjoying most the days spent on field trips. A trusted friend later recalled Rachel's comment: "Biology has given me something to write about. I will try in my writing to make animals in the woods or waters . . . as alive to others as they are to me." She confided that her goal might sound "pretentious, egotistical and silly," but she said, "I can dream."[5]

During her senior year Carson established a science club and at the end of the year graduated magna cum laude. Then, to pursue graduate study, she followed Skinker (who had left the previous year, 1928) to Johns Hopkins University and Woods Hole Marine Biological Laboratory in Massachusetts. Here Carson first saw the ocean and started her lifelong study of the sea. Johns Hopkins offered a rigorous program that pleased her. She related, "Once in a while I *don't* work in the lab all evening—mostly I do."[6]

Work as a lab assistant and part-time teacher slowed the completion of her master's degree but brought needed income to her parents, who had rented a house in Baltimore. Her sister, whose marriage had dissolved, came home with two small children, and with her father in ill health, the family depended increasingly on Rachel. She took on this financial burden as a matter of course, even though it meant giving up any hope of going for her doctorate. For the next few years she held positions as a lab assistant and a part-time instructor at Johns Hopkins and the University of Maryland.

But a teacher's salary in the midst of the depression didn't pay family expenses, especially after the death of her father in 1935. When her sister died the next year, Carson assumed responsibility for raising two orphaned nieces. She earned a few dollars writing articles on fisheries for the *Baltimore Sun* and got a part-time job at $19.25 per week writing radio broadcasts on undersea life for the Bureau of Fisheries. Her boss, the chief of the biology division, thought a particularly eloquent article more suitable for submission to the *Atlantic Monthly*. Thus, "Undersea," her first important publication, appeared in 1937 to launch a distinguished career.

Carson's article reflected both her philosophy and her style of writing:

Here in the sea mingle elements which, in their long and amazing history, have lent life and strength and beauty to a bewildering variety of living creatures. Ions of calcium, now free in the water, were borrowed years ago from the sea to form part of the protective armor of a mollusk, returned to the main reservoir when their temporary owner had ceased to have need of them, and later incorporated into the delicate statuary of a coral reef. Here are atoms of silica, once imprisoned in a layer of flint in subterranean darkness; later, within the fragile shell of a diatom, tossed by waves and warmed by the sun; and again entering into the exquisite structure of a radiolarian shell, that miracle of ephemeral beauty that might be the work of a fairy glass-blower with a snowflake as his pattern.[7]

After taking a civil service exam on which she outscored all the other applicants, Carson landed a job in 1936 as a marine biologist with the Bureau of Fisheries (later part of the Fish and Wildlife Service). Though she had encountered prejudice as a woman scientist and was only one of two women hired by the service in a professional capacity, she did not think of herself as a feminist. She later stated, "I'm not interested in things done by women or by men but in things done by people."[8]

In the ensuing years, Carson completed a manuscript that was published as *Under the Sea-Wind* just before the attack on Pearl Harbor in 1941. This, her first book, was not a commercial success—she later noted that it was received with "superb indifference." But she had written it "to make the sea and its life as vivid a reality for those who may read the book as it has become for me during the past decade." She said:

To stand at the edge of the sea, to sense the ebb and the flow of the tides, to feel the breath of a mist moving over a great salt marsh, to watch the flight of shore birds that have swept up and down the surf lines of the continents for untold thousands of years, to see the running of the old eels and the young shad to the sea, is to have knowledge of things that are as nearly eternal as any earthly life can be.[9]

Rachel Carson departed from scientific conventions, giving personal names (including Scomber the mackerel) to the creatures she described and placing the reader imaginatively in the sea environment. Her expertise at providing such an accurate portrayal of life in the sea won the acclaim of fellow scientists.

She contributed to the war effort by writing several booklets that encouraged Americans to make use of little-known fish and other seafood. Later she worked on twelve illustrated booklets on national wildlife refuges. Gradually she assumed responsibility for the publications of the Fish and Wildlife Service, advancing steadily in rank to biologist and chief editor by 1949. A coworker observed: "The tact and skill with which she tackled uninspired writers was a joy to watch. Her private views were often more pungent."[10] Manuscripts that crossed her desk emerged clear and readable, rare qualities in government documents.

Official duties left Carson little time to pursue her own creative work. She wrote an occasional article to supplement her income, receiving a most welcome five hundred dollars from the *Reader's Digest* for an article on bats. While she looked unsuccessfully for a new job free from government bureaucracy, she managed to start work on a new book. As she explained: "I am much impressed by man's dependence upon the ocean, directly, and in thousands of ways unsuspected by most people. These

Rachel Carson at work at home (Photograph by Brooks Photographers; courtesy of the Collection of American Literature, The Beinecke Rare Book and Manuscript Library, Yale University)

relationships, and my belief that we will become even more dependent upon the ocean as we destroy the land, are really the theme of the book."[11]

The book that brought Rachel Carson to international attention, *The Sea around Us,* marked a culmination of all her previous work. Since childhood she had pondered the mystery of the sea, and aided by major advances in oceanography during

World War II, correspondence with experts at home and abroad, and her own observations and experiences, she had accumulated a wealth of information. Now she wished to make this knowledge understandable and appealing "to the reader untrained in science." Research came easier to her than writing, but after three years of "just plain hard slogging," often working late at night, she completed the manuscript.

Because of the disappointing sales of her first book, she hired a literary agent, Marie Rodell, who became not only an associate but a close friend. When the *New Yorker* published a condensed version of the book in a series entitled "Profile of the Sea," Carson was catapulted overnight to national prominence. A *New York Times* reviewer stated, "Rarely does the world get a physical scientist with literary genius." *The Sea around Us,* published in 1951, stayed on the best-seller list for eighty-six weeks and was rapidly translated into more than thirty languages.

The book changed her life. Suddenly a celebrity, she endured numerous public appearances. Her earlier book, *Under the Sea-Wind,* was then reissued by a new publisher and became an instant best-seller in its own right. Carson soon gained economic independence with book royalties, resigned her position with the Fish and Wildlife Service, and realized a dream—to devote all her time to writing.

In the following years Rachel Carson continued to translate the wonders of the sea into terms understood and appreciated by the general public. *The Edge of the Sea,* based on extensive research on the Atlantic coastline, appeared late in 1955, and shortly thereafter she completed an article entitled "Help Your Child to Wonder," in which she urged readers to keep alive children's innate sense of what is "beautiful and awe-inspiring." The sounds of nature, for instance, opened the door to an unknown world:

Most haunting of all is one I call the fairy bell-ringer. I have never found him. I'm not sure I want to. His voice—and surely he himself—are so ethereal, so delicate, so otherworldly, that he should remain invisible, as he has through all the nights I have searched for him. It is exactly the sound that should come from a bell held in the hand of the tiniest elf, inexpressibly clear and silvery, so faint, so barely-to-be heard that you hold your breath as you bend closer to the green glades from which the fairy chiming comes.[12]

No wonder Carson's writings enthralled millions of readers.

But family responsibilities complicated her writing schedule. Nearly fifty, she cared for her elderly mother and a five-year-old great nephew whom she had adopted after the death of a favorite niece. In addition, the construction of her new home in a Washington suburb demanded energy. Yet she found time to relax, bird-watching in the neighboring countryside and spending quiet summers at a cottage she had built on the coast of Maine. Through such excursions she met people who became part of her small circle of close friends.

In an article in *Holiday* magazine she complained that only 6 1/2 percent of the Atlantic and Gulf Coast shorelines remained in public hands. "Somewhere," she explained, "we should know what was nature's way; we should know what the earth would have been had not man interfered."[13] She advocated the protection of selected parts of the seashore as wilderness.

Uncertain what project to pursue next, Carson pondered the effects that recent technological changes had had upon the land. Earlier she had believed that "much of Nature was forever beyond the tampering reach of man: he might level the forests and dam the streams, but the clouds and the rain and the wind were God's."[14] But the world's violent introduction to the atomic age with the bombing of Hiroshima clouded her vision of enduring life on earth. "The radiation to which we must adjust if we are to survive is no longer simply the natural background radiation of rocks and sunlight," she cautioned. "It is the result of our tampering with the atom."[15] In a revised edition of *The Sea around*

Us, she warned of the danger of dumping radioactive waste into the ocean, noting how little was known about the potential consequences: "To dispose first and investigate later is an invitation to disaster, for once radioactive elements have been deposited at sea they are irretrievable." Thus, although the sea will remain, "the threat is rather to life itself."[16]

SILENT SPRING

Carson's crusade against insecticides and herbicides, the effort for which she is best remembered, dated back to her work with the Fish and Wildlife Service. In 1945 she failed to interest the *Reader's Digest* in an article she wanted to write on the effects of DDT (dichlorodiphenyltrichloroethane). Such a project lay dormant until the idea was sparked in 1958 by a letter from a friend. Olga Huckins complained that aerial spraying the state of Massachusetts had done to control mosquitoes had killed birds and animals on her private two-acre wildlife sanctuary. So Carson began to investigate, and the more she learned, the "more appalled" she became. As she put it, "What I discovered was that everything which meant most to me as a naturalist was being threatened."[17] After several magazines refused her proposal for an article to expose the dangers of the massive use of insecticides, she decided to write a book.

Although Carson had originally hoped to complete a short manuscript by early 1959, she found the topic complex and controversial. Fortunately, she had established valuable contacts through her years of government service, and her publications opened doors that might have remained closed to someone else. Thus she gained the generous assistance of a broad circle of experts and accumulated an abundance of information. She synthesized this material, emphasizing the threat to human health "within the general framework of disturbance of the basic ecology of all living things." In a progress report to her editor she remarked that a "really damning case" could be presented "against the use of these chemicals as they are now inflicted upon us."[18]

Late in the nineteenth century, the use of chemicals to combat agricultural pests had coincided with the rise of large-scale farming in the United States. With improved transportation and new farm technology, farmers had increased production, growing specialized crops on extensive acreages. And monoculture had encouraged the spread of swarms of insects that flourished in the new environment. In response, entomology had emerged as a new branch of science and was encouraged by land-grant universities, agricultural experiment stations, and state and federal departments of agriculture. Farmers had welcomed the introduction of poisons, especially Paris green and lead arsenate.

By the 1920s farmers used calcium arsenate and aerial spraying to combat the boll weevil in cotton fields, thereby extending the use of chemical poisons from fruits and vegetables to row crops. Though the government placed limited controls on the use of insecticides, production of the chemicals accelerated rapidly, to the benefit of an emerging chemical industry.

Then the invention of DDT by a Swiss scientist in 1939 and its widespread use during World War II radically increased the use of synthetic insecticides. Americans first tested the new chemical in 1942, and DDT proved a godsend to the military in controlling lice-spread typhus in Italy, mosquito-spread malaria in the Pacific, and other insect-transmitted diseases. By the end of the war, householders and gardeners flocked to neighborhood stores eager to buy the "miracle" insecticide. Lethal to insects, apparently harmless to humans, cheap, and persistent, DDT promised major advances in public health and agricultural production as well as bug-free gardens and homes.

In 1945, articles in *Harper's, Atlantic Monthly,* the *New Yorker,* and *Time* magazine warned that DDT might be a "two-edged sword that harms as well as helps" and that much more needed to be known before it could be considered "safe for general use."[19] An article in *Reader's Digest,* however, made light of such "fantastic myths" about the dangers of DDT, citing the Department of Agriculture, the U.S. Army, and the manufacturer as authorities.[20] In spite of a few scientists' concern about its possible long-term adverse effects, no law prohibited sale or use of the chemical, and the public purchased it in increasing quantities.

Farmers, caught in a squeeze between rising production costs and falling prices for their produce, regarded capital-intensive agriculture (especially mechanization and the use of chemical fertilizers and insecticides) as the best road to profits. Both the Department of Agriculture and economic entomologists favored chemical controls over other alternatives, encouraging the development of new synthetic organic insecticides—BHC (benzene hexachloride), chlordane, aldrin, dieldrin, and others.

As a result, research on biological controls (such as predator-prey) and cultural controls (such as crop rotation) languished. Such measures required a knowledge of ecosystems, intensive labor, community cooperation, and long-term planning. In contrast, chemicals promised a quick victory over insect pests. No wonder that production of DDT increased more than eighteenfold between 1944 and the publication of *Silent Spring* in 1962. And no wonder that lobbyists for the chemical companies became leading defenders of insecticides.

Despite public enthusiasm for DDT, problems emerged. Particularly, residues on food caused concern. In response, Congress initiated hearings in 1950 to investigate the problem and then in 1954 passed the Miller amendment, which gave the Food and Drug Administration new powers to regulate tolerance levels of pesticide residues on raw agricultural products (these levels were based on safety tests conducted by the chem-

ical manufacturers). Thus, Americans assumed they were protected, and insecticide use continued to increase rapidly. But new
problems became apparent to entomologists: growing resistance to the chemicals, and the resurgence of pest populations
whose natural enemies the poisons had killed. The use of insecticides, it turned out, might be counterproductive. Even so,
the debate over the issue took place largely behind closed doors,
where chemical manufacturers, commercial farmers, and representatives of the Department of Agriculture dominated.

Not until Carson launched her campaign did the public suddenly recognize the magnitude of the problem. She prefaced
her book with an ominous quote from Albert Schweitzer that
set the tone for what was to follow: "Man has lost the capacity
to foresee and to forestall. He will end by destroying the earth."
In the opening pages she sketched a mythical Midwest town that
had been stricken by a mysterious blight: "There was a strange
stillness. . . . On the mornings that had once throbbed with the
dawn chorus of robins, catbirds, doves, jays, wrens, and scores
of other bird voices there was now no sound; only silence lay over
the fields and woods and marsh."[21] Though the town was imag-
inary, the blight was not. *Silent Spring* explained what had happened, proposed alternatives, and pled for a change of attitude.

She warned that the contamination of the earth, along with
nuclear war, constituted the most serious threat to life. In her
words: "The chemicals to which life is asked to make its adjust-
ment are no longer merely the calcium and silica and copper and
all the rest of the minerals washed out of the rocks and carried
in rivers to the sea; they are the synthetic creations of man's inventive mind, brewed in his laboratories, and having no counterparts in nature."[22] As for insecticides, she explained:

They have immense power not merely to poison but to enter into the most
vital processes of the body and change them in sinister and often deadly

ways. Thus, as we shall see, they destroy the very enzymes whose function is to protect the body from harm, they block the oxidation processes from which the body receives its energy, they prevent the normal functioning of various organs, and they may initiate in certain cells the slow and irreversible change that leads to malignancy.[23]

In the rest of her book Carson provided numerous case studies to substantiate her charges.

Future historians, she surmised, would wonder how intelligent human beings could "seek to control a few unwanted species by a method that contaminated the entire environment and brought the threat of disease and death even to their own kind."[24] It is apparent today that the reliance on chemical insecticides has created an impossible situation in which ever more toxic materials must be invented to destroy the "super races" of insects that have grown immune to existing poisons.

Carson did not oppose all uses of chemical poisons. Rather, she advocated insect control "geared to realities," in which the methods used do not "destroy us along with the insects." Noting that unknown millions of people, without their knowledge or consent, had been subjected to poisons, she said: "If the Bill of Rights contains no guarantee that a citizen shall be secure against lethal poisons distributed either by private individuals or by public officials, it is surely only because our forefathers, despite their considerable wisdom and foresight, could conceive of no such problem."[25]

The solution to her seemed clear: cooperate with the natural controls that had operated since life on earth first appeared. Carson explained the advantages of biological controls that imaginative scientists were developing—controls "based on understanding of the living organisms [the scientists] seek to control, and of the whole fabric of life to which these organisms belong."[26] Such strategies (including the use of chemicals to render insects sterile, the use of insect secretions as lures to trap them, and the encouragement of predators) offered ways for humans to reduce insect populations without endangering other species, including their own.

Carson had kept a low profile while working on *Silent Spring*, recognizing the controversial nature of the topic. When the *New Yorker* published the first of three lengthy excerpts in June 1962, however, a deluge of mail flooded her desk as well as those of many government officials. President John F. Kennedy quickly announced the formation of a special panel of scientists to investigate her claims. And when the book itself appeared on September 27, most reviewers gave it rave notices. Anthropologist Loren Eisely said the book was a "devastating, heavily documented, relentless attack upon human carelessness, greed, and irresponsibility" and that it "should be read by every American."[27]

Other Americans led by economic entomologists and representatives of the chemical industry, agribusiness, and the Department of Agriculture, had a different reaction. Their reviews called the book "unfair, one-sided, and hysterically overemphatic" and "emotional and inaccurate."[28] The biochemist William J. Darby claimed that Carson's philosophy toward nature, if heeded, would mean "the end of all human progress" and that the book "should be ignored."[29] And Representative Jamie Whitten suggested the book be moved to the "science-fiction" section of the library "in order that we may continue to enjoy the abundant life."[30]

More moderate critics defended the benefits—huge agricultural production and the eradication of diseases—that had been derived from the use of insecticides, and they chided Carson for not presenting a more balanced point of view. She remained convinced, however, that her concerns were valid, that the continued introduction of poisons into the environment held grave risks for present and future generations. The burden, she insisted, rested on manufacturers to prove the harmlessness of insecticides *before* they were used.

In spite of failing health, Carson maintained a demanding

schedule of personal appearances. By April 1963, when she appeared on "CBS Reports: 'The Silent Spring of Rachel Carson,' " more than half a million copies of her book had been sold. On the nationally televised program she more than held her own in defending her position against Dr. Robert White-Stevens, a spokesman for the chemical industry. When the President's Science Advisory Committee issued its report in May, it vindicated her position. In response, the chemical industry restated its innocence, a representative arguing that the committee's "observations and surmises" had not been substantiated by scientific investigation.

Later that year, in a short article in *Audubon* magazine, Carson renewed her campaign. "Who are we," she asked, "to say that those who come after us may never see some of today's rare and endangered species? What right do we have to destroy the scientific record contained in a living species? How do we know that we may not have great need of what it has to tell—or of the function it performs?"[31]

At almost the same time, newspapers reported five million dead fish on the lower Mississippi River, the worst in a series of incidents. After a lengthy investigation, Public Health Service officials traced the cause to endrin, an insecticide produced at a Memphis plant operated by Velsicol Chemical Corporation, a company that had tried unsuccessfully to block the publication of *Silent Spring*. The battle lines were drawn.

Carson wondered why so many people failed to recognize that they were part of the earth's ecosystem, subject to the same forces of the environment as all other species. She pondered:

What hidden fears in man, what long-forgotten experiences, have made him so loath to acknowledge first, his origins and then his relationship to that environment in which all living things evolved and coexist. The Victorians at last freed themselves from the fears and superstitions that made them recoil in shock and dismay from Darwinian concepts. And I look forward to a day when we, also, can accept the facts of our true relationship to our environment. I believe that only in that atmosphere of intellectual freedom can we solve the problems before us now.[32]

In 1964 time ran out for Rachel Carson in her battle with cancer; she died in April at the age of fifty-six. Having received numerous awards, she had taken special pride in her election to the American Academy of Arts and Letters joining forty-nine other distinguished Americans thus recognized. The academy citation read in part: "She has used her scientific knowledge and moral feeling to deepen our consciousness of living nature and to alert us to the calamitous possibility that our short-sighted technological conquests might destroy the very sources of our being."[33]

THE AFTERMATH OF SILENT SPRING

At congressional hearings in 1963, Rachel Carson had made several specific recommendations for the control of insecticide use, including (1) requiring advance notice of spraying to allow concerned parties to be heard, and providing appropriate redress for injured parties, (2) supporting new programs of education and medical research on pesticides, (3) passing legislation to restrict the sale and use of insecticides "at least to those capable of understanding the hazards and of following directions," (4) requiring the registration of chemicals by all government agencies concerned (and not just by the Department of Agriculture), (5) approving new pesticides only when no other method of insect control would suffice, and (6) conducting research on new methods of control in an attempt to minimize or eliminate the need to use chemicals.

In the late 1960s the Environmental Defense Fund, aided by such contributors as the National Audubon Society's Rachel Carson Fund, launched legal challenges to the use of insecticides. Gradually the tide turned, as the public, aroused by a large oil spill off Santa Barbara in 1969 and alarming cases of pollution elsewhere, pressured the government to take action. People recognized with growing clarity that the world's wildlife could not be protected in "preserves." DDT residues, for example, spread worldwide, concentrating in the fatty tissues of animals as the chemicals moved up the food chain, and interfering with the reproduction of such birds as eagles and peregrine falcons.

After lengthy hearings and debates, William Ruckelshaus, director of the recently established Environmental Protection Agency (EPA), ruled that DDT would be phased out of use in the United States, except for emergencies, by the end of 1972. Though newer pesticides had already largely supplanted the increasingly ineffective DDT in the marketplace, its demise as the "father of modern insecticides" had symbolic importance, for the suspension of most uses of aldrin, dieldrin, heptachlor, and chlordane soon followed. In a compromise, Congress overhauled the existing pesticide regulations, pleasing neither farmers nor environmentalists.

During the 1970s, however, the use of insecticides increased rapidly, and the number of resistant insect species nearly doubled. As chemical companies scurried to develop ever more potent poisons to combat the pests, both economic cost and environmental damaged increased. The escalation of chemical use came at a time of mounting evidence that integrated pest management (IPM), which emphasized biological controls and minimized changes in the ecosystem, offered an alternative. A study by Barry Commoner's Center for the Biology of Natural Systems revealed that organic farms in the corn belt yielded essentially the same net profits as farms dependent on chemicals.

In the 1980s, federal enforcement of pesticide regulations remained lax. When a cloud of methyl isocyanate gas (used in the manufacture of insecticides) escaped from a Union Carbide plant in Bhopal, India, in 1984, killing nearly three thousand people and injuring tens of thousands, the poison remained virtually untested. In that year the National Academy of Sciences reported that federal agencies lacked accurate health data to determine whether most of the sixty-five thousand chemicals available in the marketplace were safe or harmful. The federal government apparently believed that short-term economic benefits outweighed immediate dangers and potential long-term consequences. And herein lay much of the problem: Americans assumed that someone else protected them. But as Rachel Carson had stated, "Trusting so-called authority is not enough. A sense of personal responsibility is what we desperately need."[34] It was this sense of responsibility that had led to her commitment to inform the public.

With the passage of time, *Silent Spring* has appeared all the more prophetic: "We still talk in terms of 'conquest'—whether it be of the insect world or of the mysterious world of space. We still have not become mature enough to see ourselves as a very tiny part of a vast and incredible universe, a universe that is distinguished above all else by a mysterious and wonderful unity that we flout at our peril."[35]

Chapter 9: David Brower

In its sixtieth year, the Sierra Club—the California conservation organization established by John Muir—broke its tradition. It announced the appointment of a salaried executive director. The year was 1952; the new director, David Brower.

To his position Brower brought a deep-rooted reverence for wilderness and aesthetic preservation as well as a broad background in club affairs. He was charged with building an informed club membership by distributing publications, supporting policies, and supervising administration. During the next seventeen years he led the Sierra Club in its transformation from a small state organization to one at the forefront of the national conservation movement. Yet he was only to be fired in a storm of controversy. An outspoken and irrepressible spirit, Brower helped lead private-citizen groups in their efforts to reverse postwar environmental degradation.

SIERRA APPRENTICESHIP

Dave received an early introduction to the out-of-doors. He was born in Berkeley, California, in 1912 and during his childhood spent long hours walking in the neighboring hills. Occasionally, his parents took their four children to Lake Tahoe in their 1916 Maxwell and the family camped near the shore. They often took hiking trips in the higher mountains farther south.

Young Brower took a particular interest in butterflies, bringing caterpillars home to feed, study, and enjoy. One incident left a lasting impression on the shy boy: observing the life cycle of a caterpillar, he watched it struggle to break free of its chrysalis. Within half an hour a miraculous transformation occurred and a fully formed butterfly took flight. The well-intentioned Brower, trying to lessen the burden of the next emerging butterfly, split the chrysalis, only to find that the struggle to escape was essential to its ability to expand its wings. His interference with the natural process left the butterfly flightless, "scrambling around, grounded and doomed."

Looking back Brower stated, "It was then, perhaps, that the conservationist in me was born."[1] Nearly fifty years after the incident he reflected, "If you encounter a natural phenomenon that has had a long period of perfection, uninterrupted by technology, prior to your having discovered it, you had better respect the design that went into it and the perfection of it. If you want to change it, watch out."[2]

The Berkeley hills provided more education for Brower than did the nearby University of California. Too young by his own admission and with little money, he dropped out in his sophomore year. In the years that followed, during the Great Depression, Brower spent as much time in the Sierra Nevada as possible, taking time off from his job as a clerk in a candy company. For three summers he worked at a camp on Echo Lake, near Lake Tahoe, within easy walking distance of what was to become Desolation Wilderness. Later he spent three years as an employee of the Yosemite Park and Curry Company, the concessionaire of the national park, working first in the accounting office and then in publicity. More interested in climbing than in

Preparing for a Sierra Club high-country trip, 1940.
From left: Oliver Kehrlein, William Colby, Dick Leonard,
Dave Brower. (Courtesy, The Bancroft Library)

a career, he spent weeks at a time on backpacking trips. In the
tradition of John Muir, he explored new routes and made many
first ascents of mountain peaks.

In 1933 he joined the Sierra Club and became increasingly
involved in its activities. Since its inception in 1892, the club had
remained a California outing organization devoted primarily

to conservation of the Sierra. At first Brower gave his energy to mountaineering, paying little attention to the steady inroads of people and development in the once-untouched land. He often led parties of club members into the mountains that he knew so well, and these trips served a dual purpose for the club: to provide the shared enjoyment of a wilderness experience for compatible people and to introduce them to land the club wanted to see preserved.

Brower avidly read the *Sierra Club Bulletin*, "the way one would read the Bible," and became acquainted with the club's history, leadership, and environmental concerns.[3] After the publication of his first article on his adventures in the mountains, published in the *Bulletin* in 1935, he joined the editorial board. Thus began a lasting interest in books and publishing. Between other jobs in the late 1930s, he found half-time employment with the Sierra Club at seventy-five dollars per month, preparing a handbook for members and working on other publications. As often happened, he focused on the most pressing issue—at that time, a proposal to establish a national park in the Kings Canyon region of the Sierra—rather than on his more mundane assigned duties.

Arthur A. Blake, a club member and conservative Republican, stirred Brower's interest in conservation. Initially, Brower's enthusiasm for outdoor recreation had led him to support a proposal for an aerial tramway to transport skiers from the floor of Yosemite Valley across the pristine wilderness to a nearby peak. But Blake helped him "see the light" and "cool the early ideas [he] had about developing everything."[4] Brower threw himself wholeheartedly into the campaign for a Kings Canyon National Park; he helped produce a one-hour silent color film, which he narrated at innumerable showings, and he observed the production of a book to promote the park, Ansel Adams's *The Sierra Nevada: the John Muir Trail.* By following the production of this book, he learned how effective a publication with outstanding photographs could be in arousing public support. With the aid of Secretary of the Interior Harold Ickes, who personally courted the club's board of directors, the Sierra Club gained a signal victory in 1940 when Congress established the park.

Brower's editorial experience led him to a job with the University of California Press, where he met his future wife, Anne Hus. When World War II erupted he joined with other club members—including Richard Leonard, Einar Nilsson, and Bestor Robinson—to support the Tenth Mountain Division's logistics. Brower enlisted in the mountain troops and used his expertise in skiing and climbing to write manuals, to develop equipment and techniques, and to teach men who might serve in mountainous terrain. Now an officer, he saw action in Italy, participating in the breakthrough on the Apennine front against German forces, and learned how devastating war can be for the land as well as for people.

He returned home to find the Sierra Club in wartime hibernation. With volunteers like Brower, however, the club didn't take long to revive: it opposed proposals for allowing logging in Olympic National Park and for extending roads into the Kings Canyon wilderness. As a young member of the club's board of directors, Brower found himself increasingly at odds with its elder statesmen, including William Colby, who had served at Muir's side. Colby, quoting Muir, held that the mountains should be enjoyed and that roads in selected locations, such as Kings Canyon, should therefore be allowed. The new guard, led by Brower and Richard Leonard, thought Muir would have changed his mind if he had lived to see the postwar influx of tourists into the wilderness. By the early 1950s Brower had won out; a long-standing provision of the club's bylaws —"to render the mountains accessible"—had been deleted. The club was poised for the beginning of a new era of activism.

The growing number of controversies engaging the club's attention overwhelmed volunteers, and the board of directors appointed David Brower as the full-time and salaried executive director. He immediately encountered a formidable challenge—two proposed dams in Dinosaur National Monument—and in a struggle reminiscent of Hetch Hetchy, disagreement over the dams constituted the central environmental conflict of the 1950s.

The national monument, on the border of northwestern Colorado and eastern Utah, had been established in 1915 to protect the fossil dinosaur bones preserved in rock formations. Later, Harold Ickes had convinced FDR to enlarge the monument substantially to preserve the beautiful but little-known canyon country of the Green and Yampa rivers. It was just below the confluence of these rivers in Echo Park, in the middle of the national monument, that the Bureau of Reclamation proposed construction of a 525-foot-high dam.

The bureau was responsible for the development of the upper Colorado River basin and planned ten dams with a combined storage capacity of 48.5 million acre-feet. The Echo Park dam would provide 15 percent of the storage capacity, second only to a proposed Glen Canyon dam on the Colorado River on the Arizona-Utah border. Although alternative sites existed (outside the monument) for Echo Park and a companion dam at Split Mountain Gorge (both within the national monument), the bureau's chief argued that they "would entail a serious waste of water and power resources to the detriment of the Nation."[5]

The National Park Service, poorly informed and lacking the political clout of the rival Bureau of Reclamation, was slow to rally its supporters. By 1950, however, preservationists had been alerted to the threat. They feared that a dam at Echo Park could open a floodgate of proposals for dams in several national parks, including the Grand Canyon, Kings Canyon, and Glacier. Bernard DeVoto reflected their sentiments in an article published in July in the *Saturday Evening Post,* "Shall We Let Them Ruin Our National Parks?" The conflict was brewing as Brower entered the scene.

Brower first visited Dinosaur in 1953, having urged the Sierra Club to start rafting trips on the Yampa River. From then on, he helped generate a steady flow of publications in defense of the most scenic areas of the Colorado River. The club produced an excellent color and sound film on Dinosaur National Monument, and it was shown to many influential people. Brower enlisted author Wallace Stegner to edit the book *This Is Dinosaur.* Each member of Congress received a copy, along with a forcefully written brochure by Brower. And in the *Denver Post,* a full-page ad sponsored by the Council of Conservationists stressed the need to eliminate the Echo Park dam from the Upper Colorado Basin Project.

In a rare show of cooperation, the Sierra Club and the Wilderness Society (founded in 1935 by Aldo Leopold and others) led some twenty-five conservation organizations in launching a national campaign. Brower spent months in the nation's capital testifying before congressional committees and consulting with allies. While Howard Zahnizer of the Wilderness Society orchestrated the lobbying in Washington, Brower coordinated national publicity, commuting to the East Coast as needed. Thus, the Bureau of Reclamation and proponents of the Echo Park dam in the upper-basin states found themselves under heavy fire.

The National Park Service, having been ordered silent by the secretary of the interior, could do little more than discreetly provide information to the preservationists and watch the battle from the sidelines. But the mounting concern of citizens aroused by the preservationists more than compensated for this handicap. At one point late in the campaign, letters in support of preserving the monument outnumbered those in favor of building a dam by nearly one hundred to one.

When Douglas McKay, an Oregon Chevrolet dealer, became secretary of the interior in 1953, he asked Undersecretary Ralph Tudor to compare the evaporation rate of the proposed Echo Park dam to that at alternate dam sites. Defenders of the dam initially claimed that at least 300,000 acre-feet of water would be saved annually if a dam was constructed at Echo Park. Tudor, however, testified before a congressional committee that 165,000 acre-feet would be saved. And after a challenge from preservationists, the bureau issued a revised figure of 75,000. Brower reviewed the bureau's numbers, discovered another error, and forced Tudor to admit the figure should have been 25,000. Embarrassed and its credibility in question, the bureau began to recognize that opposition to its intrusion into Dinosaur National Monument might endanger funding for the entire Upper Colorado Basin Project.

Brower pointed out that evaporation from the proposed dams would actually waste water they were supposed to save. He and many other preservationists suggested that a higher dam at Glen Canyon would allow for added water storage and thereby eliminate the need for a dam at Echo Park. Appearing frequently at congressional hearings during the next two years, he provided expert testimony, arguing in part that the electricity to be produced by hydropower could be provided by coal or other energy sources.

The preservationists had allies, some from unexpected places. Southern California interests opposed the Upper Colorado Basin Project on principle, for they feared a loss of water and power from their fast-growing region. In addition, conservatives and representatives from states with high taxes looked warily at the price tag for the dams. They questioned government funding of new reclamation projects at a time of agricultural surplus. And it didn't help dam proponents when someone showed that the Upper Basin Project would cost sixteen times as much as the assessed value of existing farms in the region.

Ultimately, Brower and his fellow conservationists stopped a billion-dollar project dead in its tracks. When it became clear that they would remove their opposition to the Upper Colorado River Basin Project as soon as protection of Dinosaur National Monument was guaranteed, their opponents capitulated. Late in 1955 Secretary McKay announced that congressmen and senators from four upper-basin states had agreed to exclude an Echo Park dam from proposed legislation.

The victory for Brower was bittersweet. The Sierra Club had been so intent on protecting Dinosaur as part of the national park system that it had sacrificed Glen Canyon. Brower blamed himself, lamenting that he should have persuaded the club's board of directors to oppose the entire Upper Colorado Project, including the construction of the Glen Canyon Dam, which turned a part of the Colorado River into a lake (named for John Wesley Powell). But this was hindsight. At the time, he had never visited the Glen Canyon area and knew little about its unique beauty. Later he noted, "If there is any moral that is to be drawn out of my total experience in conservation, it is, don't pass judgment and give in on a place you haven't seen. Get there somehow!"[6] From this point forward, Brower took an increasingly militant stance in defense of environmental causes.

WILDERNESS PRESERVATION

During the years of struggle over Dinosaur National Monument, visitation to national parks and wilderness areas across the country continued to rise. In 1940 a population of 130 million Americans enjoyed a relatively spacious park system of 22 million acres. By 1960 the park acreage had hardly grown at all, although the population now topped 183 million. And numbers were only part of the story. An increasing percentage of Americans escaped crowded conditions in the city only to brush elbows with their urban neighbors in the out-of-doors. A report on the White Mountains of New Hampshire, for example, revealed these statistics: in 1940, hikers distributed evenly on the trail would have been nearly five miles apart; in the early 1970s the distance narrowed to seventy-three yards.

Federal agencies responded with programs to accommodate the hordes of people. In 1956 the National Park Service initiated Mission 66, a ten-year project to develop roads, visitor centers, and other facilities. And the Forest Service established a five-year plan called Operation Outdoors.

Brower and the Sierra Club took a jaundiced view of the emphasis on mass recreation and utilitarian conservation. In particular, they feared development in the scattered wilderness areas that had been established by administrative fiat since 1924. The vulnerability of the Three Sisters wilderness in Oregon made it clear that administrative rulings provided little protection. Rather, a congressional statute was needed to protect wilderness, and the Sierra Club, Wilderness Society, Audubon Society, and many other organizations devoted their energies to this end. In 1960, after several years of battling a powerful coalition of resource users, Brower commented facetiously:

If there were just a little bit of direct commercial return from wilderness—if its value could somehow be reflected on the financial pages as part of the nation's capital, rising in value fast enough to warrant a two-for-one split, if it could only be advertised in four color ads, if it were a private asset and not a public resource, if it related to the Dow-Jones average and not just to survival, if it fitted better the materialist's mores, if the developers could only speculate in its real estate and make a killing, if it meant ulcers and not just a chance for a better life—if all these

things were true, maybe the chambers of commercialism and the rough
riders of range and forest would stop stalling the WB [Wilderness
Bill]. . . . Nobody wants it but the people.[7]

To Brower, wilderness was not a matter of dollars and cents;
it was a birthright of all Americans. By what authority, he asked,
could one generation take another generation's freedom and
preclude "the right to have wilderness in their civilization . . .
the right to find solitude somewhere; the right to see, and enjoy, and be inspired and renewed, somewhere, by those places
where the hand of God has not been obscured by the industry
of man."[8] He recalled Aldo Leopold's argument that wilderness serves as an essential model of land health vital to our survival.

Addressing the National Recreation Congress in 1959,
Brower explained why the protection of wilderness was not a
threat to recreation, "as some well-meaning extremists would
have you believe." He added: "An extremist . . . is a man who
disagrees with you effectively. I should like to acknowledge my
debt to extremists everywhere. They may get us into hot water
now and then, but that's the price of staying out of water that is
perpetually lukewarm. To add a definition, extremists are the
indispensable ingredients of every needed change."[9] Such a definition aptly described Brower himself.

Brower complained that neither the Forest Service nor the
National Park Service could be depended on to protect wilderness areas within their jurisdiction. The Park Service, he claimed,
though preferable to the Forest Service, had a limited vision of
what areas might be protected as wilderness. And the Forest
Service emphasized "multiple use," a concept Brower regarded
as a political device to maximize the sale of timber and other resources. He thought the Forest Service failed to recognize that
wilderness was the highest form of multiple use—a source of
pure water, a perpetual wildlife habitat, a genetic reservoir, a

place to learn. Like John Muir, he accepted the necessity of logging most forests, but he argued that 10 percent of the land should be kept in its original state for future generations. Quoting Nancy Newhall, he noted that "wilderness holds answers to more questions than we yet know how to ask."[10]

The Wilderness Act, a compromise measure passed in 1964, designated slightly more than nine million acres of national forestland as the nucleus of a national wilderness-preservation system. Many additional acres proposed for wilderness status were excluded because stockmen, lumbermen, miners, and others wanted to develop them for commercial purposes. The act also provided that other federal lands under the Interior and Agriculture departments would be considered later for possible inclusion in the wilderness system.

THE GRAND CANYON

Brower had also been working to set aside new parklands and to protect those scenic areas already established, the most important of which was the Grand Canyon. The act establishing Grand Canyon National Park in 1919 had left the door open for development of reclamation projects "consistent with the primary purpose of said park." In 1949, when population growth and the rising demand for hydroelectric power made construction of new dams appear inevitable, Brower joined with other directors of the Sierra Club in support of a compromise—a low-level dam in the Grand Canyon that would require minimal environmental alteration. The next year Brower reversed his position and by the 1960s (after the struggle over Dinosaur and the loss of Glen Canyon) adamantly opposed any dams in the Grand Canyon. Instead, the Sierra Club urged use of the Antiquities Act to protect the entire canyon, arguing that Congress, rather than the Federal Power Commission, should ultimately decide its fate.

In a 1963 Supreme Court decision, the water of the Colorado River was divided between the lower basin states, whereupon Secretary of the Interior Stewart Udall, a native Arizonan, announced administrative plans to construct two dams in the Grand Canyon. He claimed they were needed to deliver water to central and southern Arizona for urban and agricultural use. But Brower, in one of his many appeals to Udall, warned, "I am convinced that nothing you have done, and nothing else you are hoping to do for conservation, can offset the damage that will ensue if you let Grand Canyon go down the drain and with it everything that has meaning to the National Park idea."[11]

About half of the 280 miles of the Grand Canyon lay within the national park and adjacent national monument. The proposed lower dam, at Bridge Canyon, would back water ninety-three miles into a portion of the park, and a dam upstream at Marble Canyon would affect the flow of the river through the park. In addition, conservationists feared the proposed diversion of 90 percent of the river through a tunnel to a hydroelectric plant. According to Brower, this would mean the end of the Colorado as a living river; its floodwaters would no longer cleanse the river channel or cut imperceptively deeper through the geological formations.

Proponents of the dams—including Wayne Aspinall, chair of the House Interior Affairs Committee, and Floyd Dominy, commissioner of the Bureau of Reclamation—argued that the dams were essential to the Central Arizona Project (a plan to pump water from the Colorado River to central Arizona) because more hydroelectricity was needed for periods of heaviest energy use and for revenue. They also contended that the proposed dams would leave the scenic beauty of the canyon unharmed and would provide new recreational opportunities. Brower insisted that there were alternative means of raising money for the project, including the sale of power from Hoover and other downstream dams, and that the beauty of the Grand Canyon should never be compromised.

Working with the Wilderness Society, the National Audubon Society, and many other conservation organizations, Brower took the lead in defending the Grand Canyon. Unlike Dinosaur, the Grand Canyon was revered by most Americans, including those who had never seen it, and he took advantage of their concern. In major newspapers, he ran full-page ads asking readers to write their representatives in Congress, contribute funds to the defense of the canyon, and join the Sierra Club. Thousands responded.

Brower believed that the debts incurred from his expensive newspaper ads could be repaid after the crisis had passed. And he thought that by adhering to a vague Internal Revenue Service (IRS) rule that precluded the club from "substantial" attempts to influence legislation, the club's effectiveness would be limited. Better to lose tax deductions, he thought, than to lose the Grand Canyon.

On June 9, 1966, a provocative ad prepared by the San Francisco agency of Freeman, Mander, and Gossage appeared in four national newspapers, declaring in bold print, "Now only you can save Grand Canyon from being flooded . . . for profit." The next day the IRS sent a letter to club headquarters in San Francisco announcing that its tax deductible status was in question. This action sharply reduced large gifts and bequests.

But the threat would not silence Brower, and a series of full-page ads followed, including one that read, "Should we also flood the Sistine Chapel so tourists can get nearer the ceiling?" Sympathy for the Sierra Club grew, and membership doubled in the next three years. Although the club eventually lost its tax-deductible status, it gained the freedom to lobby as hard as it pleased. As Brower noted, the American public "did not wish the tax man to jeopardize the world's only Grand Canyon."[12]

Brower coordinated the work of an array of authors, scientists, photographers, and other professionals—most of whom donated their time and talents. The impressive result was a seemingly endless stream of publications, including two films and three books: *The Place No One Knew: Glen Canyon on the Colorado; Time and the River Flowing: Grand Canyon;* and *Grand Canyon of the Living Colorado.* In addition, the club lobbied relentlessly and gave expert testimony at public hearings.

Brower had two main arguments: the dams would intrude on the national park, and they were unnecessary. The only purpose of the dams, he explained repeatedly, was to generate electricity, partly to pump water and partly for sale to finance the Central Arizona Project. But alternative sources of energy, namely nuclear (which Brower later opposed) and coal, were available and cost less per kilowatt hour. He also stated that it made more sense to use federal funds directly for construction of the Central Arizona Project than to use them for dams in the Grand Canyon, especially because there was doubt whether the dams would ever pay for themselves.

Furthermore, the proposed dams would waste water, the most precious commodity in the arid Southwest. The waters of the Colorado River were already overcommitted, and existing dams (particularly Hoover and Glen Canyon) could hold many years' worth of normal runoff. In fact, Hoover Dam had been full only once or twice in its lifetime, and Glen Canyon Dam lost so much water to evaporation and seepage into porous sandstone that its usefulness could be justifiably challenged. Moreover, the evaporating water left behind salts and other impurities that later plagued downstream users. The Sierra Club argued that the Central Arizona Project could succeed quite well without either dam, just as the upper Colorado Basin project had not suffered from the loss of the proposed Echo Park dam.

Finally, dam proponents offered a compromise: they would build a small Bridge Canyon dam, and Marble Canyon would be included in the national park. At a congressional hearing, Representative Morris K. Udall of Arizona (brother of the secretary of the interior) complained about the "impossibly ada-mant noncompromising position of the Sierra Club." Brower responded:

> Mr. Udall, you are not giving us anything that God didn't put there in the first place. . . . If there are no other ways to go about getting your water, I would still say that the compromise should not be made—that Arizona should be subsidized with something other than the world's Grand Canyon, or any part of it. . . .
>
> We have no choice. There have to be groups who will hold for these things that are not replaceable. If we stop doing that, we might as well stop being an organization and conservation organizations might as well throw in the towel.[13]

Brower's persistence paid off. Several supporters of the dams, including Secretary Udall, recognized belatedly that the dams were not necessary. And when Congress finally author-ized a $1.3 billion Colorado River Bill in 1968, the two Grand Canyon dams had been deleted from the plans. The Central Arizona Project then proceeded with power derived from a steam power plant that used fossil fuels. Much of the credit for saving the Grand Canyon went to David Brower, whom *Life* magazine called "his country's No. 1 working conservation-ist."[14]

THE BROWER CONTROVERSY AND BEYOND

Brower's use of expensive, full-page ads to instigate public in-volvement in the Grand Canyon affair got him into hot water with the Sierra Club's board of directors and the Internal Rev-enue Service. This problem and other incidents divided the club's leadership, eventually resulting in a showdown over Brower's future as the club's executive director.

The controversy actually began in the late 1950s when Brower attacked the motives of Forest Service officials who had authorized logging of a forest of rare Jeffrey pines just east of the Sierra Nevada. A majority of the club's board of directors, accustomed to cooperation and friendship between club leaders and federal officials, passed a regulation forbidding criticism of the "motives, integrity, or competence of an official or bureau." The resolution also cautioned against lobbying activity that might endanger the tax-exempt status of the club. Soon thereafter, Brower succeeded in urging the board to establish the Sierra Club Foundation to provide protection against the Internal Revenue Service.

It was Brower's stand on a proposed power plant along the coast of California, however, that proved his undoing. The Pacific Gas and Electric Company had purchased eleven hundred acres of the Nipomo Dunes, on an uninhabited part of the California coast, for a nuclear power plant. Because the company had been defeated in an earlier effort to build a similar plant at Bodega Bay, north of San Francisco, it took objections seriously. Thus, when the Sierra Club's board of directors agreed to support an alternate site, on the coast at Diablo Canyon, if Pacific Gas and Electric would make the Nipomo Dunes (later a state park) available for acquisition by the state, the company readily agreed.

Brower protested the approval of the proposed plant at Diablo Canyon, arguing that the board had acted before it knew the quality of the land affected. Many club members maintained that the board was honor-bound to support the original Diablo Canyon vote, but Brower countered that the biggest mistake of all would be "letting the face of the coast be despoiled to save [their] own."[15] The issue split the board and led to a referendum submitted to the entire membership, and ultimately the board's position was upheld. During the campaign over the referendum, Brower allowed a so-called half-*Bulletin* to be published, which gave only his side of the debate, after material from the opposition had not met the deadline for election written matter. This alienated a number of club leaders, including his long-time friends Richard Leonard and Ansel Adams. And seven past presidents joined a few other members in a stinging letter to the board, calling Brower's leadership "irresponsible and uncompromising."[16] Brower replied with a conciliatory letter and weathered the storm. Undaunted, however, he continued his opposition to Diablo Canyon and late in September 1968, after an election that changed the composition of the board of directors, won a vote opposing any power plants along the "wild, natural, native, pristine, scenic, or pastoral shores of the United States."

The dispute within the club over Diablo Canyon was a clash over method. Should the club negotiate with its adversaries and reach agreement through quiet diplomacy and compromise, or should it take a firm stand and stick to its guns? Historically, the club had used both approaches, and so had David Brower. But the compromise that had led to the Glen Canyon Dam taught him a bitter lesson, and in the 1960s Brower took a harder line, which included opposing a compromise with Pacific Gas and Electric over the Diablo Canyon nuclear site.

He later concluded that many of his growing problems resulted from personality conflicts, particularly with the club president, Edgar Wayburn. Brower lacked the tact necessary for smooth personal relations, paid little attention to detail, did not watch budgetary commitments closely enough, and pushed ahead on his own in times of battle, leaving others behind. His imagination ran ahead of the club's ability to pay the bills, and he took on more tasks than anyone could hope to accomplish.

Many prominent club members objected that Brower and his staff had taken control from the thousands of volunteers who had formerly provided the backbone for club accomplishments. Brower responded that volunteers were valuable but that the tasks then facing the club called for full-time professionals. He remarked privately, "We're still trying to operate like a volunteer fire department long after we know the conflagration was too big for that."[17] Without new leadership, he claimed, there would have been dams in the Grand Canyon and no Redwood National Park.

Brower continued to use a limited administrative discretionary fund of $25,000. Each time he took action that had not been specifically authorized in advance—for instance, paying $1,500 to continue litigation over a proposed hydroelectric power plant at Storm King Mountain (on the Hudson River), sending two people to the Yukon River to battle the proposed Ramparts Dam, or establishing a London office to permit use of a $75,000 grant for the publication of two books on the Galapagos Islands—he drew mounting opposition.

The growing debts of the club contributed to a conflict that had to be resolved. When total expenditures in 1957 had not yet reached $100,000, the club broke even; ten years later, when the budget passed $2,000,000, the club faced a rapidly increasing deficit. Much of the blame fell on Brower's award-winning exhibit-format series—superbly (and expensively) produced publications that spread the Sierra Club's environmental message. As a result of this publication program, the organization's deficit grew to $129,000 in the first ten months of 1968. Late that year, three members of the board of directors asked for Brower's dismissal, charging him with financial irresponsibility and objecting to a proposed allocation of a small percentage of royalties to his own discretionary fund. Brower countered that the future growth of the club depended largely on an expanding publication program and that caution would keep the club from realizing its potential as a protector of the environment. One board member told a newspaper editor: "There's a recklessness to Dave that's terrifying. It's like driving down a city street with a man who's going 90 miles an hour. For a couple of blocks you may be O.K., but pretty soon you're gonna hit something. Well, that scares the hell out of me. But you know what?

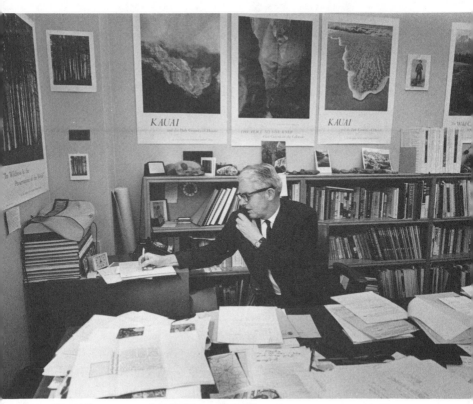

David Brower at work in his Sierra Club office,
1968 (Photograph by Joe Monroe)

I think Dave likes it."[18] Brower's critics feared there would be no club at all if he was allowed to continue.

In January 1969, Wayburn (president of the club) suspended Brower's financial authority because Brower had placed and charged to his discretionary fund a $10,500 ad, "Earth National Park," in the *New York Times*. The ad, which proposed the idea that the entire planet be viewed as a kind of "conservation district within the Universe," requested contributions for an international series of exhibit-format books (perhaps one hundred volumes over twenty to thirty years) that would help protect the earth's wild places. After unsuccessfully contesting Wayburn's authority, Brower took a leave of absence. A thoroughly divided Sierra Club prepared for a crucial election to fill five seats on the fifteen-member board of directors and for a direct membership vote on the Diablo Canyon issue.

Before the Diablo Canyon dispute, club elections had been staid affairs in which an established coterie of board members were normally reelected. As one person aptly put it, the club's government had been a kind of "consultative oligarchy." Club members were remarkably homogeneous—well-educated, professional, upper-middle-class—and they accepted the board's leadership on good faith. But those days had passed. Earlier, in an attempt to bolster its political clout during the Grand Canyon struggle, the club had conducted a nationwide campaign for new members; as a result, membership had neared seventy-eight thousand and the number of paid personnel had mushroomed to seventy-eight. Thus, the club faced the problems of any burgeoning bureaucracy.

The election in April 1969 reflected these growing pains as well as the controversies surrounding Brower's leadership. Brower campaigned vigorously, telling voters their choice was between an older, largely quiescent "society of companions on the trail" and a vibrant, risk-taking international organization. He stated in a press release:

The local problems in California and America are growing at a geometric rate none of us imagined ten years ago, and now it is the entire environment that is the proper province of conservationists—the population explosion must concern us, [as must] pollution, oxygen depletion, and urban decline, as well as the saving of the few remaining untouched wild areas. . . . Furthermore, the club must decide if it is to meet these threats to our environment with modern communication tools that industry and government have perfected. That means offices; radio, television, and films; an educational publishing and advertising pro-

216

gram; and conservation lobbying commensurate with the enormous need.[19]

In defense of the methods he promoted, Brower could point to the tenfold increase in membership under his leadership. Ironically, 1968 had been the club's most successful year in Congress, seeing the establishment of the Redwood and North Cascades national parks, the expansion of the Land and Water Conservation Fund, the creation of a scenic-rivers system, national trails system, and estuarine study system, and the defeat of both proposed dams in the Grand Canyon. The club continued many battles after 1968, opposing such projects as a hydroelectric plant at Storm King and the Disney corporation's proposed winter resort at Mineral King in the Sierra.

Brower had many prominent supporters, including William O. Douglas, justice of the Supreme Court, biologist Paul Ehrlich, entertainer Arthur Godfrey, and author Joseph Wood Krutch. But he also had influential opponents, such as author Wallace Stegner, who criticized Brower in his widely-circulated article, "Bitten by Worm of Power."

The election returns surprised Brower; he and four pro-Brower candidates met defeat, as did his Diablo Canyon policy by a three-to-one margin. Without access to club publications and with enough money for only one mailing, his campaign had suffered more than he had realized. For two weeks he tried to hang on to his office, but the new board forced his resignation.

In spite of dire predictions of what would happen in the event of Brower's defeat, the Sierra Club, under its new executive director, Michael McCloskey, continued to play a leading role in the conservation movement. By the time McCloskey moved from his executive directorship to become staff chairman of the club in the mid-1980s, membership had topped 350,000 and a staff of 200 operated with a $20 million budget. The small group of largely volunteer conservationists of the 1950s had been

The Diablo Canyon nuclear power plant (Courtesy of the Sierra Club)

transformed into a major enterprise with regional offices across the country, sophisticated fund-raising campaigns, and wilderness outings throughout the world. Eventually, a trouble-plagued Diablo Canyon nuclear plant was constructed at a cost of $5.6 billion, an amount twelve times greater than original estimates.

As for Dave Brower, he barely paused for breath before founding two new organizations: the John Muir Institute, a non-profit establishment for promoting environmental research and education, in 1968; and Friends of the Earth (FOE), an aggressive lobbying group concerned with world environmental problems, in 1969. A subsidiary group of FOE, the League of Conservation Voters, supported candidates sympathetic to the environmental cause. In 1972 Brower attended the Stockholm Conference as the FOE representative and in the ensuing years traveled to many countries. By the early 1980s, twenty-six sister organizations of FOE had been established in twenty-four foreign countries.

Of future generations Brower said: "Their genes are in our custody, and guarding them is our greatest responsibility. After all, we do not inherit the land from our fathers. . . . we borrow it from our children."[20] Predictably, Brower took on more than he could manage in his crusade to defend the world's ecosystems. In 1979 he resigned as president of FOE and became titular chairman, a position he later lost. But in 1981 he formed yet another organization, Earth Island Institute, which sought to inculcate an ecological conscience in many sectors of society.

Early in the 1980s, attempting to unite the environmental and peace movements, Brower helped initiate a series of biennial conferences on the fate of the earth. He also returned to the board of directors of the Sierra Club, having been placed on the ballot by petition. And at the age of seventy-two he founded the Brower Concern, an organization intended to catalyze discussion of the most pressing global problems, particularly the threat of nuclear war. Accused by his opponents of using emotional appeals to attract support for his cause, Brower defended his tactics: "After all," he stated, "people who don't believe in emotion can be thankful their parents didn't share that problem. Otherwise they wouldn't be here."[21]

Russell Train, chairman of the president's Council on Environmental Quality, said it best: "Thank God for Dave Brower. He makes it so easy for the rest of us to be reasonable. Somebody has to be a little extreme. Dave is a little hairy at times, but you do need somebody riding out there in front."[22]

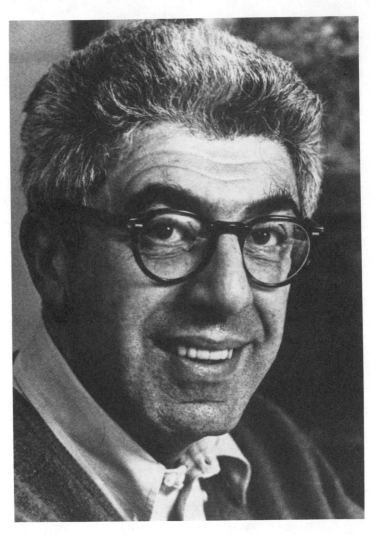

Barry Commoner (Courtesy of Barry Commoner)

Chapter 10: Barry Commoner

In 1976 an audience in upstate Michigan had heard David Brower speak in behalf of the environment and then Leonard Woodstock of the United Automobile Workers defend the needs of labor. Now Barry Commoner, a fifty-eight-year-old professor of biology, arose to try to reconcile the desire for a clean environment with the need for jobs. "There are deep, inherent flaws in the capitalist system," he noted, that result in the exploitative use of resources and the neglect of labor.[1] Commoner blamed such problems on the single-minded pursuit of profit and believed they could be solved through "democratic socialism," a system in which social rather than private investment decisions prevail.[2]

Commoner's participation in this meeting of auto workers, community leaders, and environmentalists was representative of his commitment to inform citizens about the environment and how they might better care for it. Called the "Paul Revere of Ecology" and "a professor with a class of millions" by *Time* magazine,[3] he helped instigate the environmental movement of the 1960s and 1970s. Commoner drew public attention to pollution and other dangers to the environment that resulted primarily from the application of technology developed after World War II. Although his bid to establish a new political party in the 1980 presidential election failed, he remains dedicated to helping find ways to meet human needs while minimizing damage to the environment.

EARLY LIFE

Commoner grew up in Brooklyn. Born in 1917 to hardworking Russian immigrants, (his mother was a seamstress and his father a tailor), he knew poverty. But contrary to report, he did not grow up among tenements or join a street gang. Rather, Barry he lived at the edge of town, where he watched the construction of an elevated railway at one end of his block and explored a swamp stretching to Jamaica Bay at the other. Across the street from the family's row house was a goat farm.

At home the boy was introduced to books and ideas. His mother, whom he taught English, avidly read Yiddish literature. And an uncle and his poet wife lived with the family for a time, often inviting their literary friends to visit. When Barry researched a school assignment on Cotton Mather, his uncle provided access to the stacks of the New York Public Library, where he was chief of the Slavonic division; he also gave him a microscope. On weekends while in high school, young Commoner explored Brooklyn's Prospect Park, collecting specimens to study.

Commoner worked his way through Columbia University, graduating in 1937 with honors in zoology. Next he tackled Harvard and in 1941, the year of Pearl Harbor, received his doctorate. Only in his midtwenties, he had begun his academic career as an instructor at Queens College in New York. The war interceded, however, and he spent the next four years in active duty in the U.S. Naval Reserve. His wartime experience in mil-

itary research led to his central concern—the social consequences of scientific research.

RADIOACTIVE FALLOUT AND THE
RESPONSIBILITY OF SCIENTISTS

The navy assigned Commoner to assist in aircraft application of
DDT, the "miracle" chemical that worked wonders to protect
American troops from insect-borne diseases on Pacific islands.
Told that DDT had an unprecedented ability to kill any insect
and that it was totally harmless to people, Commoner discovered undesired side effects only from experience. When personnel at an experimental rocket station off the New Jersey coast
complained of clouds of flies, planes sprayed the island and
nearby water with DDT. Within hours the flies had died. But
within a week, tons of decaying fish had washed up on the beach,
attracting vast swarms of flies from the mainland.

As the war ended, Commoner was assigned to the staff of a
Senate Military Affairs Subcommittee investigating the relationship between science and social policy. One facet of the subcommittee's work was to discuss the atomic bomb and chemical
warfare. Thus, Commoner helped arrange for presentations by
Robert Oppenheimer and other physicists who had fathered the
bomb. Opinions differed among the scientists. Some regretted
their participation in the Manhattan Project, which had developed the bombs dropped on Hiroshima and Nagasaki, whereas
others took a practical stand and simply wondered how the proliferation of atomic weapons could be prevented. Though in a
secondary role, Commoner helped push for civilian control of
atomic energy, emphasizing its peaceful uses. Through these
discussions he was introduced to public-policy issues arising out
of scientific research.

After his military service ended in 1946, he served briefly as
associate editor of *Science Illustrated* and in this position learned

about the public-information aspects of science education and developed his writing skills. He then accepted a position as professor of plant physiology at Washington University in St. Louis. Just entering his professional career, he was not entrenched in any particular school of thought or professional identity, and this may help explain his emergence as a maverick among his fellow scientists. Trained as a cellular biologist, he pursued biochemical and biophysical research on the subjects of free radicals and the tobacco mosaic virus. Commoner later startled many of his colleagues by arguing that DNA's role as a determinant of heredity had been exaggerated and that those who focused their research on molecules neglected the study of the "natural complexity of biological systems." His defense of "classical biology" and a "holistic" approach eventually contributed to his identification as an ecologist.

Events far beyond his laboratory, atmospheric testing of nuclear weapons, led to Commoner's emergence as a "politico-scientist." The Atomic Energy Commission (AEC), created in 1946, had been placed in charge of developing military and peaceful uses of atomic and nuclear energy. By 1951 the United States had set off sixteen test explosions, and the Soviet Union nearly as many. Because of the secrecy that surrounded such tests, the public heard little from the government except assurances that all tests were harmless and restricted to remote sites. But in the spring of 1953, physicists near Troy, New York, reported highly radioactive fallout that had apparently had come to earth in a rainstorm after drifting across the country from a nuclear test site in Nevada.

That same year the AEC offered reassurances that nuclear explosions created "no immediate or long-range hazard to human health." However, one of the radioactive elements in the fallout, iodine-131, drifted east from Nevada into Utah grasslands, and through the milk from cows that ate the grass it concentrated in children's thyroid glands. Another radioactive isotope, strontium-90, concentrated in people's bones, creating a serious potential for cancer. Then, in 1954, fallout from an American H-bomb test fell on and eventually killed several of the twenty-three crewmen of the *Lucky Dragon,* a Japanese fishing boat.

Three years later, the AEC carried out a series of sixteen nuclear tests in Nevada. At one ("Smoky"), over one thousand infantrymen took positions in trenches about five miles from a tall tower on which a forty-four-kiloton bomb was exploded. Ninety minutes after the blast the troops waged a mock battle next to ground zero, and one soldier, Paul Cooper, described the site as "cherry hot" (twenty years later he died of leukemia).[4] Said Commoner: "The AEC . . . turned me into an ecologist."[5]

As the dangers of nuclear testing became apparent, the curtain of secrecy slipped. In 1956 Commoner provided information on fallout for a letter from a group of scientists to presidential candidate Adlai Stevenson, whose attack on atmospheric testing marked the first time a scientific issue played an important role in a presidential campaign. In the same year, Commoner initiated a petition that was circulated among scientists at home and abroad to protest nuclear testing.

In 1958 he helped form the St. Louis Committee for Nuclear Information (CNI), an organization that pioneered public education about fallout and other scientific issues of public concern. "I was making speeches in every church and hall in St. Louis," Commoner noted, "describing the facts of atmospheric testing."[6] Soon after the CNI was established, Margaret Mead and Rene Dubos started a similar group in New York, and other groups were formed across the country under the auspices of the Scientists' Institute for Public Education.

The fallout issue led Commoner to investigate a growing concern, the responsibility of scientists in the management of public affairs. Nuclear fallout posed a unique problem in the history of humanity, because it affected literally every person on earth as well as those to be born for generations to come.

In an article published in *Science* in 1958, Commoner reported that data presented at Congressional hearings indicated that fallout from previous tests might account "for the birth of from 2500 to 13,000 genetically defective children and for 25,000 to 100,000 cases of leukemia and bone tumor (considered together) during the next generation."[7] He questioned:

It is not clear who is expected to make this decision [about nuclear testing] and thereby assume, in an unprecedented degree, the grave moral burden carried by those who must judge the social worth of human life. Should this judgment be made by experts with special competence? If so, where should their expertness lie? In nuclear physics, radiochemistry, biology, medicine, sociology, military strategy? On the other hand, should a responsibility of this weight be reserved to elected officials, in order to ensure that the decisions will reflect the ethical views of our society?[8]

Commoner called for more research, a systematic method of reporting on fallout worldwide, and a broad educational campaign to bring this information to the public. It was the scientist's responsibility, he maintained, to provide the "necessary facts and the means for understanding them to the public."[9] Only then would citizens have sufficient information to make independent judgments.

The council of the American Association for the Advancement of Science (AAAS) appointed Commoner as one of five members of an Interim Committee on the Social Aspects of Science. In its preliminary report, the committee pointed out the rapid application of scientific research in "antibiotics, synthetic polymers, nuclear energy, transistor electronics, microwave techniques, electronic computers."[10] Business used research to spur industrial development, and the federal government focused on national security. As a result, basic research suffered, physics and chemistry prospered at the expense of the biological and social sciences, and science departments at colleges and universities depended increasingly on federal grants. The committee warned of an "impending crisis in the relationship between science and American society"—a warning reflected in President Dwight D. Eisenhower's "farewell address" in 1961, in which he discussed the growth of a "military-industrial complex" in the United States.

Part of the problem, Commoner observed, stemmed from unequal development among branches of science. Physicists, for example, had unleashed the bomb and its radioactive material, but biologists and physicians had no means to deal with the problems from the radioactive dust that fell to the earth.

Later, the National Aeronautics and Space Administration (NASA) focused on a single project: taking a man to the moon and back by 1970. The quest for national prestige and military advantage, rather than the desire to contribute to knowledge, determined what scientific projects were undertaken. Commoner criticized the space program, arguing that "as long as half the world is hungry and all the world in daily fear of destruction, the responsibility of science to man is to be found first on the planet on which he lives."[11]

From his perspective, because science had the potential for greatly improving human life as well as for endangering it, social agencies had to determine the best use of scientific knowledge. Accordingly, the scientist had the responsibility to "bring the facts and their estimates of the result of proposed actions before the people."[12] Then the people could decide which avenues to pursue.

In 1966 Commoner summarized his conclusions in his first book, *Science and Survival*. Written in a clear, nontechnical style, it reached a wide audience. Commoner noted that humans pay a price for every intrusion into the natural environment. In each case, he explained, they are like the "sorcerer's apprentice," experimenting on themselves. Fortunately, the sustained efforts of citizens and scientists like Commoner contributed to the Nuclear Test Ban Treaty of 1963, in which the United States and the Soviet Union agreed to stop atmospheric testing of nuclear weapons. Commoner later labeled this the first victory "in the campaign to save the environment—and its human inhabitants—from the blind assaults of modern technology."[13]

THE ENVIRONMENTAL MOVEMENT

This victory for the environment came none too soon. The late 1940s and the 1950s had witnessed a baby boom and rapid expansion of the national economy, and though the people of the United States had enjoyed unequaled productivity and prosperity, they had neglected their own habitat. The waters of many American rivers and lakes had become hazardous as they filled with raw sewage and industrial wastes. The air above major cities had become choked with a variety of noxious gases and grit. And on the farmlands and in the forests, people were using ever-increasing amounts of chemicals without being aware of their long-term effects.

Both the Truman and Eisenhower administrations were slow to respond to the decline of the nation's environmental health. They supported programs that would develop resources and provide the greatest short-term growth for the largest number of people. Slums, smog, and segregation were accepted without serious question as long as the gross national product continued its steady climb. The government focused on major development programs—an interstate highway system, the space program—not on such issues as urban rejuvenation, racial integration, and the environment. Americans still believed that Middle Eastern oil was inexhaustible and forever inexpensive and that applied scientists could produce substitutes or develop

Garbage dumped into the San Francisco Bay, 1969 (Courtesy of the Sierra Club)

alternative products should the country ever encounter shortages.

In spite of failures in conservation, the nation enjoyed a high standard of living, and few Americans expressed concern about the future. As a result, summarized the historian Elmo Richardson caustically, when Americans faced an ecological crisis, "they had nothing more to draw upon to cope with that threat than the economic materialism, the bureaucratic inertia, and the political gamesmanship practiced by the men of the Truman-Eisenhower era."[14]

Still, the concern for conservation had never died. David Brower and the Sierra Club had shown surprising strength in the 1950s in arousing public involvement when Dinosaur National Monument had been threatened, and membership in preservation organizations had begun a steady climb. With the help of Rachel Carson, Barry Commoner, and others, Americans awoke in the 1960s to the dangers of pollution and its implications for the quality of life. But by the 1970s, toxic chemicals threatened life itself. Jogging, health-food stores, organic gardening, and holistic medicine all experienced a rapid rise in popularity, whereas smoking in public became an antisocial act in some parts of the country. Americans recognized that their own health depended on the health of the environment in which they lived, and they increasingly questioned the standards by which corporations and government agencies (witness Love Canal) determined safe levels of pollutants. The contaminated environment was being linked to cancer, heart disease, genetic and reproductive problems, and deteriorating immune systems.

The environmental movement that emerged in the 1960s and early 1970s differed markedly from those that had preceded it, which had focused on efficient resource management. The new movement had much broader concerns, particularly over the environmental quality of communities. And whereas the older movements had depended on the federal administration for leadership, the new movement had its origin and strength at the grass-roots level. People in communities organized to protect their open space and to prevent such major intrusions as strip mining or construction of high-megawatt power plants.

Ecology became a heavily used (and misused) term, as students learned of carbon cycles and the intricacies of an ecosystem. Many people worried about the viability of the biological processes upon which human institutions and life itself depended. Earth Day, a day of national "teach-ins" on campuses across the country, marked the zenith of public concern for planet Earth.

In response, Congress passed an impressive array of legislation culminating in 1969 with the approval of the National Environmental Policy Act (NEPA). This legislation required federal agencies to prepare statements indicating the effect on the environment for all federal projects that might have significant environmental consequences and to consider alternatives to mitigate damage. The regulation of environmental quality became institutionalized with the creation of the Environmental Protection Agency (EPA) under an executive-branch reorganization plan in 1970.

THE CLOSING CIRCLE

Barry Commoner played an instrumental role in the growth of the new environmental movement, and he helped lay the groundwork for Earth Day in 1970. He called Americans "unwitting" victims of ignorance. We had become dependent on the automobile long before we understood the health hazards of smog in our cities. We had given up soap in favor of detergents before we recognized that they pollute our water supplies. We had developed insecticides only to discover that they threaten more than the lives of pests. In a series of technological changes, synthetics replaced cotton and wool, trucks displaced railroads, and chemical fertilizers were used instead of animal manure. Such changes reflected a shift from natural to synthetic, from energy-conserving to power-consumptive, and from resusable to disposable.

In his second and best-known book, *The Closing Circle* (1971), Commoner explored how human acts had "broken out of the circle of life." He concluded that the chief reason for the environmental crisis that had engulfed the United States in recent years was the "sweeping transformation of productive technologies since World War II."[15] Recognizing that increased population and affluence affected the level of pollution, he stated that productive methods developed since 1946 accounted for 80 to 85 percent of the total output of pollutants. To support his contention he cited spectacular increases in the manufacture of such products as synthethic fibers (up 5,980 percent), plastics (up 1,960 percent), and synthetic organic chemicals (up 950 percent). At the same time, Commoner pointed out, there had been a decline in the production of environmentally benign goods such as cotton fiber (down 7 percent), returnable beer bottles (down 36 percent) and in the nonpolluting horsepower generated by work animals (down 87 percent). Whereas the average consumer required about the same amount of food, clothing, and housing as previously, the individual's demand on the natural environment had increased abruptly.

The new products were not assimilated in natural environmental cycles and thus became pollutants. For example, high-compression engines caused nitrogen and oxygen to combine as nitrogen oxides, the key ingredients in smog. Likewise, large electric power plants created sulfur dioxides and nitrogen oxides. And new farm technologies upset natural cycles: insecticides disrupted the balance between pests and their predators, and excessive amounts of inorganic fertilizers contributed to water pollution.

Commoner asked if ecological stresses were so strong that, if not relieved, they would "degrade the ecosystem to make the earth uninhabitable by man." In a qualified answer, he judged that environmental degradation, at least in industrialized countries, could "destroy the capability of the environment to support a reasonably civilized human society."[16] The point in time at which ecological degradation might become irreparable, he guessed, might be twenty to fifty years from when he wrote *The*

Closing Circle. Yet he warned that any projections of future trends were suspect. Basically optimistic, he maintained that catastrophes could be avoided by farsighted corrective action.

Commoner chided his fellow scientists for their reductionist bias and increasingly narrow fields of specialization. He thought that biologists, for instance, studied cells and molecules isolated from the living organisms of which they were a part. He believed that scientists had become isolated and neglected the study of environmental problems. In 1965, in an effort to address these issues, he had founded the Center for the Biology of Natural Systems at Washington University. The staff, drawn from such diverse fields as biophysics, sanitary engineering, anthropology, and economics, focused on practical problems that needed solutions. Commoner championed a holistic approach and the application of science to "real problems in the real world."

For example, he took interest in nearby Decatur, Illinois, a city of one hundred thousand surrounded by farmland, where the local health department had discovered that the city water supply contained a high level of nitrate, hazardous to people when converted to nitrite. Commoner's group discovered that farmers, to maximize their economic return and remain competitive, used more inorganic nitrogen fertilizer on their crops than the plants could use efficiently. As a result, the excess nitrogen drained into rivers and local water supplies. It was left to the people of Decatur and Illinois how best to reduce nitrogen use to a safe level while protecting the economic interests of farmers, on whom the community depended.

Commoner publicized the much-heralded "death" of Lake Erie. Throughout recorded history the lake had maintained a biological balance, supporting a large fish population in its clear waters. Surrounded by half a dozen major cities, the lake served as a valuable resource for some 13 million people. Then, increasingly in the twentieth century, the lake suffered from eutrophication. Excess nitrates and phosphates discharged into its waters, causing algal blooms that, when they decomposed, depleted the oxygen necessary to sustain life in the lake. As a result, many fish died and parts of the once-beautiful lake had the appearance of pea soup. Commoner emphasized that the deterioration of Lake Erie was solely the result of human intervention.

At the end of *The Closing Circle,* Commoner explored the links between the environmental crisis and our economy, posing two key questions:

1. To what extent are the fundamental properties of the private enterprise system incompatible with the maintenance of ecological stability, which is essential to the success of any *productive system?*

2. To what extent is the private enterprise system, at least in its present form, inherently incapable of the massive undertakings required to "pay the debt to nature" already incurred by the environmental crisis—a debt which must soon be repaid if ecological collapse is to be avoided?[17]

In response to his own questions, Commoner noted that increased labor productivity resulting from new technologies paid higher profits than the technologies they replaced, which caused less pollution. Thus, the drive to increase productivity had the unintended result of increasing pollution. And the costs of this pollution were borne by society, not by those who produced it. In brief, as Commoner stated, "there is no such thing as a free lunch."

He concluded that the economic system had to be based on social goals rather than private gain—that ecological considerations had to guide economic and political decisions. The costs to clean up the environment and convert to ecologically sound technological practices would be enormous—hundreds of billions of dollars—and would absorb the resources and capital of the nation for at least a generation. In addition, he warned, the added burden of paying the "environmental debt to nature" would fall heaviest on those least able to pay it—the poor. To Commoner the United States had two options: "rational, social organization of the use and distribution of the earth's resources, or a new barbarism."[18]

He sympathized little with environmentalists who appeared to advocate restricting people's choices through some form of coercion. For example, he criticized Garrett Hardin's article "The Tragedy of the Commons," in which Hardin argued that people needed to restrict access to the "commons" (air, water, and so on) through "mutual coercion, mutually agreed upon." Commoner regarded the British study *Blueprint for Survival* as a plan for regimentation and criticized the computer-based study *Limits to Growth*, commissioned by the Club of Rome, a worldwide group of prominent industrialists, economists, and scientists, for omitting options that could resolve environmental problems before ecocatastrophes occurred. Even so, he never made clear how his own policies could be implemented without some sort of coercion and loss of political liberty.

Commoner's sharpest disagreement was with Paul Ehrlich of Stanford University, author of *The Population Bomb*. Ehrlich had awakened public attention to the dangers of rapid population growth and the need for stabilizing it. Commoner, because he believed that technology holds the key to environmental degradation, said relatively little about population. In an extensive critique, Ehrlich and John Holdren, a physicist at the California Institute of Technology, called *The Closing Circle* "inexplicably inconsistent and dangerously misleading."[19] Basically, they argued that Commoner did not adequately support his thesis and neglected the importance of population growth and rising affluence as causes of environmental decline. Ehrlich thought that population growth had already reached a point at which a substantial increase in the world's death rate from overpopulation was inevitable; Commoner thought this view in error and intimated that Ehrlich had a fixation on the need for population control. To Commoner, controlling population growth meant some measure of political repression, and he abhorred any form of birth control that was not voluntary and self-initiated. Strong-willed and with a sense of mission, both men held to their positions, and the debate, often rancorous, did little to clarify the issues or aid the reputation of either.

Commoner did agree that third-world countries faced immediate threats because of overpopulation, but he argued that the solution was economic development rather than stringent population-control measures. A believer in the theory of demographic transition, he thought that third-world countries, with high birth and death rates, could follow the population trends of industrialized countries, where an increase of wealth led to reduced mortality and a willingness of couples to have fewer children. He blamed high birthrates on poverty and cited colonial exploitation and the maldistribution of wealth as the root of much of the problem.

Placing the issue in a broader context, Commoner noted:

To claim that many people go hungry and cold in the world because there is not adequate food and fuel has no more basis in fact than the claim that some people in the United States are poor because there is not enough wealth to go around. The basic fault that gives rise to these calamitous problems is the unequal distribution of wealth—between rich countries and poor ones, and, within each country, between rich people and poor people. Their origins will not be found in the earth's ecosystem or in the present state of its available resources.[20]

Addressing the Environment Forum at the United Nations Conference on the Human Environment in Stockholm in 1972, Commoner concluded that to solve the environmental crisis humanity must first solve the problems of "poverty, racial injustice and war." In brief, "a peace among men must precede the peace with nature."[21]

Because the availability of resources and the production of goods and services depend on energy, it is not surprising that after the oil embargo of 1973–74 Americans turned their attention to the energy question. It came as a shock in the United States when the flow of Middle Eastern oil suddenly stopped and long lines of impatient drivers had to wait hours for a few gallons of gasoline.

Americans had long assumed the presence of unlimited, cheap energy. After all, we had made the transition from wood and waterpower to coal and then to petroleum and natural gas. After World War II, we had launched an aggressive policy in the Middle East to ensure that our energy needs would be met. The United States, the most energy-intensive nation on earth, had committed itself to massive energy consumption.

Even in the 1960s when OPEC (the Organization of Petroleum Exporting Countries) was created and concerns about pollution dampened enthusiasm about burning fossil fuels, Americans remained confident about the future. Utility companies could turn to the presumably cheap, safe, and unlimited energy available from nuclear power plants—at least, such was the forecast of the Atomic Energy Commission and the utility companies.

The American public shouldn't have been so complacent, for the days of cheap energy were already numbered before the Yom Kippur (Arab-Israeli) War of 1973 led to the oil embargo. Increased consumption, coupled with reduced exploration for oil and production of oil at home, had left the country vulnerable. Then, suddenly, we faced an "energy crisis." No one knew how to solve the problem, for energy could not be separated from environmental concerns and economic realities. In his newest book, *The Poverty of Power* (1976), Commoner explained, "Proponents of one solution become opponents of the others.

Policy stagnates and remedial action is paralyzed, adding to the confusion and gloom that beset the country."[22]

To Commoner, the fundamental flaw in American society was the design of the country's economic system. The private-enterprise system failed to meet such essential social needs as renewable and nonpolluting energy and resources; efficient and minimally harmful technologies in agriculture, transportation, and manufacturing; and production processes that allow for safe and rewarding jobs while requiring limited capital.

He attributed these failures to the desire to maximize profits regardless of the cost in energy, capital, or environmental health. The petrochemical industry, more than any other, revealed what had gone wrong; this most capital-intensive and laborsaving of major manufacturing industries had remained profitable to private investors as long as the public had absorbed such "externalities" as pollution, unemployment, and danger in the workplace.

Commoner believed that over several decades Americans could come to depend on renewable resources if they understood the benefits and liabilities of the various available energy sources and if they based policy decisions on social needs rather than on private profits. He argued that much could be accomplished by pursuing energy efficiency—by using the minimum energy necessary to accomplish each task. To achieve this goal would necessitate a phasing out of nuclear power plants, an example of thermodynamic overkill, generating temperatures in the range of one million degrees fahrenheit to produce steam for electricity. Nuclear energy had other problems as well: it posed threats to safety, resulted in cost overruns, produced radioactive waste, and made possible the proliferation of nuclear weapons. And Commoner regarded coal, gaseous and liquid fuel made from coal (synthetic fuel), and shale oil as inefficient, polluting, and potentially dangerous to human health.

Instead, he advocated solar energy because it is renewable,

available, environmentally safe, and, in the long run, inexpensive. Although the transition to a renewable resource base would take several decades, such feasible and well-known practices and developments as organic farming and electrified railroads could be pursued immediately. And natural gas could provide a safe transition fuel, particularly because a heating system that burned natural gas could also burn methane, produced from organic matter. Cogeneration (the use of electricity and waste heat) promised major savings, and solar electrical cells (photovoltaics) could become economically attractive.

It galled Commoner that the federal government continued to subsidize the nuclear and synthetic-fuel power industries. In 1976, speaking on the nuclear-power industry, he complained: "It is a lopsided partnership between the private and public sectors, in which the rewards have been private and the huge risks— the hazards to life, the waste of billions of dollars, the rising cost of power, the impending collapse of the nuclear-power program, and the ensuing economic chaos—have been assigned to the public."[23]

Though *The Poverty of Power* received wide praise, several reviewers considered Commoner absolutist and visionary in his insistence on solar energy. They noted his weakness in economic theory and his tendency to present only the evidence that supported his point of view. *Forbes* magazine caustically labeled Commoner "a second-rate scientist and a no-rate economist." In the *Sierra Club Bulletin*, the reviewer Richard Tybout stated that Commoner confused thermodynamic efficiency with economic efficiency and called the book "economic nonsense." And Kenneth Boulding described it as a "political tract," referring to the last chapter as a "naive exposition of a vulgar Marxist economics" and lamenting, "It is distressing when a good man writes a bad book." Undaunted, Commoner replied, "I've never had a course in economics, but an economist is not a biologist either, and one of us has to step across the line to get at the big issues."[24]

In *The Politics of Energy* (1979), Commoner completed his criticism of the government's environmental policy and of large-scale, centralized energy production. He called President Jimmy Carter's National Energy Plan deceitful and a hoax because of its dependence on coal and nuclear power. He argued that the cost of producing oil or any other nonrenewable resource would grow exponentially. And he criticized proposals for a breeder-based energy system because of its very grave environmental hazards, said that embarking on a transition to fusion power was like "building a bridge across a chasm without first locating the other side," and advocated the use of public funds "to establish new, competitive solar industries." Commoner stressed the need for a strategy of "social governance," although he never explained how social governance would work or how it might affect democratic institutions.[25] A reviewer aptly called the book "an energy platform for a third party."[26]

THE CITIZENS' PARTY AND BEYOND

Increasingly, Commoner saw solar conversion as more a political than a technical or economic problem. Solar energy was feasible now, if the government would give it a helping hand. He argued that big oil companies, electric utility companies, and the two major political parties stood in the way of such a policy. Therefore, he joined with other dissidents to form the Citizens' party, described by *Newsweek* as an "antibusiness amalgam of environmentalists, consumerists, antinuclear activists and minority-rights advocates."[27]

The founders of the party had no hope of winning at the national level, but they dreamed that a presidential candidate, as an initial step, might gain 5 percent of the vote and thus qualify the party for matching federal funds. The first task was to decide on a strategy and qualify candidates for the ballot in as many states as possible. When 262 delegates from some thirty states

240

gathered in Cleveland in April 1980 for the founding convention, they faced an uphill battle. Perhaps half of the delegates had joined the party only in recent weeks, and no one could agree on a platform.

Believing strongly in internal democracy and an ideology that combined populism and social democracy, party members submitted position papers and resolutions to form the basis of a party platform to be voted on by the entire membership by mail (Commoner later described this as "an insane idea, which utterly failed"[28]). Instead of operating from a confusing and unworkable national platform, local state groups wrote their own statements of party goals. In brief, the Citizens' party stood for public control (but not necessarily ownership) of energy industries, an end to nuclear power plants, the use of solar energy and conservation practices, sharp and immediate reductions in defense spending, active support for human rights at home and abroad, the provision of work for anyone who wanted it, the establishment of stable prices for necessities such as food, housing, fuel, and medical care, and limitations on the power of corporations.

Commoner agreed to be the party's presidential nominee, with LaDonna Harris, an Indian-rights activist from Oklahoma, as the vice-presidential candidate. Because the party spent almost all of its limited funds gathering signatures to get on state ballots, Commoner relied on local party members to organize his itinerary as he traveled from one community to the next.

Professing faith in the future, Commoner compared the Citizens' party to the Republican party of 1854. A third party could succeed, he maintained, when the two major parties proved incapable of confronting the critical issues of the times. In Lincoln's day the issue was slavery. In 1980, Commoner insisted, the issue was that owners of capital made major decisions for American society based "on the sole criterion of maximizing profit."[29] Someone needed to look after the welfare of the people, the creation of jobs, the protection of the environment, and the conservation of energy.

Commoner's greatest disappointment in the campaign was his failure to gain the attention of the national media. He attributed the problem to the mentality demonstrated by a reporter in Albuquerque, New Mexico, who asked him, "Are you really a serious candidate or are you just running on the issues?"[30] Because he had no chance of winning, the major television networks and newspapers ignored him.

The election results in November were predictable: Commoner had attracted fewer than 250,000 votes nationwide. The public-interest groups he had counted on gave little support, apparently more interested in lobbying parties in power than in helping to build a new political organization. Although most observers saw the election as an overwhelming defeat, Commoner considered the scattered success of local party candidates as an omen for the future. He split from the party, however, to support the presidential candidacy of Jesse Jackson in 1984, believing that Jackson's "rainbow coalition" most closely represented the ideals of the Citizens' party.

Ronald Reagan's presidency began on an inauspicious note. According to a *Los Angeles Times* editorial, "Ronald Reagan's very first act as President in January, 1981, was to turn up the thermostat at the White House."[31] His administration's cavalier attitude toward environmental issues was reflected in the appointment of James G. Watt as secretary of the interior and Anne M. Gorsuch (later Burford) as head of the Environmental Protection Agency. Watt, a westerner dedicated to reducing government protection and regulation of federal lands, promoted private development of federal resources and worked to weaken environmental standards. Gorsuch implemented sharp funding reductions in the EPA, especially for research, monitoring, and enforcement, and was forced to resign amidst accusations that the agency had made "sweetheart deals" with corporations in administering a $1.6 billion "superfund" to clean up toxic wastes. Energy subsidies helped encourage the investment of private capital in increasingly expensive and uncompetitive power plants, thus adding to the national deficit and unemployment.

After Reagan was elected, Commoner moved his Center for the Biology of Natural Systems to Queens College, where he had first taught. This move, after he had spent thirty-four years at Washington University in St. Louis, was undoubtedly spurred on by conflicts with the university administration. Commoner's success in raising grant money for his center had given him unusual independence, and the fact that he led campus opposition, both locally and nationally, to American involvement in the Vietnam War may have made fund-raising by the university more difficult.

New York City offered opportunities to confront environmental and energy problems of urban dwellers, especially the poor. Here, he and his staff launched into a flurry of activities including the study of environmentally safe methods of disposing of municipal garbage, the development of a neighborhood energy cooperative using cogenerators to provide both heat and electricity to row houses, the organization of workshops to train people on optimum weatherization techniques, and the creation of a computer network for public education on environmental and energy issues. The center remained dedicated to solving the "real problems" of urban and rural communities.

As he neared his seventieth birthday, Commoner reflected on the environmental movement that he had helped create:

What happened in 1970 was a kind of inchoate outburst of people's feelings that the environment is important and had been neglected. There was damned little organization at first; everybody was sounding off in

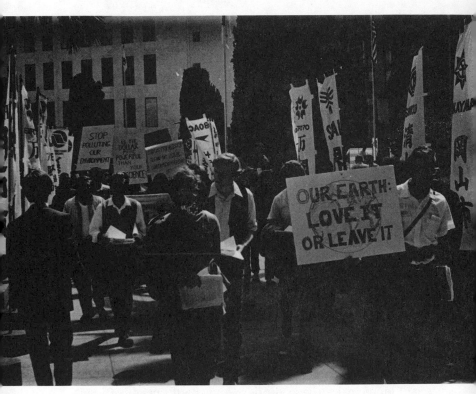

Environmentalists' protest march in San Francisco
(Courtesy of the Sierra Club)

one direction or another. What really held it together was the very simple
moral statement that future generations depend on the environment and
we have been blind as to what's been happening to it.[32]

He could point to several accomplishments, including the
rapid increase in knowledge about the state of the environment, the proliferation of environmental organizations at the
local, state and national level, and the expenditure of billions of
dollars in clean-up campaigns. Yet much of what had been accomplished, such as bringing about the use of scrubbers in power
plants and of catalytic devices on automobiles, represented only

a quick fix. The 1980s were a decade of stagnation in the improvement of environmental quality, partly because of severe budget cuts to the federal agencies responsible for enforcing environmental standards.

The few substantive improvements in recent years, Commoner claimed, resulted from stopping the process that had produced the pollutant in the first place. Thus, strontium 90 in milk was reduced by ending nuclear atmospheric testing; lead was reduced in the environment through its removal from most gasoline; mercury was reduced in surface water by eliminating its use in the production of chlorine; and dangerous chemicals were reduced by prohibiting the use of DDT, PCB (polychlorinated biphenyls), and other substances. In brief, Commoner summarized, "all the really successful environmental improvements have been achieved by altering" the technology of production.[33]

Commoner recognized the formidable obstacles to major changes in the system of production. Production decisions were based primarily on the desire for short-term economic profit, and corporations dominated the political system. In addition, environmentalists remained divided on the best strategies for change. Commoner believed that the important social issues in American society—"human rights; the quality of life; health; jobs; peace; survival"—had a common root. What the nation needed was to recognize the key issue: how the choice of production technologies is to be determined."[34]

Barry Commoner, as much as anyone, educated this country's citizens about the plight of the environment in the post–World War II era. As a scientist dedicated to informing the public and as a citizen willing to enter politics, he helped raise the environmental awareness and political consciousness of Americans.

Conclusion

Conservation in the United States made major strides between the time Thoreau's first book lay unsold on a shelf in Concord, Massachusetts, and the time Rachel Carson's *Silent Spring* reached the best-seller list. What began as a sentimental and romantic interest in nature became a national movement that enlisted poet and politician, student and scientist.

Thoreau preached the value of unspoiled wilderness fifty years before Americans began to realize that the frontiers of their country had disappeared. Marsh introduced the rudiments of ecology decades before Leopold brought the full force of science to the defense of wilderness. Olmsted introduced the idea of city planning a century before Congress created a Department of Urban Affairs. And Mather sought to set aside national parks and attract people to them fifty years before Brower warned of their overuse.

Several groups of people carried the conservation movement forward. Some believed they were waging a democratic crusade against big business, monopolists, and land grabbers. Others conceived of conservation as the application of scientific knowledge to resource management. And still others saw their efforts as a moral or religious crusade to protect the natural environment or as an attempt to avoid ecological disruptions and maintain environmental health.

Thus, the movement to conserve and preserve the land gained the support of individuals and groups with widely divergent attitudes. All these groups, like Muir and Pinchot, realized that America's resources are limited and need to be used in the country's best interest. The major differences of opinion were (and still are) over what constitutes the highest or best use.

As the twenty-first century draws near, the success of the conservation movement remains uncertain. Despite apparent abundance in the United States and advances in saving forests and watersheds, parklands and farmlands, fish and other wildlife; despite the increased crop yield per acre on farms, board-foot yield per tree in the forests, foot-acres of water storage per watershed, and recreation and park acreage per state, we are in jeopardy.

Today's problems are of a new order. Rachel Carson noted in *Silent Spring*, "Along with the possibility of the extinction of mankind by nuclear war, the central problem of our age has . . . become the contamination of man's total environment."[1] A lexicon of new terms—dioxin, vinyl chloride, PCB—has entered our vocabulary. While chemistry has worked wonders in saving lives, alleviating pain, bolstering food production, and providing numerous useful products, its waste products pose severe risks. And environmentally caused cancers proliferate. In addition, the effects of new technology are ominous. For example, the burning of fossil fuels threatens a greenhouse effect, with potential melting of the polar ice caps and unknown alteration of the global climate. And lakes and forests suffer the effects of acid rain.

Less noticed, but just as important, this country's renewable resource base is endangered. California agriculture—long a showcase of productivity and profit—illustrates part of the problem. In a recent year, agriculture consumed 87 percent of the state's water supply; used exorbitant quantities of energy to grow crops for livestock; depended on the heavy use of chemicals; destroyed native grasses, wetlands, and free-flowing streams; lost topsoil to erosion, and in other ways left the land depleted. Most people took little notice as the best farmlands were converted to urban development, as land ownership became concentrated in fewer and fewer hands, and as the health of the land gradually deteriorated, crippling its ability for self-renewal.

There are several beliefs about the environment that must be questioned in much the way that Powell questioned the existence of a western garden land. One is the myth that nature is hostile and must be conquered. In the place of this myth we should cultivate what Leopold called an "ecological conscience." Then there is the related nineteenth-century myth that people are separate from nature and that their happiness depends on material progress alone. A little late, but perhaps not too late, Americans are realizing that too much "progress" is not the answer to their quest for physical and mental well-being. As Thoreau asked, "What is the use of a house if you haven't a tolerable planet to put it on?"[2]

Rachel Carson and Barry Commoner helped explain the complexity of today's environmental problems and why no quick solutions exist. We have no means to extract the chemical pollutants that have entered underground water supplies; we do not know the long-range consequences of the buildup of carbon dioxide in the atmosphere from burning fossil fuels; we do not know how to protect ourselves from radiation poisoning, whether caused by nuclear power plant accidents or by war.

Lester Brown of the Worldwatch Institute warned in 1985 that the world is not living within its means and that its "security and future well-being may be threatened less by the conflicts among nations than they are by the deteriorating relationship between ourselves . . . and the natural systems and resources that sustain us."[3] What is needed, he continued, are policies that respect the carrying capacity of ecosystems and preserve the biological diversity of the earth.

Brown expressed hope for the future because "every threat to sustainability has been successfully addressed by at least a few countries." Population control, soil conservation, reforestation, recycling, and a shift to renewable energy all are possible and have been achieved in one place or another. The resources and technology necessary to tackle environmental problems exist; what is missing, according to Brown, is "awareness and political will."[4]

Changes can be made if exceptional individuals—the Marshes, Leopolds, and Carsons of our time—join forces with concerned and educated citizens to help decide today, in the political arena, the kind of world we shall have tomorrow.

Notes

INTRODUCTION

1. William Bradford, *Of Plymouth Plantation, 1620–1647,* new ed. (New York: Alfred A. Knopf, 1979), p. 62.
2. Stewart L. Udall, *The Quiet Crisis* (New York: Holt, Rinehart and Winston, 1963), p. 19.

CHAPTER ONE: THE FORERUNNERS

1. Joseph Wood Krutch, *Henry David Thoreau* (New York: William Morrow, 1948), p. 63.
2. Walter Harding, *The Days of Henry Thoreau* (New York: Alfred A. Knopf, 1965), p. 292.
3. Brooks Atkinson, ed., *Walden and Other Writings of Henry David Thoreau,* (New York: Random House, 1937), pp. 4–5.
4. Bradford Torrey and Francis H. Allen, eds., *The Journal of Henry David Thoreau* (Boston: Houghton Mifflin, 1906), 8: 220–21.
5. Roderick Nash, *Wilderness and the American Mind,* rev. ed. (New Haven: Yale University Press, 1973), p. 92.
6. Krutch, *Henry David Thoreau,* p. 115.
7. Atkinson, *Walden and Other Writings,* p. 288.
8. Krutch, *Henry David Thoreau,* p. 4.

9. Torrey and Allen, *Journal of Henry David Thoreau,* 12: 387.

10. Quoted in Krutch, *Henry David Thoreau,* p. 84.

11. Atkinson, *Walden and Other Writings,* p. 290.

12. "The Beginning of Central Park," *Nineteenth Annual Report, 1914, of the American Scenic and Historic Preservation Society* (Albany: J. B. Lyon, 1914), p. 515.

13. Lewis Mumford, *The Brown Decades* (New York: Dover Publications, 1971), p. 39.

14. Frederick Law Olmsted, Jr., and Theodora Kimball, eds., *Frederick Law Olmsted: Landscape Architect, 1822–1903* (New York: Benjamin Blom, 1970), p. 46.

15. F. L. Olmsted and Calvert Vaux, *Description of a Plan for the Development of Central Park* (New York, 1858), pp. 7, 8.

16. Charles E. Beveridge, *Creating Central Park, 1857–1861* (Baltimore: Johns Hopkins University Press, 1983), vol. 3 of *The Papers of Frederick Law Olmsted,* ed. David Schyler, p. 3.

17. "The Yosemite Valley and the Mariposa Big Trees: A Preliminary Report," *Landscape Architecture* 43 (1952): 17.

18. Ibid., p. 22.

19. Charles Capen McLaughlin, "Selected Letters of Frederick Law Olmsted" (Ph.D. diss., Harvard University, 1960), p. 73.

20. Elizabeth Stevenson, *Park Maker: A Life of Frederick Law Olmsted* (New York: Macmillan, 1977), p. 404.

21. Mumford, *The Brown Decades,* p. 43.

22. Ibid., p. 35.

23. David Lowenthal, *George Perkins Marsh: Versatile Vermonter* (New York: Columbia University Press, 1958), pp. vii–viii.

24. Ibid., pp. 17–18.

25. David Lowenthal, "Introduction," in George Perkins Marsh, *Man and Nature* (Cambridge: The Belknap Press of Harvard University Press, 1965), p. xii.

26. George P. Marsh, *Report Made under Authority of the Legislature of Vermont, on the Artificial Propagation of Fish* (Burlington, Vt.: Free Press Print, 1857), p. 17.

27. Lowenthal, *George Perkins Marsh,* p. 237.

28. Marsh, *Man and Nature,* pp. 18, 28.

29. George Perkins Marsh, *Address Delivered before the Agricultural Society of Rutland County, September 30, 1847* (Rutland, Vt.: 1848), p. 18.

30. Lowenthal, *George Perkins Marsh,* p. 252.

31. Marsh, *Man and Nature,* p. 34.
32. Lowenthal, *George Perkins Marsh,* p. 259.
33. Marsh, *Man and Nature,* pp. 36, 43.
34. Ibid., p. 36.
35. Ibid., p. 42.
36. Gifford Pinchot, *Breaking New Ground* (New York: Harcourt, Brace, 1947), p. xvi.
37. Hans Huth, *Nature and the American* (Berkeley: University of California Press, 1957), p. 169.
38. Stewart L. Udall, *The Quiet Crisis* (New York: Holt, Rinehart and Winston, 1963), p. 82.

CHAPTER TWO: JOHN WESLEY POWELL

1. J. W. Powell, *Exploration of the Colorado River of the West* (Washington, D.C.: Government Printing Office, 1875), p. 80.
2. U.S. Congress, House, *Geographical and Geological Surveys West of the Mississippi,* 43d Cong., 1st sess., 1873–74, H. Rept. 612, p. 53.
3. National Academy of Sciences, *A Report on the Surveys of the Territories,* 45th Cong., 3d sess., 1878, H. R. Misc. Doc. 5, pp. 3, 5.
4. J. W. Powell, "Institutions for the Arid Lands," *Century* 40 (May 1890): 113.
5. 51st Cong., 1st sess., 1890, S. Rept. 1466, p. 60.

CHAPTER THREE: GIFFORD PINCHOT

1. William Henry Harbaugh, *Power and Responsibility: The Life and Times of Theodore Roosevelt* (New York: Farrar, Straus & Giroux, 1961), p. 334.
2. Theodore Roosevelt, *An Autobiography* (New York: Macmillan, 1913), p. 429.
3. Gifford Pinchot, *Biltmore Forest* (Chicago: Lakeside, 1893), pp. 44–45.
4. Ibid., p. 49.
5. Gifford Pinchot, *The Fight for Conservation* (New York: Doubleday, Page, 1910), p. 38.
6. *United States Statutes at Large,* 26:1103.
7. Theodore Roosevelt, *State Papers as Governor and President, 1899–1909* (New York: Charles Scribner's Sons, 1925), p. 120.

8. Jenks Cameron, *The Development of Forest Control in the United States* (Baltimore: Johns Hopkins University Press, 1928), p. 239.

9. Pinchot, *The Fight for Conservation,* p. 58.

10. Samuel P. Hays, *Conservation and the Gospel of Efficiency* (Cambridge: Harvard University Press, 1959), p. 67.

11. Gifford Pinchot, *Breaking New Ground* (New York: Harcourt, Brace, 1947), p. 320.

12. Ibid., p. 322.

13. Pinchot, *The Fight for Conservation,* pp. 43–46.

14. Ibid., pp. 4, 20.

15. Pinchot, *Breaking New Ground,* p. 505.

16. Ibid., p. 32.

CHAPTER FOUR: JOHN MUIR

1. John Muir, *The Mountains of California* (London: T. Fisher Unwin, 1894), pp. 251–54.

2. John Muir, *The Story of My Boyhood and Youth* (Boston: Houghton Mifflin, 1912), p. 33.

3. Ibid., p. 223.

4. Ibid., pp. 275–76.

5. Linnie Marsh Wolfe, *Son of the Wilderness: The Life of John Muir* (Madison: University of Wisconsin Press, 1978), p. 89.

6. John Muir, *The Story of My Boyhood and Youth and A Thousand-Mile Walk to the Gulf* (Boston: Houghton Mifflin, 1916), p. 324.

7. Ibid., p. 343.

8. Ibid., pp. 354–55.

9. Ibid.

10. Ibid., p. 357.

11. Udall, *Quiet Crisis,* p. 110.

12. Michael P. Cohen, *The Pathless Way: John Muir and American Wilderness* (Madison: University of Wisconsin Press, 1984), p. 81.

13. Huth, *Nature and the American,* p. 151.

14. Stephen Fox, *John Muir and His Legacy: The American Conservation Movement* (Boston: Little, Brown, 1981), p. 83.

15. William Frederic Badè, *The Life and Letters of John Muir,* 2 vols. (Boston: Houghton Mifflin, 1924), 2:59.

16. Frederick Turner, *Rediscovering America: John Muir in His Times and Ours* (New York: Viking, 1985), p. 227.

17. Wolfe, *Son of the Wilderness,* p. 190.

18. Robert Engberg, "John Muir's 'Great Evils from Destruction of Forests,'" *Pacific Historian* 25 (Winter 1981): 14.

19. Herbert F. Smith, *John Muir* (New York: Twayne, 1965), p. 121,

20. John Muir, *Our National Parks* (Boston: Houghton Mifflin, 1901), p. 1.

21. Ibid., p. 13.

22. Udall, *Quiet Crisis,* p. 119.

23. Muir, *Our National Parks,* p. 331.

24. Ibid., p. 340.

25. Ibid., p. 359.

26. Ibid., pp. 364–65.

27. Ibid., p. 363.

28. Wolfe, *Son of the Wilderness,* p. 290.

29. Ibid., p. 291.

30. Ibid., p. 292.

31. Badè, *Life and Letters* 2:413.

32. Ibid., p. 356.

33. Ibid., p. 417.

34. Ibid., p. 420.

35. *Proceedings of a Conference of Governors,* 60th Cong., 2d sess., 1909, H. Doc. 1425, p. 153.

36. Ibid., pp. 156–57.

37. Badè, *Life and Letters* 2:389.

38. John Muir, *The Writings of John Muir,* vol. 5, *The Mountains of California II* (Boston: Houghton Mifflin,1916), p. 291.

39. Badè, *Life and Letters* 2:386.

40. Wolfe, *Son of the Wilderness,* p. 337.

CHAPTER FIVE: STEPHEN MATHER

1. Robert Shankland, *Steve Mather of the National Parks,* 2d rev. ed. (New York: Alfred A. Knopf, 1954), p. 7.

2. Ibid., p. 8.

3. Ibid., p. 57.

4. Ibid., p. 6.

5. *United States Statutes at Large,* 39:535.

6. *Report of the Secretary of the Interior, 1918,* 65th Cong., 3d sess., H. Doc. 1455, p. 110.

7. "Report of the Director of the National Park Service," in *Reports of the Department of the Interior, 1919,* 66th Cong., 2d sess., H. Doc. 409, p. 963.
8. Shankland, *Steve Mather,* p. 216.
9. *Report of the Secretary, 1918,* pp. 112–13.
10. Shankland, *Steve Mather,* p. 215.
11. *United States Statutes at Large,* 34: 225.
12. Shankland, *Steve Mather,* p. 161.
13. Ibid., p. 247.
14. Ibid., facing p. 307.

CHAPTER SIX: ALDO LEOPOLD

1. Aldo Leopold, *A Sand County Almanac* (New York: Oxford University Press, 1949), pp. 201–3.
2. Roderick Nash, *Wilderness and the American Mind* (New Haven: Yale University Press, 1967), p. 183.
3. Aldo Leopold, "Wilderness as a Form of Land Use," *Living Wilderness* 43 (December 1979):12.
4. Susan Flader, *Thinking like a Mountain* (Columbia: University of Missouri Press, 1974), p. 98.
5. Aldo Leopold, "The Wilderness and Its Place in Forest Recreational Policy," *Journal of Forestry* 19 (1921): 718.
6. Susan L. Flader, "Aldo Leopold and the Wilderness Idea," *Living Wilderness* 43 (December 1979): 5.
7. Ibid., p. 6.
8. Aldo Leopold, *A Sand County Almanac and Other Essays from Round River* (New York: Oxford University Press, 1966), p. 130.
9. Flader, "Aldo Leopold," p. 7.
10. Aldo Leopold, "Why the Wilderness Society?" *Living Wilderness* 1 (December 1935): 10.
11. Clay Schoenfeld, "Aldo Leopold Remembered," *Audubon* 80 (May 1978): 29.
12. Ibid., p. 32.
13. Anthony Wolff, "Introduction," in Susan Flader, *The Sand Country of Aldo Leopold* (San Francisco: Sierra Club, 1973).
14. Leopold, *Sand County Almanac,* pp. 203–4, 214–15; *Sand County Almanac and Other Essays,* p. 177.
15. Leopold, *Sand County Almanac,* p. 217.

16. Ibid., p. 110.
17. Ibid., p. 109.
18. Ibid., pp. 204–5.
19. Schoenfeld, "Aldo Leopold Remembered," p. 37.
20. Aldo Leopold, "The Green Lagoons," *American Forests* 51 (August 1945): 414.
21. Leopold, *Sand County Almanac*, p. 193.
22. Ibid., p. 194.
23. Ibid., pp. 173, 176–77.
24. Ibid., p. vii.
25. Ibid., pp. 195–96.
26. Ibid., p. 199.
27. Ibid., pp. 200–201.
28. Ibid., p. 221.
29. Leopold, *Sand County Almanac and Other Essays*, p. 187.
30. Leopold, *Sand County Almanac*, p. 214.
31. Ibid., pp. 224–25.

CHAPTER SEVEN: HAROLD ICKES

1. Harold L. Ickes, *The Autobiography of a Curmudgeon* (New York: Reynal and Hitchcock, 1943), p. 9.
2. Ibid., p. 33.
3. Donald C. Swain, *Federal Conservation Policy, 1921–1933* (Berkeley: University of California Press, 1963), p. 163.
4. Donald D. Shipley, "A Study of the Conservation Philosophies and Contributions of Some Important American Conservation Leaders" (Ph.D. diss., Cornell University, 1953), p. 228.
5. Harold L. Ickes, *The New Democracy* (New York: W. W. Norton, 1934), p. 19.
6. Ibid., p. 74.
7. Ruth Gruber, "Ickes: American Legend," *Nation* 174 (April 19, 1952): 363.
8. T. W. Watkins, "The Terrible-Tempered Mr. Ickes," *Audubon* 86 (March 1984): 100.
9. "The Most Exciting Moments in My Life," MS, box 120, Harold L. Ickes Papers, Library of Congress, Washington, D.C.
10. Arthur M. Schlesinger, Jr., *The Coming of the New Deal* (Boston: Houghton Mifflin, 1958), pp. 282–83.

11. Ibid., p. 283.
12. David Cushman Coyle, Conservation: An American Story of Conflict and Accomplishment (New Brunswick: Rutgers University Press, 1957), p. 120.
13. "National Parks," *Science* 89 (February 24, 1939): 171.
14. Harold L. Ickes, "My Twelve Years with F. D. R.," *Saturday Evening Post* 220 (June 12, 1948): 111.
15. Ibid.
16. Ickes, *New Democracy,* p. 96.
17. Form letter from Gifford Pinchot, July 9, 1935, "Conservation 1935–1937" folder, box 155, Ickes Papers, Library of Congress.
18. *The Secret Diary of Harold L. Ickes,* 3 vols. (New York: Simon and Schuster, 1953–54), 3: 131.
19. Ibid.
20. Edgar B. Nixon, ed., *Franklin D. Roosevelt and Conservation* (General Services Administration, National Archives and Records Service, Franklin D. Roosevelt Library), p. 541.
21. Linda J. Lear, "Harold Ickes and the Oil Crisis of the First Hundred Days," *Mid America* 63 (January 1981): 13.
22. Harold L. Ickes, "My Twelve Years with FDR, " *Saturday Evening Post* 121 (July 17, 1948): 102.
23. Gruber, "Ickes: American Legend," p. 363.

CHAPTER EIGHT: RACHEL CARSON

1. U. S. Congress, Senate, Committee on Government Operations, *Interagency Coordination in Environmental Hazards (Pesticides): Hearings before the Subcommittee on Reorganization and International Organization,* 88th Cong., 1st sess., June 4, 1963, p. 206.
2. Ibid., 2d sess., April 16, 1964, p. 2005.
3. Paul Brooks, *Speaking for Nature* (San Francisco: Sierra Club Books, 1980), p. 276.
4. Theme attached to Dorothy Thompson Seif, "Letters from Rachel Carson: A Scientist Sets Her Course," MS, Rachel Carson Council, Chevy Chase, Maryland.
5. Ibid., p. 35.
6. Ibid., p. 70.
7. R. L. Carson, "Undersea," *Atlantic Monthly* 160 (September 1937): 325.

8. "The Gentle Storm Center: Calm Appraisal of 'Silent Spring,' " *Life* 53 (October 12, 1962): 105.

9. Rachel L. Carson, *Under the Sea-Wind* (New York: Simon and Schuster, 1941), p. xiii.

10. Paul Brooks, *The House of Life: Rachel Carson at Work* (Boston: Houghton Mifflin, 1972), p. 78.

11. Ibid., p. 110.

12. Rachel Carson, "Help Your Child to Wonder," *Woman's Home Companion* 83 (July 1956): 48.

13. Rachel Carson, "Our Ever-Changing Shore," *Holiday* 24 (July 1958): 120.

14. Frank Graham, Jr., *Since "Silent Spring"* (Boston: Houghton Mifflin, 1970), p. 13.

15. Rachel Carson, *Of Man and the Stream of Time* (Graduation address delivered at Scripps College, Claremont, Calif., 1962), p. 10.

16. Rachel L. Carson, *The Sea around Us,* rev. ed. (New York: Oxford University Press, 1961), p. xiii.

17. Brooks, *House of Life,* p. 233.

18. Ibid., p. 244.

19. "DDT Dangers," *Time* 45 (April 16, 1945): 91–92.

20. Lois Mattox Miller, "What You Should Know about DDT," *Reader's Digest* 47 (November 1945): 84.

21. Rachel Carson, *Silent Spring* (Boston: Houghton Mifflin, 1962), p. 2.

22. Ibid., p. 7.

23. Ibid., pp. 16–17.

24. Ibid., p. 8.

25. Ibid., pp. 12–13

26. Ibid., p. 278.

27. Loren Eisely, review of *Silent Spring,* by Rachel Carson, *Saturday Review* (September 29, 1962): 18–19, 34; Philip Sterling, *The Life of Rachel Carson* (New York: Thomas Y. Crowell, 1970), p. 171.

28. "Pesticides: The Price for Progress," *Time* 80 (September 28, 1962): 45, 48.

29. William H. Darby, review of *Silent Spring,* by Rachel Carson, *Chemical and Engineering News* 40 (October 1, 1962): 60.

30. Jamie L. Whitten, *That We May Live* (Toronto: D. Van Nostrand, 1966), p. 141.

31. Rachel Carson, "Rachel Carson Answers Her Critics," *Audubon* 65–66 (September–October 1963): 262.

32. Rachel L. Carson, "The Pollution of Our Environment," [l963–64?], p. 19, MS, box V:2, Rachel Carson Papers, Collection of American Literature, Beinecke Rare Book and Manuscript Library, Yale University, New Haven, Connecticut. © by Roger Christie and quoted by permission of Frances Collin.

33. Brooks, *House of Life*, p. 323.

34. "Gentle Storm Center," p. 105.

35. Carson, *Of Man and the Stream of Time*, p. 8.

CHAPTER NINE: DAVID BROWER

1. "Relevance 1919," box 2, "Assorted Maps and Articles" folder, David Brower Papers, Bancroft Library, University of California, Berkeley.

2. Susan Schrepfer, *David R. Brower: Environmental Activist, Publicist, and Prophet* (Berkeley: Regional Oral History Office, The Bancroft Library, University of California, 1980), p. 15.

3. Ibid., p. 12.

4. Ibid., p. 18.

5. Clayton R. Koppes, "Oscar L. Chapman: A Liberal at the Interior Department, 1933–1953" (Ph.D. diss., University of Kansas, 1974), p. 343.

6. Schrepfer, *David R. Brower*, pp. 47–48.

7. Entry for 3/13 in Notebook XIII, 2/9/60–10/31/60, box 5, Brower Papers.

8. David R. Brower, "Wilderness—Conflict and Conscience," *Sierra Club Bulletin* 42 (June 1957): 2.

9. "The Meaning of Wilderness to Recreation" (Paper prepared for the Forty-first National Recreation Congress, Chicago, October 1, 1959), box 1, "Adecology" folder, Brower Papers.

10. Ansel Adams and Nancy Newhall, *This Is the American Earth* (San Francisco: Sierra Club, 1960), p. 62.

11. Brower to Udall, April 29, 1966, box 166, "Grand Canyon National Park" folder, Sierra Club Papers, Bancroft Library, University of California, Berkeley.

12. MS, n.d., box 1, "Sierra Club–Misc. Corresp." folder, Brower Papers.

13. "Regional Disputes, Lobbying Shape Colorado River Bill," *Congressional Quarterly Weekly Report*, no. 44 (November 1, 1968), p. 3024.
14. "Knight Errant to Nature's Rescue," *Life* 60 (May 27, 1966): 37.
15. Brower to George Marshall, March 2, 1967, box 208, folder 3 on Diablo Canyon, Sierra Club Papers.
16. Susan R. Schrepfer, *Richard M. Leonard: Mountaineer, Lawyer, Environmentalist* (Berkeley: Regional Oral History Office, The Bancroft Library, University of California, 1975), p. 446.
17. "What's Eating the SC?" entry for 2/26 in Notebook XLIV, 2/10/69–6/30/69, box 3, Brower Papers.
18. Robert A. Jones, "Fratricide in the Sierra Club," *Nation* 208 (May 5, 1969): 568.
19. Press release, February 7, 1969, box 205, Sierra Club Papers.
20. "Dave Brower: The Environmentalist and the Bomb," *Mother Earth News,* no. 77 (September–October 1982): 96.
21. Ibid., p. 94.
22. John McPhee, *Encounters with the Archdruid* (New York: Farrar, Straus and Giroux, 1971), p. 57.

CHAPTER TEN: BARRY COMMONER

1. Alan Anderson, Jr., "Scientist at Large," *New York Times Magazine,* November 7, 1976, p. 59.
2. Barry Commoner, "Environmental Growth and Environmental Quality: How to Have Both," *Social Policy* 16 (Summer 1985): 26.
3. "Paul Revere of Ecology," *Time* 95 (February 2, 1970): 58.
4. Barry Commoner, "Hiroshima at Home," *Hospital Practice* 13 (April 1978): 58.
5. Barry Commoner, "Beyond the Teach-in," *Saturday Review* 53 (April 4, 1970): 51.
6. Anderson, "Scientist at Large," p. 60.
7. Barry Commoner, "The Fallout Problem," *Science* 127 (May 2, 1958): 1023.
8. Ibid., p. 1024.
9. Ibid., p. 1025.
10. "Social Aspects of Science," *Science* 125 (January 25, 1957): 143.
11. Barry Commoner, "The Responsibility of Science to Man," *Perspectives in Biology and Medicine* 8 (Autumn 1964): 92.
12. "Social Aspects of Science," p. 146.

13. Barry Commoner, *The Closing Circle* (New York: Alfred A. Knopf, 1971), p. 56.
14. Elmo Richardson, *Dams, Parks and Politics* (Lexington: The University of Kentucky Press, 1973), p. 201.
15. Commoner, *Closing Circle*, pp. 12, 177.
16. Ibid., p. 217.
17. Ibid., p. 257.
18. Ibid., p. 296.
19. Paul R. Ehrlich and John P. Holdren, "Critique," *Bulletin of the Atomic Scientists* 28 (May 1972): 16.
20. Barry Commoner, *The Poverty of Power* (New York: Alfred A. Knopf, 1976), p. 233.
21. Barry Commoner, "The Meaning of the Environmental Crisis," paper presented June 5, 1972, MS, box 138, Barry Commoner Papers, Library of Congress, Washington, D.C.
22. Commoner, *Poverty of Power,* p. 1.
23. Ibid., p. 120.
24. "A Latter Day Wizard of Oz," *Forbes* 118 (July 1, 1976): 26; Tybout review in the *Sierra Club Bulletin* 62 (March 1977): 33; Boulding review in *Coevolution Quarterly,* Summer 1977, pp. 36–37; Commoner quote in Anderson, "Scientist at Large," p. 59.
25. Barry Commoner, *The Politics of Energy* (New York: Alfred A. Knopf, 1979), pp. 49, 53, 82.
26. Mark Northcross, review of *The Politics of Energy,* by Barry Commoner, *Progressive* 43 (September 1979): 53.
27. "Dr. Ecology for President," *Newsweek* 95 (April 21, 1980): 48.
28. Frank Smallwood, *The Other Candidates: Third Parties in Presidential Elections* (Hanover, N.H.: University Press of New England, 1983), p. 217.
29. Ibid., p. 212.
30. Ibid., p. 220.
31. "Conservation, Reagan Style," *Los Angeles Times,* March 28, 1986.
32. Beverly Beyette, "Environmentalists: Three Who Believe," *Los Angeles Times,* June 6, 1985.
33. Barry Commoner, "A Reporter at Large: The Environment," *New Yorker* (June 15, 1987): 57.
34. Ibid., p. 70.

1. Carson, *Silent Spring,* p. 8.
2. David Brower, "Irreplaceables, Foundations and Conventional Heresy," *Sierra Club Bulletin* 49 (December 1964), p. 10.
3. Lester R. Brown, *State of the World, 1985* (New York: W. W. Norton, 1985), p. 223.
4. Quoted in A. Kent MacDougall, "Worldwatch Spotlights Future Ecological Crises," *Los Angeles Times,* July 14, 1985.

Bibliographical Essay

Literature on American environmental history has expanded rapidly in the last quarter century. The following references are provided only as an introduction to the field and an indication of the works I found most useful in completing this book.

For short essays on individuals and environmental topics, see Richard C. Davis, ed., *Encyclopedia of American Forest and Conservation History*, 2 vols. (New York: Macmillan, 1983). Most entries include brief bibliographical references. Ronald J. Fahl, *North American Forest and Conservation History: A Bibliography* (Santa Barbara, Calif.: ABC-Clio Press, 1977), is the best guide to published works. An updated computerized data base of Fahl's work, containing more than eleven thousand citations since 1975, is available from the Forest History Society in Durham, North Carolina. Also see Roderick Nash's bibliography in *The American Environment: Readings in the History of Conservation*, 2d ed. (Reading, Mass.: Addison-Wesley, 1976); Loren C. Owings, *Environmental Values, 1860–1972* (Detroit: Gale Research, 1976); Mary Anglemyer, *A Search for Environmental Ethics: An Initial Bibliography* (Washington, D.C.: Smithsonian Institution Press,

1980); and Anglemyer, *The Natural Environment: An Annotated Bibliography on Attitudes and Values* (Washington, D.C.: Smithsonian Institution Press, 1984).

Bibliographical essays on environmental history include Gordon B. Dodds, "The Historiography of American Conservation: Past and Prospects," *Pacific Northwest Quarterly* 56 (April 1965): 75–81; Thomas LeDuc, "The Historiography of Conservation," *Forest History* 9 (October 1965): 23–28; Lawrence Rakestraw, "Conservation Historiography: An Assessment," *Pacific Historical Review* 41 (August 1972): 271–88; William Lang, "Using and Abusing Abundance: The Western Resource Economy and the Environment," in Michael P. Malone, ed., *Historians and the American West* (Lincoln: University of Nebraska Press, 1983); and Richard White, "American Environmental History: The Development of a New Historical Field," *Pacific Historical Review* 54 (August 1985): 297–335.

John Opie provides an assessment of the field in "Environmental History: Pitfalls and Opportunities," *Environmental Review* 7 (1983): 8–16, reprinted in Kendall E. Bailes, ed., *Environmental History: Critical Issues in Comparative Perspective* (Lanham, Md.: University Press of America, 1985). See also Donald Worster, "History as Natural History: An Essay on Theory and Method," *Pacific Historical Review* 53 (February 1984): 1–19. Wilbur R. Jacobs calls for new approaches to the writing of western and frontier history in two provocative articles: "Frontiersmen, Fur Traders, and Other Varmints: An Ecological Appraisal of the Frontier in American History," *AHA Newsletter* 8 (November 1970): 5–11, and "The Great Despoliation: Environmental Themes in American Frontier History," *Pacific Historical Review* 47 (February 1978): 1–26. The *Journal of Forest History*, which contains valuable bibliographical information, and the *Environmental Review* are the two best journals in environmental history.

Joseph M. Petulla's textbook, *American Environmental History*

(San Francisco: Boyd & Frazer, 1977) emphasizes economic history and the history of technology. And in *American Environmentalism: Values, Tactics, Priorities* (College Station: Texas A & M University Press, 1980), Petulla traces the historical roots of the modern environmental movement. Donald Worster, in *Nature's Economy: The Roots of Ecology* (San Francisco: Sierra Club Books, 1977), discusses the history of ecological thought in the United States. And James B. Trefethen offers a short, well-illustrated discussion of land use in *The American Landscape: 1776–1976, Two Centuries of Change* (Washington, D.C.: Wildlife Management Institute, 1976). Even briefer is Roderick Nash, *The American Conservation Movement* (St. Charles, Mo.: Forum, 1974). In addition, Stewart Udall, *The Quiet Crisis* (New York: Holt, Rinehart and Winston, 1963); Frank Graham, Jr., *Man's Dominion: The Story of Conservation in America* (Philadelphia: J. B. Lippincott, 1971); and William K. Wyant, *Westward in Eden: The Public Lands and the Conservation Movement* (Berkeley: University of California, 1982), provide lively accounts of conservation history.

For the best study of federal land policy, see Paul W. Gates, *History of Public Land Law Development* (Washington, D.C.: Government Printing Office, 1968). Dyan Zaslowsky, *These American Lands: Parks, Wilderness, and the Public Lands* (New York: Henry Holt, 1986), assesses past and current management policies. Still useful are Russell B. Nye, "The American View of Nature," in *This Almost Chosen People* (East Lansing: Michigan State University Press, 1966), and Arthur A. Ekirch, Jr., *Man and Nature in America* (New York: Columbia University Press, 1963). Hans Huth, *Nature and the American: Three Centuries of Changing Attitudes* (Berkeley: University of California Press, 1957), and Roderick Nash, *Wilderness and the American Mind,* rev. 3d ed. (New Haven: Yale University Press, 1982), remain standards in the field.

The best analysis of Indian and colonial land use is William

Cronon, *Changes in the Land: Indians, Colonists, and the Ecology of New England* (New York: Hill and Wang, 1983). For a comparable study, see Richard White, *Land Use, Environment, and Social Change: The Shaping of Island County, Washington* (Seattle: University of Washington Press, 1980). Lee Clark Mitchell, *Witnesses to a Vanishing America: The Nineteenth Century Response* (Princeton: Princeton University Press, 1981), focuses on attitudes toward the disappearance of wilderness. Donald J. Pisani, "Forests and Conservation, 1865–1890," *Journal of American History* 72 (September 1985): 340–59, discusses the growing fear of a timber famine in the late nineteenth century. And Susan L. Flader provides an overview in "Scientific Resource Management: An Historical Perspective," *American Forests* 82 (July 1976): 28–31, 57–58 and (August 1976): 49–56.

A number of biographies (cited below) have been written about leading American conservationists, and a few studies discuss several individuals. Paul Brooks, *Speaking for Nature* (San Francisco: Sierra Club Books, 1980), is an engaging discussion of leading nature writers from Thoreau to the present. In addition, Peter Wild, in *Pioneer Conservationists of Western America* (Missoula, Mont.: Mountain Press, 1979) and *Pioneer Conservationists of Eastern America* (Missoula, Mont.: Mountain Press, 1986), deals with more than thirty individuals. Richard H. Stroud, ed., presents very brief biographical sketches in *National Leaders of American Conservation* (Washington, D.C.: Smithsonian Institution Press,1985); this work updates and replaces Henry Clepper, ed., *Leaders of American Conservation* (New York: Ronald, 1971).

THOREAU, OLMSTED, MARSH

More than one hundred doctoral dissertations and close to one hundred biographical and critical book-length studies have been written on Thoreau. For an excellent selective bibliography, see

Walter Harding and Michael Meyer, *The New Thoreau Handbook* (New York: New York University Press, 1980). The notes and selected bibliography of Edward Wagenknecht, *Henry David Thoreau* (Amherst: University of Massachusetts Press, 1981), are also useful. Biographies of Thoreau include Henry Seidel Canby, *Thoreau* (Boston: Houghton Mifflin, 1939); Joseph Wood Krutch, *Henry David Thoreau* (Westport, Conn.: Greenwood, 1948); and Walter Harding, *The Days of Henry Thoreau* (New York: Alfred A. Knopf, 1965). Also see Sherman Paul, *The Shores of America: Thoreau's Inward Exploration* (Urbana: University of Illinois Press, 1958). For brief evaluations of Thoreau as a conservationist, see Philip Whitford and Kathryn Whitford, "Thoreau: Pioneer Ecologist and Conservationist," *Scientific Monthly* 73 (November 1951): 291–96; Kathryn Whitford, "Thoreau and the Woodlots of Concord," *New England Quarterly* 23 (September 1950): 291–306; William J. Wolf, *Thoreau: Mystic Prophet Ecologist* (Philadelphia: Pilgrim Press Book, 1974), pp. 145–66; and Kurt Kehr, "Walden Three: Ecological Changes in the Landscape of Henry David Thoreau," *Journal of Forest History* 27 (January 1983): 28–33. Princeton University Press is publishing Thoreau's works in approximately twenty-five volumes, which will supersede a 1906 edition of twenty volumes published by Houghton Mifflin.

Two excellent biographies of Olmsted complement each other: Laura Wood Roper, *FLO: A Biography of Frederick Law Olmsted* (Baltimore: Johns Hopkins, 1973), and Elizabeth Stevenson, *Park Maker: A Life of Frederick Law Olmsted* (New York: Macmillan, 1977). For a briefer appraisal of Olmsted's professional accomplishments, see John Emerson Todd, *Frederick Law Olmsted* (Boston: Twayne, 1982). Albert Fein, *Frederick Law Olmsted and the American Environmental Tradition* (New York: George Braziller, 1972), is a well-illustrated presentation of many of his plans and projects. Johns Hopkins University Press is publishing eight volumes of selected documents: *The Papers of Frederick Law Olmsted,* edited by David Schyler; volume 3 is Charles E. Beveridge's *Creating Central Park, 1857–1861* (1983). Another collection of documents is Frederick Law Olmsted, Jr., and Theodore Kimball, eds., *Frederick Law Olmsted: Landscape Architect, 1822–1903* (New York: Benjamin Blom, 1970), which also focuses on Central Park.

David Lowenthal, *George Perkins Marsh: Versatile Vermonter* (New York: Columbia University Press, 1958), is the definitive biography. For a brief account see Lowenthal's "George Perkins Marsh: The Magnificent Amateur," *American Forests* 83 (September 1977): 8–11, 44–48. Suzanne Fries Liebtrau's dissertation, "Trailblazers in Ecology—The American Ecological Consciousness, 1850–1864," (University of Michigan, 1973), is also helpful. Marsh's conservation ideas prior to *Man and Nature* (Cambridge: The Belknap Press of Harvard University Press, 1965) are reflected in his *Address before the Agricultural Society of Rutland County* (Rutland, Vt.: 1847) and *Report Made under Authority of the Legislature of Vermont, on the Artificial Propagation of Fish* (Burlington, Vt.: Free Press Print, 1857).

JOHN WESLEY POWELL

Three biographies of Powell are William C. Darrah, *Powell of the Colorado* (Princeton: Princeton University Press, 1951); Wallace Stegner, *Beyond the Hundredth Meridian: John Wesley Powell and the Second Opening of the West* (Boston: Houghton Mifflin, 1954); and John U. Terrell, *The Man Who Rediscovered America: A Biography of John Wesley Powell* (New York: Weybright and Talley, 1969). A briefer sketch is given in chapter 15 of William H. Goetzmann, *Exploration and Empire: The Explorer and the Scientist in the Winning of the American West* (New York: Alfred A. Knopf, 1966). Powell's role in science is discussed by A. Hunter Dupree, *Science in the Federal Government: A History of Policies and Activities to 1940* (Cambridge: Belknap Press of Harvard University Press, 1957); Thomas G. Manning, *Government in Science: The U.S. Geological Survey, 1867–1894* (Lexington: University of Kentucky Press, 1967); and John Joseph Zernel, "John Wesley Powell: Science and Reform in a Positive Context" (Ph.D. diss., Oregon State University, 1983). Joseph A. Miller, "Congress and the Origins of Conservation: Natural Resource Policies, 1865–1900" (Ph.D. diss., University of Minnesota, 1973), contains considerable material on Powell. And for useful bibliographical guides to water use in the West, see Gordon B. Dodds, ed., "Conservation and Reclamation in the Trans-Mississippi West: A Critical Bibliography," *Arizona and the West* 13 (Summer 1971): 143–71, and Lawrence B. Lee, *Reclaiming the American West: An Historiography and Guide* (Santa Barbara, Calif.: ABC-Clio Press, 1980). Powell's land and water policies are set forth in his 1878 report and three articles: "The Irrigable Lands of the Arid Region," "The Non-Irrigable Lands of the Arid Region," and "Institutions for the Arid Lands," in *Century* 39 (March 1890): 766–76; 39 (April 1890): 915–22; and 40 (May 1890): 111–16.

GIFFORD PINCHOT

The Gifford Pinchot Papers are located in the Library of Congress. Hazel Dawson, *Gifford Pinchot: A Bio-Biography* (Department of the Interior, Information Services Division, Office of Library Services, 1971), lists works by Pinchot, official publications attributed to him and those co-written by him, and publications about him. Pinchot presented his conservation beliefs and principles in *The Fight for Conservation*, reprint ed. (Seattle: University of Washington Press, 1967), and he defended his career as a forester in *Breaking New Ground* (New York: Harcourt, Brace, 1947).

For an overview of American forest history, see Thomas C. Cox et al., *This Well-Wooded Land: Americans and Their Forests from Colonial Times to the Present* (Lincoln: University of Nebraska

Press, 1985). M. Nelson McGeary, *Gifford Pinchot* (Princeton: Princeton University Press, 1960), is a biography; and Harold T. Pinkett, *Gifford Pinchot: Private and Public Forester* (Urbana, Ill.: University of Illinois Press, 1970), focuses on his forestry career. The *Journal of Forestry* 63 (August 1965) contains several articles on Pinchot by people who worked with him. Harold K. Steen, *The U.S. Forest Service: A History* (Seattle: University of Washington Press, 1976), places Pinchot's role in forestry in historical perspective; and James L. Penick, Jr., *Progressive Politics and Conservation: The Ballinger-Pinchot Affair* (Chicago: University of Chicago Press, 1968), discusses that controversy. Samuel P. Hays, *Conservation and the Gospel of Efficiency: The Progressive Conservation Movement, 1890–1920* (Cambridge: Harvard University Press, 1959), describes Pinchot's contributions as part of a movement toward centralization, efficiency, and order. The same time period is covered by Elmo R. Richardson, *The Politics of Conservation: Crusades and Controversies, 1897–1913* (Berkeley: University of California Press, 1962). Hays's chapter, "Gifford Pinchot and the American Conservation Movement," in Carroll W. Purcell, Jr., ed., *Technology in America: A History of Individuals and Ideas* (Cambridge: MIT Press, 1981), relates Pinchot's scientific forestry movement to recent environmental concerns.

JOHN MUIR

William F. Kimes and Maymie B. Kimes, *John Muir: A Reading Bibliography* (Palo Alto, Calif.: William P. Wreden, 1977), lists over three hundred books, articles, and other items written by Muir as well as the major collections of Muir's manuscripts and correspondence. Also see Ann T. Lynch, "Bibliography of Works by and about John Muir, 1869–1978," *Bulletin of Bibliography* 36 (April–June 1979): 71–80, 84. The most important collection of Muir papers is located at the Holt-Atherton Pacific Center for Western Studies, University of the Pacific, Stockton, California. Linnie Marsh Wolfe's biography, *Son of the Wilderness: The Life of John Muir* (New York: Alfred A. Knopf, 1945), and William Frederic Badè, *The Life and Letters of John Muir*, 2 vols. (Boston: Houghton Mifflin, 1923–24), are still useful. A brief biography is T. H. Watkins and Dewitt Jones, *John Muir's America* (New York: Crown, 1976). Muir's political activities as a founder and leader of the Sierra Club are traced in Holway R. Jones, *John Muir and the Sierra Club: The Battle for Yosemite* (San Francisco: Sierra Club, 1965).

With the recent availability of Muir's papers, a number of new books on Muir have been published. Stephen Fox, *John Muir and His Legacy* (Boston: Little, Brown, 1981), provides a brief biography, a history of the conservation movement since 1880, and an analysis of the motives and significance of the preservationists who followed Muir. Michael P. Cohen, *The Pathless Way: John Muir and the American Wilderness* (Madison: University of Wisconsin Press, 1984), explains the development of Muir's ideas and values and offers a personal response to them. Frederick Turner, *Rediscovering America: John Muir in His Time and Ours* (New York: Viking, 1985), is another biography. Special issues of the *Pacific Historian* 25 (Summer 1981) and 29 (Summer–Fall 1985) contain articles by Muir scholars.

STEPHEN MATHER

The only biography of Mather is Robert Shankland's *Steve Mather of the National Parks*, rev. ed. (New York: Alfred A. Knopf, 1954). Horace M. Albright, *The Birth of the National Park Service: The Founding Years, 1913–1933* (Salt Lake City: Howe Brothers, 1985), presents a first-person account. The first half of Donald C. Swain's *Wilderness Defender: Horace M. Albright and Conservation* (Chicago: University of Chicago Press, 1970) deals extensively with Mather's administration. In "The Passage of the National Park Service Act of 1916," *Wisconsin Magazine of History* 50 (1966): 4–20, Swain explains efforts to establish a park service. Thomas R. Cox, "From Hot Springs to Gateway: The Evolving Concept of Public Parks, 1832–1976," *Environmental Review* 5 (1981): 14–26, discusses historical changes and regional differences as they apply to the meaning of parks in America. John Ise, *Our National Parks: A Critical History* (Baltimore: Johns Hopkins, 1961), focuses on legislative and administrative history. Alfred Runte, *National Parks: The American Experience,* 2d ed., rev. (Lincoln: University of Nebraska Press, 1987), argues that most American national parks were created from worthless lands as scenic monuments rather than as recreation or wilderness areas. For brief histories of the national parks, see Robert W. Righter, *The National Parks in the American West* (St. Louis: Forum, 1979), and Joseph L. Sax's special supplement, "America's National Parks: Their Principles, Purposes and Prospects," *Natural History* 85 (October 1976). Among critiques of management of the national parks are F. Fraser Darling and Noel D. Eichhorn, *Man and Nature in the National Parks: Reflections on Policy* (Washington, D.C.: Conservation Foundation, 1967); the Conservation Foundation, *National Parks for the Future* (Washington, D.C.: Conservation Foundation, 1972); and Joseph L. Sax, *Mountains without Handrails: Reflections on the National Parks* (Ann Arbor: University of Michigan Press, 1980). Ronald A. Forestra's *America's National Parks and Their Keepers* (Washington, D.C.: Resources for the Future, 1984) emphasizes the recent history of the National Park Service.

ALDO LEOPOLD

Curt Meine provides an excellent biography, *Aldo Leopold: His Life and Work* (Madison: University of Wisconsin Press, 1987). Susan L. Flader explains Leopold's conservation philosophy in *Thinking like a Mountain: Aldo Leopold and the Evolution of an Eco-*

logical Attitude toward Deer, Wolves, and Forests (Columbia: University of Missouri Press, 1974). Also see Flader, *The Sand Country of Aldo Leopold* (San Francisco: Sierra Club, 1973). Two other books on Leopold are J. Baird Callicott, ed., *Companion to a Sand County Almanac* (Madison: University of Wisconsin Press, 1987), and Thomas Tanner, ed., *Aldo Leopold: The Man and His Legacy* (Ankeny, Iowa: Soil Conservation Society of America, 1987). Roderick Nash has a chapter on Leopold in his *Wilderness and the American Mind*, rev. 3d ed. (New Haven: Yale University Press, 1982). Articles on Leopold include Paul L. Errington, "In Appreciation of Aldo Leopold," *Journal of Wildlife Management* 12 (October 1948): 341–50; Clay Schoenfeld, "Aldo Leopold Remembered," *Audubon* 80 (May 1979): 29–37; Susan Flader, "Aldo Leopold and the Wilderness Idea," *Living Wilderness* 43 (December 1979): 4–8; and Boyd Gibbons, "Aldo Leopold: A Durable Scale of Values," *National Geographic* 160 (November 1981): 682–708.

HAROLD ICKES

The Harold L. Ickes Papers are deposited in the Library of Congress. For the prelude to the New Deal, see Donald C. Swain, *Federal Conservation Policy, 1921–1933* (Berkeley: University of California Press, 1963), and Kendrick A. Clements, "Herbert Hoover and Conservation, 1921–33," *American Historical Review* 89 (February 1984): 67–88. A. L. Reisch Owen, *Conservation under F.D.R.* (New York: Praeger, 1983), is an overview. Richard Lowitt, *The New Deal and the West* (Bloomington: Indiana University Press, 1984), focuses on public lands and deals extensively with Ickes. Clayton R. Koppes's dissertation, "Oscar L. Chapman: A Liberal at the Interior Department, 1933–1953" (University of Kansas, 1974), also includes many references to Ickes; and Koppes's article "Environmental Policy and American Liberalism: The Department of the Interior, 1933–1953,"

Environmental Review 7 (Spring 1983): 17–41, provides an interpretive survey. For a discussion of conservation policy after the New Deal, see Elmo Richardson, *Dams, Parks and Politics: Resource Development and Preservation in the Truman-Eisenhower Era* (Lexington: University of Kentucky Press, 1973). An interview with Ickes by Marquis James, "The National Domain and the New Deal," *Saturday Evening Post* 206 (December 23, 1933): 10-11, 55, reveals Ickes's attitudes at the time he became secretary of the interior.

The early career of Ickes is discussed in Linda J. Lear, *Harold L. Ickes: The Aggressive Progressive, 1874–1933* (New York: Garland, 1981); she also has a full biography of Ickes nearly completed. John Maze and Graham White conjecture on Ickes's controversial behavior in "Harold L. Ickes: A Psychohistorical Perspective," *Journal of Psychohistory* 8 (1981): 421–44, and at greater length in *Harold Ickes of the New Deal: His Private Life and Public Career* (Cambridge: Harvard University Press, 1985). Two useful dissertations are Mont J. Harmon, "Harold L. Ickes: A Study in New Deal Thought" (University of Wisconsin, 1953), and Mark L. Jacobs, "Harold Ickes: Progressive Administrator" (University of Maine, 1973). See also Harmon, "Some Contributions of Harold L. Ickes," *Western Political Quarterly* 7 (June 1954): 238–52, and T. H. Watkins, "The Terrible-Tempered Mr. Ickes," *Audubon* 86 (March 1984): 93-111. For a discussion of aesthetic conservation, see Donald C. Swain, "Harold Ickes, Horace Albright, and the Hundred Days: A Study in Conservation Administration," *Pacific Historical Review* 34 (November 1965): 455–65; Swain, "The National Park Service and the New Deal, 1933–1940," *Pacific Historical Review* 41 (1972): 312–32; and Barry Macintosh, "Harold L. Ickes and the National Park Service," *Journal of Forest History* 29 (April 1985): 78–84. Ickes's role in reclamation is discussed in Donald C. Swain, "The Bureau of Reclamation and the New Deal, 1933–1940," *Pacific Northwest Quarterly* 61 (July 1970): 137–46, and Linda J. Lear,

"Boulder Dam: A Crossroads in Natural Resource Policy," *Journal of the West* 24 (October 1985): 82–94. For a discussion of his efforts to transfer the Forest Service to the Department of the Interior, see Richard Polenberg, *Reorganizing Roosevelt's Government: The Controversy over Executive Reorganization, 1936–1939* (Cambridge: Harvard University Press, 1966). Oil policy is addressed in Linda J. Lear, "Harold L. Ickes and the Oil Crisis of the First Hundred Days," *Mid America* 63 (January 1981): 3–17; Stephen J. Randall, "Harold Ickes and the United States Foreign Petroleum Policy Planning, 1939–1945," *Business History Review* 57 (Autumn 1983): 367–87; and Michael B. Stoff, *Oil, War, and American Security: The Search for a National Policy on Foreign Oil, 1941–1947* (New Haven: Yale University Press, 1980).

Harold L. Ickes, *The Autobiography of a Curmudgeon* (New York: Reynal and Hitchcock, 1943), while valuable for details unavailable elsewhere, should be used with caution; Ickes used it to defend himself against his critics. Also see Harold L. Ickes, *The Secret Diary of Harold L. Ickes*, 3 vols. (New York: Simon and Schuster, 1953–54).

RACHEL CARSON

Rachel Carson's papers are located in the Beinecke Rare Book and Manuscript Library, Yale University, New Haven, Connecticut. This extensive collection has not been fully processed or cataloged and is therefore difficult to use. A specialized collection on toxicology, as well as limited material on Carson, is located in the Rachel Carson Council Library, Chevy Chase, Maryland. Most important is Dorothy Thompson Seif's manuscript, "Letters from Rachel Carson: A Young Scientist Sets Her Course." The best study of Rachel Carson and her career is Paul Brooks, *The House of Life: Rachel Carson at Work* (Boston: Houghton Mifflin, 1972), republished in a paperback edition as *Rachel Carson at Work: The House of Life* (Boston: G. K. Hall,

1985). Philip Sterling, *The Life of Rachel Carson* (New York: Thomas Y. Crowell, 1970), contains biographical material, and Carol B. Gartner, *Rachel Carson* (New York: Frederick Ungar, 1983), discusses her literary accomplishments. See also Peter Wild, "After *Silent Spring,* the Issue Became Life Itself," *High Country News* 11 (February 9, 1979): 1, 6–7.

Several studies deal with the history of insecticide use: Frank Graham, Jr., *Since "Silent Spring"* (Boston: Houghton Mifflin, 1970); James Whorton, *Before "Silent Spring": Pesticides and Public Health in Pre-DDT America* (Princeton: Princeton University Press, 1974); Thomas R. Dunlap, *DDT: Scientists, Citizens, and Public Policy* (Princeton: Princeton University Press, 1981); John H. Perkins, *Insects, Experts, and the Insecticide Crisis: A Quest for New Pest Management Strategies* (New York: Plenum, 1982); and Perkins, "Insects, Food and Hunger: The Paradox of Plenty for U. S. Entomology, 1920–1970," *Environmental Review* 7 (Spring 1983): 71–96. Ralph H. Lutts, "Chemical Fallout: Rachel Carson's *Silent Spring,* Radioactive Fallout, and the Environmental Movement," *Environmental Review* 9 (Fall 1985): 210–25, discusses how concern about nuclear fallout has affected attitudes toward agricultural insecticides.

Books critical of *Silent Spring* include Jamie L. Whitten, *That We May Live* (Toronto: D. Van Nostrand, 1966); Rita Gray Beatty, *The DDT Myth: Triumph of the Amateurs* (New York: John Day, 1973); and George Claus and Karen Bolander, *Ecological Sanity* (New York: David McKay, 1977). On the other side, Robert Van den Bosch, *The Pesticide Conspiracy* (Garden City, N.J.: Doubleday, 1978), attacks the pesticide industry. More tempered is Robert L. Rudd, *Pesticides in the Living Environment* (Madison: University of Wisconsin Press, 1964). Carson responded briefly in "Rachel Carson Answers Her Critics," *Audubon* 65 (September–October 1963): 262–65. For her testimony in 1963, see U.S. Congress, Senate, Committee on Government Operations, *Interagency Coordination in Environmental Hazards (Pesticides):*

Hearings before the Subcommittee on Reorganization, Research, and International Organization, 88th Cong., 1st sess., 1964, pp. 206–48. For a brief statement of her environmental philosophy, see Rachel Carson, *Of Man and the Stream of Time*, a graduation address at Scripps College, Claremont, California, 1962.

Among reflections on Carson's contributions to environmentalism are "Rachel Carson Dies of Cancer: 'Silent Spring' Author Was 56," *New York Times*, April 15, 1964, p. 1; Shirley A. Briggs, "Remembering Rachel Carson," *American Forests* 76 (July 1970): 8–11; Wayne Handley, *Natural History in America: From Mark Catesby to Rachel Carson* (New York: Quadrangle, 1977): pp. 324–39; Paul R. Ehrlich, "Paul R. Ehrlich Reconsiders *Silent Spring*," *Bulletin of the Atomic Scientists* 35 (October 1979): 34–36; and Philip M. Boffey, "20 Years after 'Silent Spring': Still a Troubled Landscape," *New York Times*, May 25, 1982, p. C1.

DAVID BROWER

No biography of Brower has been written, and no bibliography about him has been compiled. Brower plans to write an autobiography, but he has been too busy to make much progress. Two collections in the Bancroft Library of the University of California (Berkeley)—the Sierra Club Papers and the David Brower Papers—provide the best sources of material on Brower's life and environmental concerns.

Susan R. Schrepfer conducted two lengthy and informative interviews, both available from the Regional Oral History Office of the Bancroft Library: "David R. Brower: Environmental Activist, Publicist, and Prophet"(1980), and "Richard M. Leonard: Mountaineer, Lawyer, Environmentalist" (1975). Both deal extensively with the history of the Sierra Club and the controversy over Brower's dismissal. The Brower interview contains a list of books published under Brower's direction. Other interviews with Brower include Charles N. Conconi, "An Interview with David Brower: Founder of Friends of the Earth," *Environ-mental Quality* 4 (April 1973): 19–26, 69; "The Plowboy Interview: Dave Brower," *Mother Earth News*, no. 21 (May 1973): 6–12; and "Dave Brower: The Environmentalist and the Bomb," *Mother Earth News*, no. 77 (Sept.–Oct. 1982): 94–96. The Sierra Club's oral history project includes interviews with William E. Siri, Bestor Robinson, Edgar Wayburn, and Michael McCloskey.

John McPhee, *Encounters with the Archdruid* (New York: Farrar, Straus and Giroux, 1971), helps explain Brower's conservation philosophy, and Bill Devall, "David Brower," *Environmental Review* 9 (Fall 1985): 238–53, emphasizes Brower's concerns in the 1970s and 1980s. Devall analyzes club politics in "The Governance of a Voluntary Organization: Oligarchy and Democracy in the Sierra Club" (Ph.D. diss., University of Oregon, 1970). Frank Graham, Jr., "Dave Brower: Last of the Optimists?" *Audubon* 84 (September 1982): 62–73, provides a sketch of Brower at the age of seventy, as does Brower's article "In Wilderness Wanders David Brower, Still Seeking to Preserve the World," *California Magazine* 9 (September 1984): 115–21, 167. The *Sierra Club Bulletin* (renamed *Sierra*) presents a wealth of information on the club and includes several articles by Brower.

BARRY COMMONER

Commoner's papers, to 1979, are deposited in the Library of Congress; his more recent papers are available at the Center for the Biology of Natural Systems, Queens College, Flushing, New York. No biography of him has been written, and no complete list of his numerous publications exists. However, the Center for the Biology of Natural Systems has an updated bibliography of Commoner's most important scientific studies.

Among Commoner's most useful articles are "Social Aspects of Science," *Science* 125 (January 25, 1957): 143–47; "The

Fallout Problem," *Science* 127 (May 2, 1958): 1023–26; "Integrity of Science," *Science Journal* 2 (April 1966): 75–79; "Ecosystems Are Circular," *American Forests* 80 (April 1974): 8–11, 76–79, and (May 1974): 20–22, 60–62; "The Promise and Perils of Petrochemicals," *New York Times Magazine*," September 25, 1977, pp. 38–46, 70–71; and "Economic Growth and Environmental Quality: How to Have Both," *Social Policy* 16 (Summer 1985): 18–26. Most of the material in these articles is incorporated into his books.

Several interviews with Commoner contain valuable information; they include Anne Chisholm, *Philosophers of the Earth: Conversations with Ecologists* (London: Sidgwick & Jackson, 1972), pp. 122–39; Lawrence Weschler, "An Interview with Barry Commoner," *Rolling Stone*, May 1980, pp. 44–48; Frank Smallwood, *The Other Candidates: Third Parties in Presidential Elections* (Hanover, N.H.: University Press of New England, 1983), pp. 208–25; and Sam Totten and Martha Wescott Totten, *Facing the Danger: Interviews with 20 Antinuclear Activists* (Trumansburg, N.Y.: Crossing, 1984), pp. 25–29. Articles written about Commoner include Alan Anderson, Jr., "Scientist at Large," *New York Times Magazine*, November 7, 1976, and Peter Wild, "Barry Commoner Boils Ecology Down to Basics: 'There's No Free Lunch,' " *High Country News* 11 (October 19, 1979). A feature article in *Time*, "Fighting to Save the Earth from Man," 95 (February 2, 1970): 56–63, emphasizes Commoner and other ecologists.

For a discussion of the conservation movement of the 1960s and 1970s, see Donald Fleming, "Roots of the New Conservation Movement," in Fleming, ed., *Perspectives in American History* (Cambridge: Harvard University, Charles Warren Center for Studies in American History, 1972), 6:7–91; Samuel P. Hays, *Beauty, Health, and Permanence: Environmental Politics in the United States, 1955–1985* (New York: Cambridge University Press, 1987); Hays, "The Structure of Environmental Politics since

World War II," *Journal of Social History* 14 (Summer 1981): 719–38; and Hays, "From Conservation to Environment: Environmental Politics in the United States since World War II," *Environmental Review* 6 (Fall 1982): 14–41. The Commoner-Ehrlich debate is in the *Bulletin of the Atomic Scientists* 28 (May 1972): 16–56. For indictments of the environmental movement, including Commoner, see John Maddox, *The Doomsday Syndrome* (New York: McGraw-Hill, 1972), and George Claus and Karen Bolander, *Ecological Sanity* (New York: David McKay, 1977). David L. Sills provides a more balanced analysis in "The Environmental Movement and Its Critics," *Human Ecology* 3 (January 1975): 1–41.

CONCLUSION

Books on current environmental problems and prospects for their solution have proliferated in recent years. Among the more useful global assessments are Barbara Ward and René Dubos, *Only One Earth* (New York: Ballantine, 1972); Erik P. Eckholm, *Losing Ground* (New York: W. W. Norton, 1976); Richard J. Barnet, *The Lean Years* (New York: Simon and Schuster, 1980); and Lester R. Brown, *Building a Sustainable Society* (New York: W. W. Norton, 1981). Since 1984, Brown and the Worldwatch Institute have published an annual volume, *State of the World* (New York: W. W. Norton), which is rapidly gaining a global audience.

Index

Brower, David (*cont.*)
  ness, 204–7; after World War
  II, 200; youth of, 196–97
Brown, Lester, 248–49
Bryant, William Cullen, 19
Bureau of Land Management,
  175
Bureau of Reclamation, 59, 70,
  158, 164, 167; and Echo Park
  controversy, 201, 202–3
Burford, Anne M., 242
Butler, James, 89

Cameron, Ralph H., 129
Carr, Ezra, 89, 92
Carr, Jeanne, 89, 92, 95
Carson, Rachel, 6, 230, 248; as
  author, 181–85; at congressional hearings, 177, 193;
  death of, 193; *Edge of the Sea,
  The,* 184; as editor, 182; education of, 179–80; and family
  responsibilities, 180, 185; and
  Fish and Wildlife Service,
  181, 182, 184; "Help Your
  Child to Wonder," 184; as
  marine biologist, 181; and
  protection of shorelines, 185;
  and radiation, 185–86; recognition of, 193; *Sea Around Us,
  The,* 183–84, 185–86; *Silent
  Spring,* 177, 189–92, 195,
  247; as teacher, 180; "Undersea," 181; *Under the Sea-Wind,*
  181–82, 184; youth of, 179
Central Arizona Project, 208,
  210, 211
Central Park, 16, 19–22, 25
Civilian Conservation Corps
  (CCC), 160, 163–64

Cleveland, Grover, 66, 99, 102
Club of Rome, 235
Colby, William, 104, 108, 200
Colorado River: and dams, 156,
  203, 204, 208, 210; and Powell expeditions, 39, 41–43, 44;
  and Supreme Court decision
  (1963), 208; and Upper Basin
  Project, 202, 203–4, 210. *See
  also* Dams
Commoner, Barry, 6, 194, 221,
  248; academic career of, 222,
  223, 224, 243; and atomic energy, 223; and Center for the
  Biology of Natural Systems,
  194, 233, 243; and Citizens'
  party, 240–42; *Closing Circle,
  The,* 231, 234, 235; contribution of, 245; criticisms of,
  239; economic theory of,
  234–35, 238, 245; as editor,
  223; education of, 222; and
  Ehrlich, 235–36; and energy,
  238, 240; and environmental
  movement, 231, 243–45; and
  Jesse Jackson, 242; and Lake
  Erie, 233–34; military service
  of, 222–23; and New York
  City, 243; and nuclear weapons testing, 224–26, 228; on
  political coercion, 235; *Politics
  of Energy, The,* 240; and pollution, 230, 233–34; and population, 235–36; *Poverty of Power, The,* 237, 239; and
  responsibility of scientists,
  223–28, 233; *Science and Survival,* 227; and St. Louis Committee for Nuclear Information, 225; youth of, 222

284

Congress: and Ballinger-Pinchot controversy, 82, 83; and Civilian Conservation Corps (CCC), 160; and colonial conservation laws, 5; and Colorado River Bill (1968), 211; and Commission on Fish and Fisheries, 6; and conservation legislation (1968), 217; defeat of land law reforms by, 52, 73; and Environmental Protection Agency (EPA), 231; and Giant Forest, 115; and Governors' Conference, 78; hearings on insecticides, 193; and Hetch Hetchy, 109; and Kings Canyon National Park, 200; and land-disposal policies, 3; and Mather memorial, 133; and memorial on forestry (1873), 37; and Miller amendment, 188; and National Conservation Commission, 77; National Environmental Policy Act (NEPA), 231; and national park roads, 128; National Park Service Act, 116; and national planning, 170; opposition to Pinchot and Roosevelt, 73–74, 79; and pesticide regulations, 194; and Powell proposals, 50–51; and recession of Yosemite Valley, 105; and regulation of forest reserves (1897), 66; Reorganization Act, 171; support of Powell, 44; and Tennessee Valley Authority (TVA), 160; Transfer Act, 70; and western surveys,

48; Yosemite National Park, 96. *See also* Land laws
Conservation, 101; advances in, 246–47; of arid West, 44; and Ballinger-Pinchot controversy, 80–83; citizen organizations, 6, 244; in colonial era, 5; crusade for (1908), 61–62; decline of, 79, 172, 175; in Europe, 34, 36; Franklin Roosevelt and, 160, 175–76; federal agencies and, 59; individuals and, 7; and legacy of Ickes, 175–76; Leopold's philosophy of, 142–45,148, 149–51; movement (first), 75–80, 82, 83, 155; movements compared, 230; Muir's philosophy of, 101; National Conservation Association, 81; in nineteenth century, 5–6; North American Conference, 79; opposition to Pinchot-Roosevelt program, 73–74; Pinchot's philosophy of, 64, 66, 76, 83, 101, 109; preservation and preservationists, 66, 101, 107, 109, 123–24, 203, 230; second movement (1930s), 6, 170; Theodore Roosevelt and, 68, 77; third movement (1960s–70s), 6, 135, 177, 230–31, 243–45; from TR to FDR, 155–56; utilitarian, 32, 54, 83, 101, 107, 123–24, 131–32, 205. *See also* Pollution
Coolidge, Calvin, 124, 155, 161

Dams: Bridge Canyon, 208, 210;

Dams (*cont.*)
and Dinosaur National Monument, 201; Echo Park, 201, 202, 203, 210; Glen Canyon, 167, 201, 203, 204, 210, 213; Grand Canyon, 207–11 passim, 217; Grand Coulee, 167, 168; Hetch Hetchy, 106–10; Hoover (Boulder), 155–56, 167, 168, 208–9, 210; Marble Canyon, 208, 210; Muscle Shoals, 160; in national parks, 201–2; proliferation of, 167; Ramparts, 214; Split Mountain, 201; on Tennessee River, 161; in Upper Colorado River Basin, 201; and Yellowstone, 119–20
DDT, 186, 187–88, 194, 223
Deforestation: in Alps, 33–34; about Mediterranean, 33; results of, 35–36, 65; in Vermont, 31, 33
Department of Agriculture, 74; and CCC, 164; and forestry, 65, 66; and government reorganization, 170; and insecticides, 188, 189, 191; and national parks, 116, 124; and Wilderness Act, 207
Department of Conservation, 171, 172
Department of the Interior, 71, 158, 176; and CCC, 164; and forestry, 65, 66; and Forest Service, 81, 83; and government reorganization, 170–71; and Hetch Hetchy, 107; history of, 158–59; Ickes's re-

form of, 159; and national forests, 124; and Wilderness Act, 207
Dinosaur National Monument, 201, 203, 204, 230
Downing, Andrew Jackson, 20
Dry farming, 47, 48, 57
Dust Bowl, 5, 164

Earth Day, 231
Echo Park controversy, 201–4
Ecological conscience, 143, 149
Ecology, 6, 230; and Marsh, 27, 34; and Mather, 132
Ehrlich, Paul, 217, 235–36
Eisely, Loren, 191
Eisenhower, Dwight D., 227, 228, 230
Emerson, Ralph Waldo, 9, 10, 92
Energy: atomic, 223; and Boulder Canyon Project, 155–56, 167; and Carter's National Energy Plan, 240; and Central Arizona Project, 208, 210; and Commoner, 238–40; and control of hydroelectric dam sites, 77; and Diablo Canyon, 212–13, 218; and Division of Power, 170; and federal dams, 167; government subsidies of, 239; and Hetch Hetchy, 109; Ickes and public power, 162, 170; and Nipomo Dunes, 212; nuclear, 212–13, 218, 238, 239, 240; and oil embargo, 237; and petroleum, 172–74; solar, 238–39, 240; and World War II, 173–74

Environmental Defense Fund, 193
Environmental movement (1960s-70s), 135, 177, 230–31, 243
Environmental Protection Agency (EPA), 194, 231, 242–43
Europe: attitude of settlers from, 2; concern with conservation, 34, 36; forestry in, 62; parks in, 19, 20

Fall, Albert B., 121, 155
Fire: control of, 78; in forest reserves and parks, 98; in Sierra, 94; Indian use of, 1; and Powell, 49; and Thoreau, 15
Fish and Wildlife Service, 171, 181, 182, 184
Fish culture, 6; Marsh report on, 31–32
Fisher, Walter L., 83, 108
Forest reserves, 70, 102; army protection of, 99; expansion of, 66; Muir's concern for, 98, 100, 102; renamed national forests, 70–71. *See also* National forests
Forestry: and Adirondack state forest preserve, 26; American Forest Congress, 70; American Forestry Association, 65; and Biltmore estate, 26; Bureau of, 67; Division of, 65, 67; in Europe, 62, 63; Forest Commission, 65, 98; Marsh and, 37; Muir and, 95, 100, 102; before 1901, 65; Olmsted and, 26; Pinchot's idea

of, 63–64, 75; Powell and, 49, 56; regulation of forest reserves (1897), 66; rider of 1891 (forest reserves), 65; Theodore Roosevelt's message to Congress on, 68; Yale school of, 67. *See also* Forest reserves; Forest Service; National forests
Forest Service, 59, 66, 164; creation of, 70–71; and Department of the Interior, 81, 83; efficiency of, 74; and government reorganization, 171; and Indian lands, 81; and Leopold, 136–38; and National Park Service, 116, 123–24, 132, 137, 206; and Operation Outdoors, 205; Pinchot's proposed organization for, 66; preservation and recreational interests of, 124; principles of, 71; and Taft, 81; *Use Book,* 74; timber-cutting policy of, 71; and wilderness, 138, 139. *See also* National forests
Friends of the Earth (FOE), 218–19

Garfield, James R., 73, 80, 81; and Hetch Hetchy, 107, 108
General Land Office, 48, 51, 81, 100, 158; and forest reserves, 65, 67
Geological Survey, 52–57, 58, 59, 158
Glavis, Louis, 82, 169
Gorsuch, Anne M., 242

Government: reorganization of, 170–72; science sponsored by, 52–54, 58; support of economic growth by, 4. *See also* Congress; *names of individual agencies*

Governor's Conference on the Conservation of Natural Resources, 61, 77, 78, 79, 107

Grand Canyon, 128; Cameron and, 129; and dams, 207–11, 217; naming of, 42; national monument, 104; national park, 122, 129, 207; Powell and, 39, 42–44

Grasslands: in arid West, 47; Bureau of Land Management and, 175; CCC and, 164; control of, 78; Division of Grazing and, 164; Grazing Service and, 165; and nuclear-weapons testing, 224; overgrazing of, 33, 54, 79; Pinchot's management of, 71; Powell and, 56; in Sierra, 94; and Taylor Grazing Act, 59, 165, 175

Grazing. *See* Grasslands

Harding, Warren, 121, 155
Harrison, Benjamin, 65
Hayden, Ferdinand, 48, 51, 52
Hetch Hetchy, 106–10, 116, 119
Homestead Act, 3, 46
Hoover, Herbert, 119, 156, 161
Hunting: Leopold and, 136–37, 147; Muir and, 87; Thoreau and, 15

Ickes, Harold L., 6; character of, 159–60; and Chicago politics, 153–54; and CCC, 164; and civil rights, 157–58; on conservation, 155; conservation legacy of, 175–76; education of, 153; and fascism, 172; and Franklin Roosevelt, 171, 173, 174; and government reorganization, 170–72; on individualism and environmental decline, 157; later years of, 175; law practice of, 154; marriage and family of, 154, 175; and national parks, 165–66, 200, 201; and national planning, 169–70; New Democracy, The, 158, 169–70; as petroleum administrator, 172–74; as a political reporter, 153–54; as a Progressive, 152, 154; and PWA, 162, 168–69; and reclamation, 167–68; resignation of, 169, 171, 174–75; on resource scarcity, 174; as secretary of the interior, 152, 154, 158–72 passim, 175; and soil conservation, 165; and TVA, 162; youth of, 153

Indians: and Antiquities Act, 125; and Bureau of Ethnology, 52, 58, 59; and Bureau of Indian Affairs, 44, 158; and CCC, 164; and Dawes Act, 157; and Ickes, 157; land use by, 1–2; management of reservation lands, 81; and Powell, 43, 44, 52

Insecticides, 186–92, 193–95, 223, 232

Irrigation, 47, 49, 50, 108; and

Boulder Canyon Project, 155–56; in California, 95; and Colorado–Big Thompson project, 166; and Ickes, 167–68; Powell proposal for, 50–51, 55–56; and Theodore Roosevelt, 68; and Reclamation Act, 70; survey, 55–57, 58, 66; and Yellowstone, 119–20. *See also* Dams; Reclamation

Johnson, Robert Underwood, 96

King, Clarence, 48, 52, 53

Lake Erie, 233–34
Land ethic, 135, 149–51
Land laws: Act of 1901, 106–7; Antiquities Act, 125; defeat of reform of, 52; deficiency of, in arid West, 47; and forest lands, 65; fraudulent use of, 3–4; Homestead Act, 3, 46; Louisiana Purchase, 3; misuse of, 99, 100; need for revision of, 72–73, 78; opposition to, 3; Ordinance of 1785, 3; Reclamation Act, 70; rider of 1891 (forest reserves), 65; Swamp Land Act, 3; Taylor Grazing Act, 59, 165, 175; Timber and Stone Act, 4; Timber Culture Act, 6; Wilderness Act, 138, 207. *See also* Congress; Public lands; *names of individual acts*
Landscape architecture: and Downing, 20; and Olmsted, 16, 20–21, 23, 25, 26; and Olmsted, Jr., 116

Lane, Franklin K.: and Hetch Hetchy, 107, 109; and Mather, 111, 113, 118, 119, 120
League of Conservation Voters, 219
Leopold, Aldo, 7, 246, 248; death of, 142; family of, 142; Forest Service career of, 136, 137–38; *Game Management*, 139; and hunting, 136–37, 147; land ethic of, 135–36, 149–51; conservation philosophy of, 142–45, 149–51; and recreation, 137, 146–47; *Sand County Almanac, A*, 135, 142, 147; and sand county shack, 140; in Southwest, 136–38; as teacher-scholar, 139, 150; and U.S. Forest Products Laboratory, 138; and wilderness, 137–38, 140, 145–49, 206; and Wilderness Society, 140; and wildlife management, 139–40, 148; and Wisconsin Conservation Act, 139; youth of, 136

McFarland, J. Horace, 107, 115–16, 120
McGee, W J, 59, 76, 77
Marsh, George Perkins, 6, 246; and balance in nature, 34; and camels, 31; in Congress, 30; description of, 32; and ecology, 27, 34; education of, 29; and government regulations, 32, 36; hope for future, 36; and impact of humans, 35–36; intellect and interests

Roosevelt, Franklin D. (FDR), 6, 152; and CCC, 162–63; conservation legacy of, 175–76; death of, 174; and historic preservation, 165; and Ickes, 154, 171, 173, 174; and national planning, 170; support of conservation, 160; and TVA, 161–62; and wildlife, 172

Roosevelt, Theodore (TR), 6, 80, 106, 152, 155; and Governors' Conference, 61–62; and Ickes, 154; and importance of conservation, 77; and Inland Waterways Commission, 76–77; and Muir, 102–4, 107; and Muscle Shoals, 160; and National Conservation Commission, 77; and national forests, 74, 104; and national parks and monuments, 104; and North American Conservation Conference, 79; opposition to, 73–74, 78, 79, 81; outdoor interests of, 68; and Pinchot, 62, 68–70, 81, 107; and Public Lands Commission, 73; and Taft, 80

Sargent, Charles S., 65, 99, 102–3, 104, 107
Save-the-Redwoods League, 122
Schurz, Carl, 49
Sierra Club, 98, 230; accomplishments of (1968), 217; Brower and, 196, 198–99, 211–17, 219; creation of, 97, 198–99; and Diablo Canyon, 212–13, 216, 217; and Echo Park Controversy (Dinosaur), 202, 204; Foundation, 212; and Glen Canyon, 204; and Grand Canyon, 207–11; growth of, 216, 217–18; and Internal Revenue Service, 209, 211, 212; and Kings Canyon, 200; McCloskey and, 217; Mather and, 113; and recession of Yosemite Valley, 104–5; after World War II, 200; and wilderness, 205; and Yosemite National Park, 102

Sierra Nevada, 91, 94, 95; Mather's trip to, 114–15; Muir's travel in, 93, 94; and Sierra Club, 97, 198–99

Smithsonian Institution, 30–31, 41, 52

Soil: Conservation Service, 165; erosion, 2, 78, 79, 137, 155, 165; Erosion Service, 170

Stewart, William, 55, 56, 57, 58

Taft, William Howard, 79, 80–83, 108
Teapot Dome, 155
Tennessee Valley Authority (TVA), 77, 160–62, 168
Thoreau, Henry David, 6, 37, 92, 246, 248; "Civil Disobedience," 13; death of, 16; education of, 9; Emerson's influence on, 10; and family business, 10, 14; and government, 12–13; and hunting and fishing, 15; journal writing of, 10; legacy of, 16; and

920
STR

Strong, Douglas
Hillman.

Dreamers &
defenders

$9.95